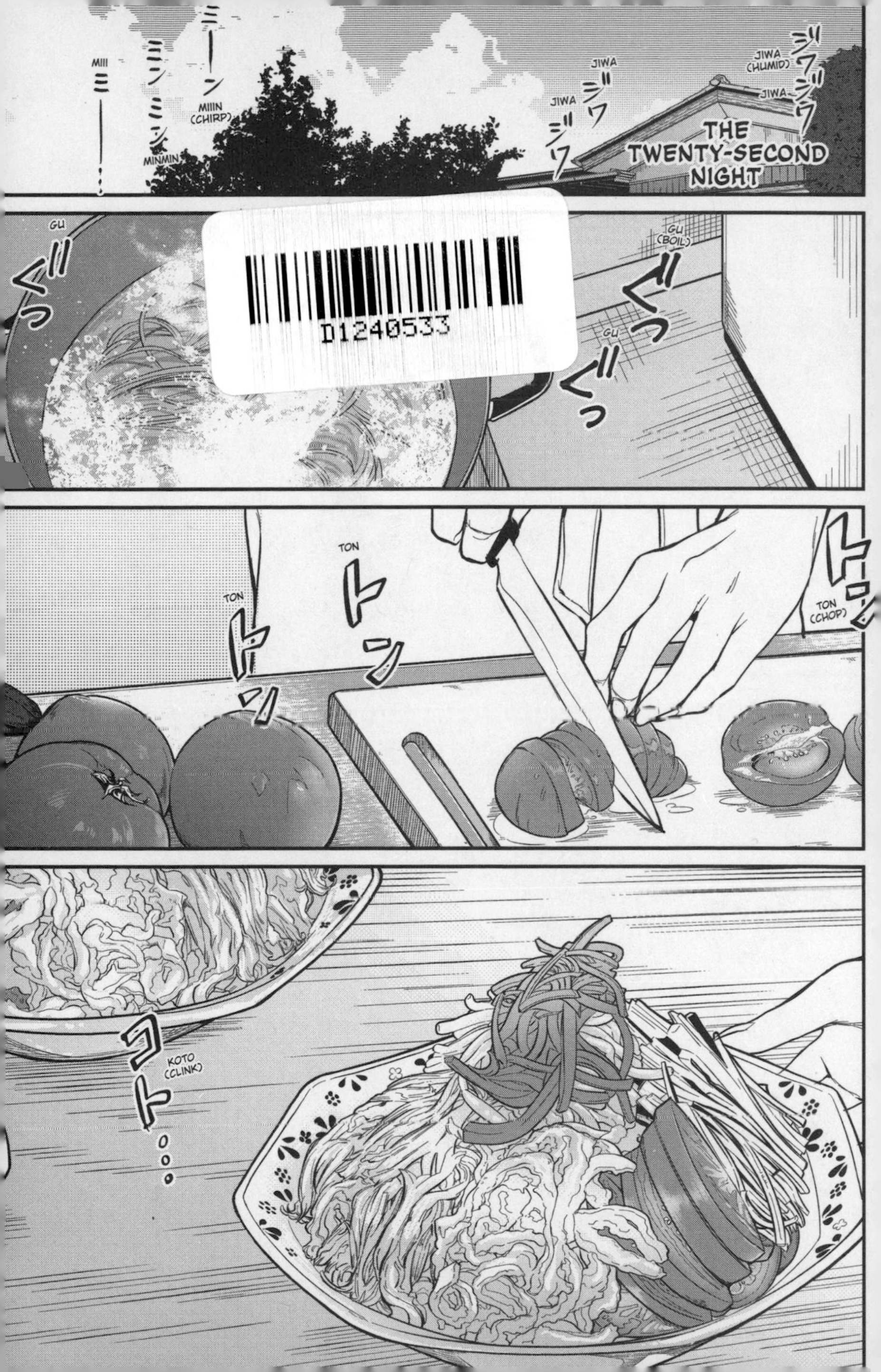

ジワジワ
JIWA (HUMID)
JIWA
THE TWENTY-SECOND NIGHT
JIWA ジワ
JIWA ジワ
ミーン ミンミン
MIIIN (CHIRP)
MINMIN
ミー…
MIII
GU (BOIL)
GU
ぐつぐつ
ぐつ
GU
トン
TON (CHOP)
TON
TON
コト…
KOTO (CLINK)

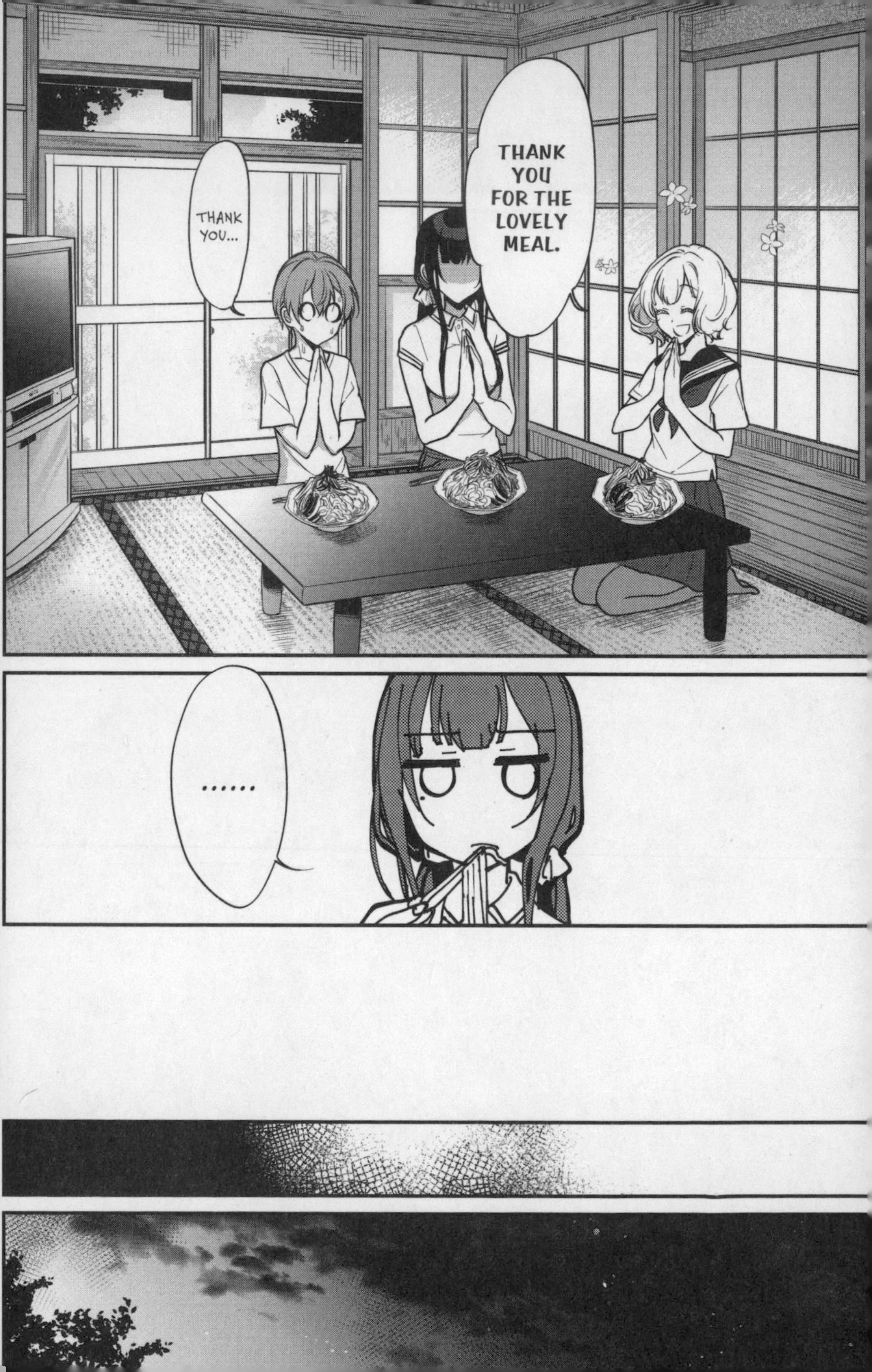
THANK YOU FOR THE LOVELY MEAL.
THANK YOU...
......

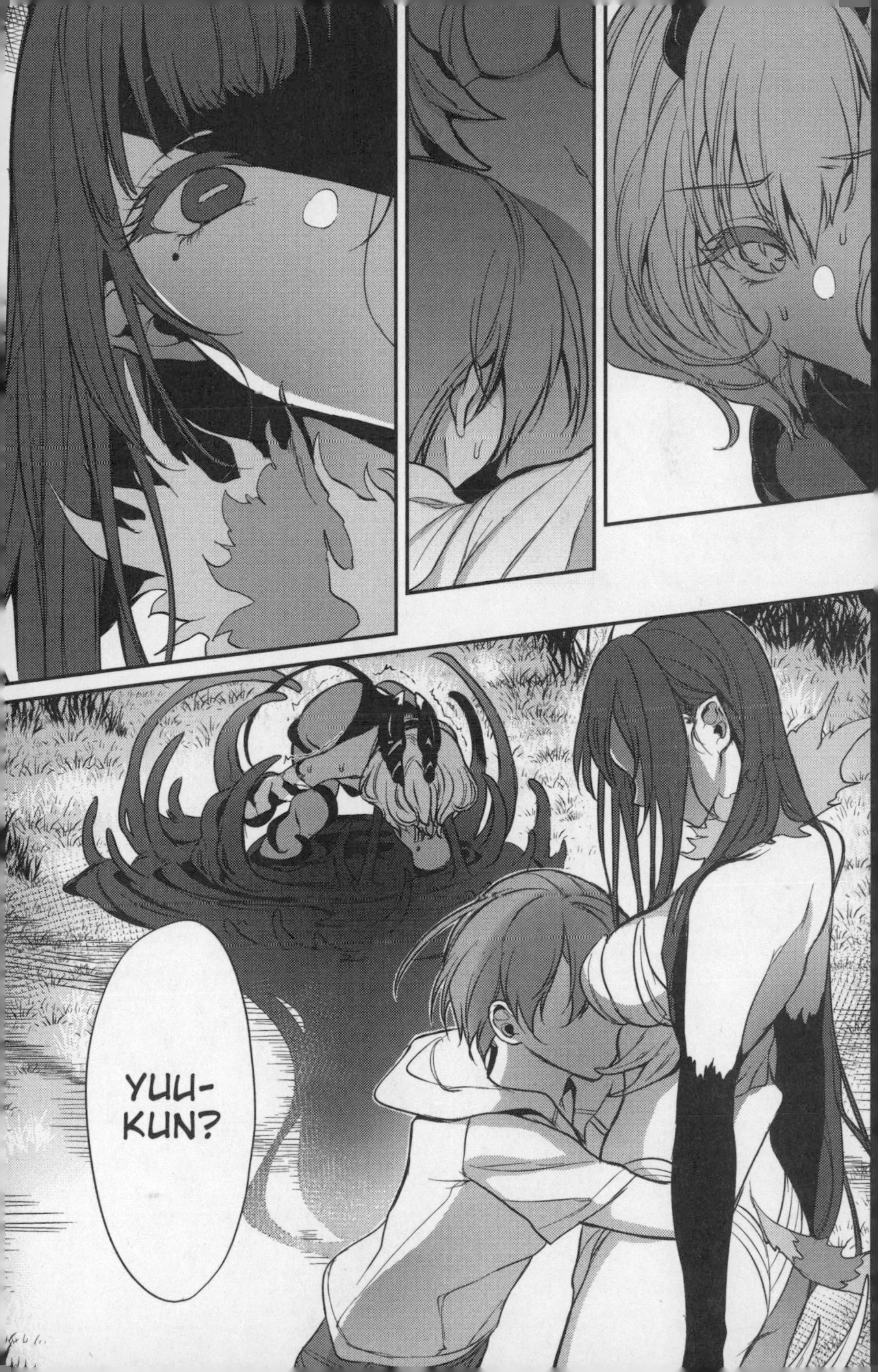
YUU-KUN?

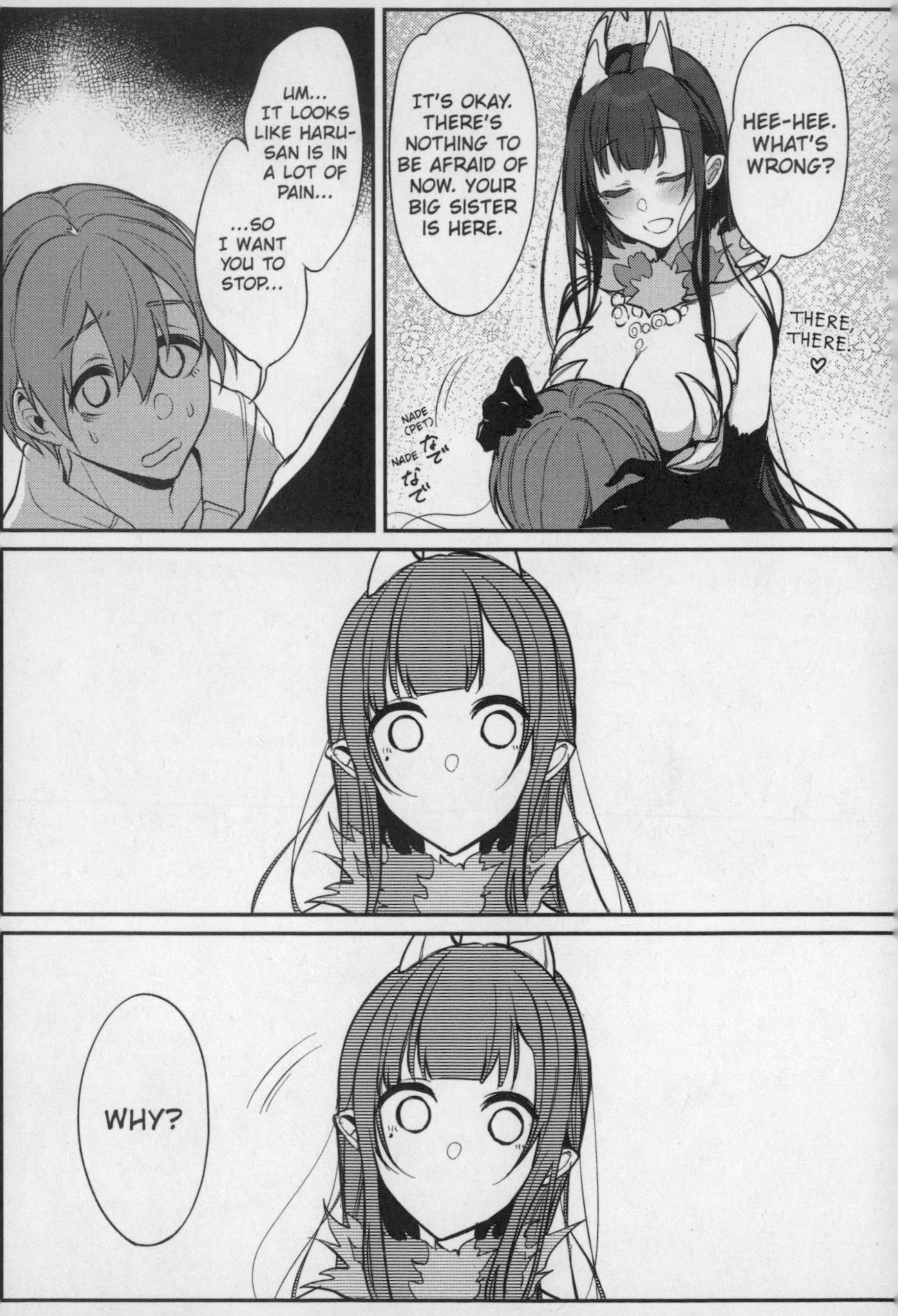
HEE-HEE. WHAT'S WRONG?
IT'S OKAY. THERE'S NOTHING TO BE AFRAID OF NOW. YOUR BIG SISTER IS HERE.
THERE, THERE. ♥
NADE (PET) NADE なでなで
UM... IT LOOKS LIKE HARU-SAN IS IN A LOT OF PAIN...
...SO I WANT YOU TO STOP...
WHY?

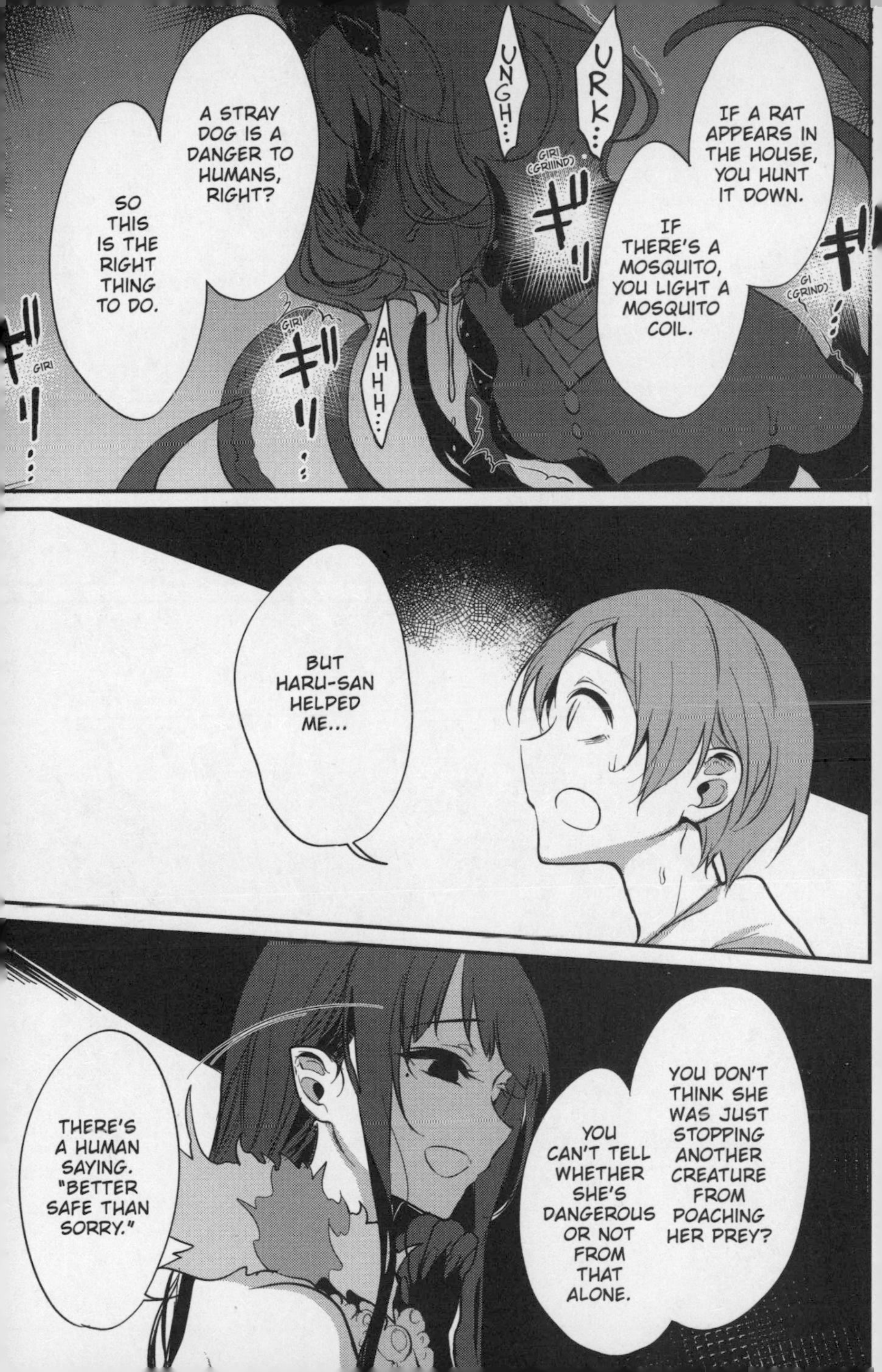
GI (GRIND)
IF A RAT APPEARS IN THE HOUSE, YOU HUNT IT DOWN.
IF THERE'S A MOSQUITO, YOU LIGHT A MOSQUITO COIL.
URK...
GIRI (GRIIIND)
UNGH...
A STRAY DOG IS A DANGER TO HUMANS, RIGHT?
SO THIS IS THE RIGHT THING TO DO.
AHHH...
GIRI
GIRI
BUT HARU-SAN HELPED ME...
YOU DON'T THINK SHE WAS JUST STOPPING ANOTHER CREATURE FROM POACHING HER PREY?
YOU CAN'T TELL WHETHER SHE'S DANGEROUS OR NOT FROM THAT ALONE.
THERE'S A HUMAN SAYING. "BETTER SAFE THAN SORRY."

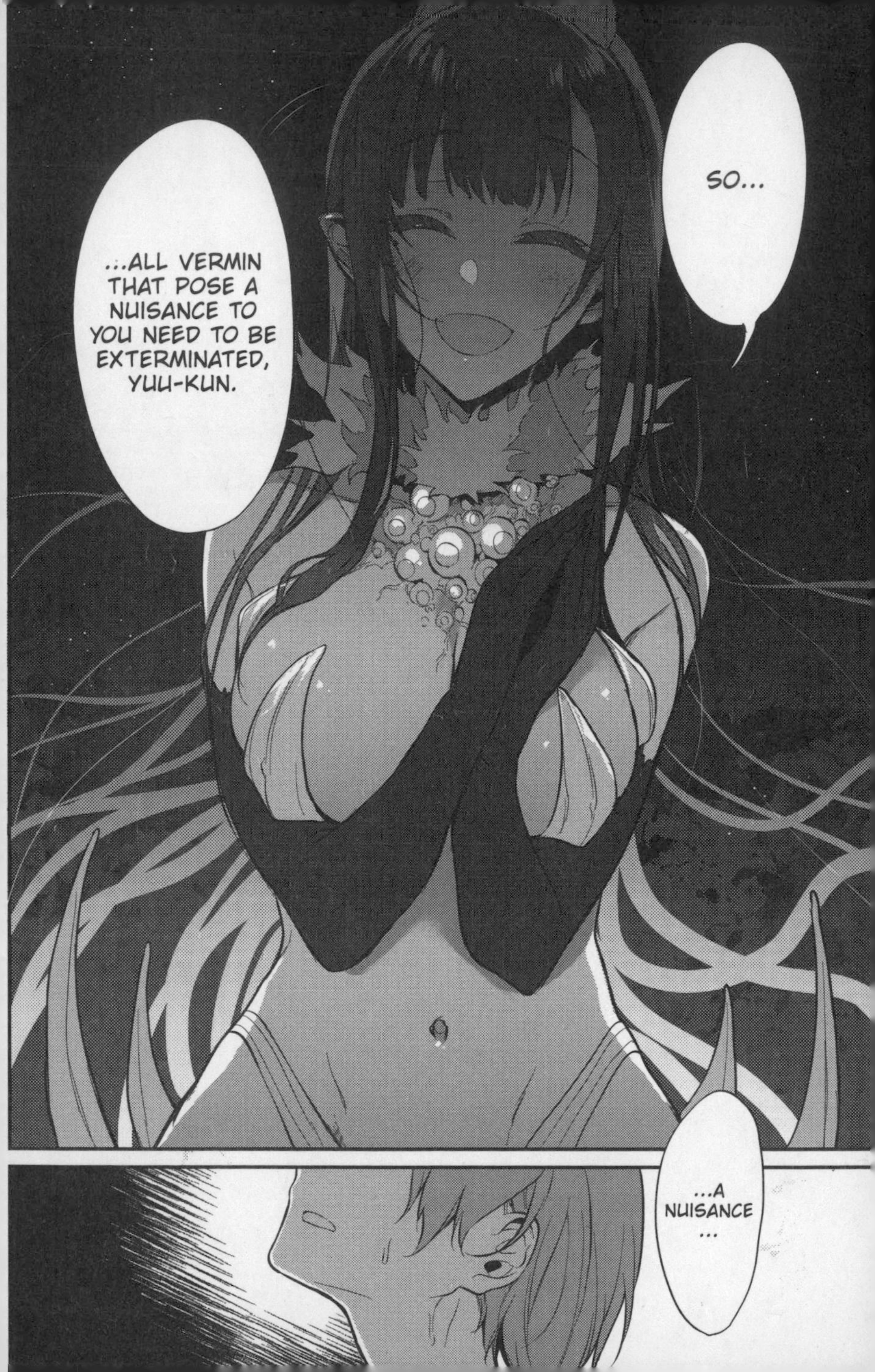
SO...
...ALL VERMIN THAT POSE A NUISANCE TO YOU NEED TO BE EXTERMINATED, YUU-KUN.
...A NUISANCE ...

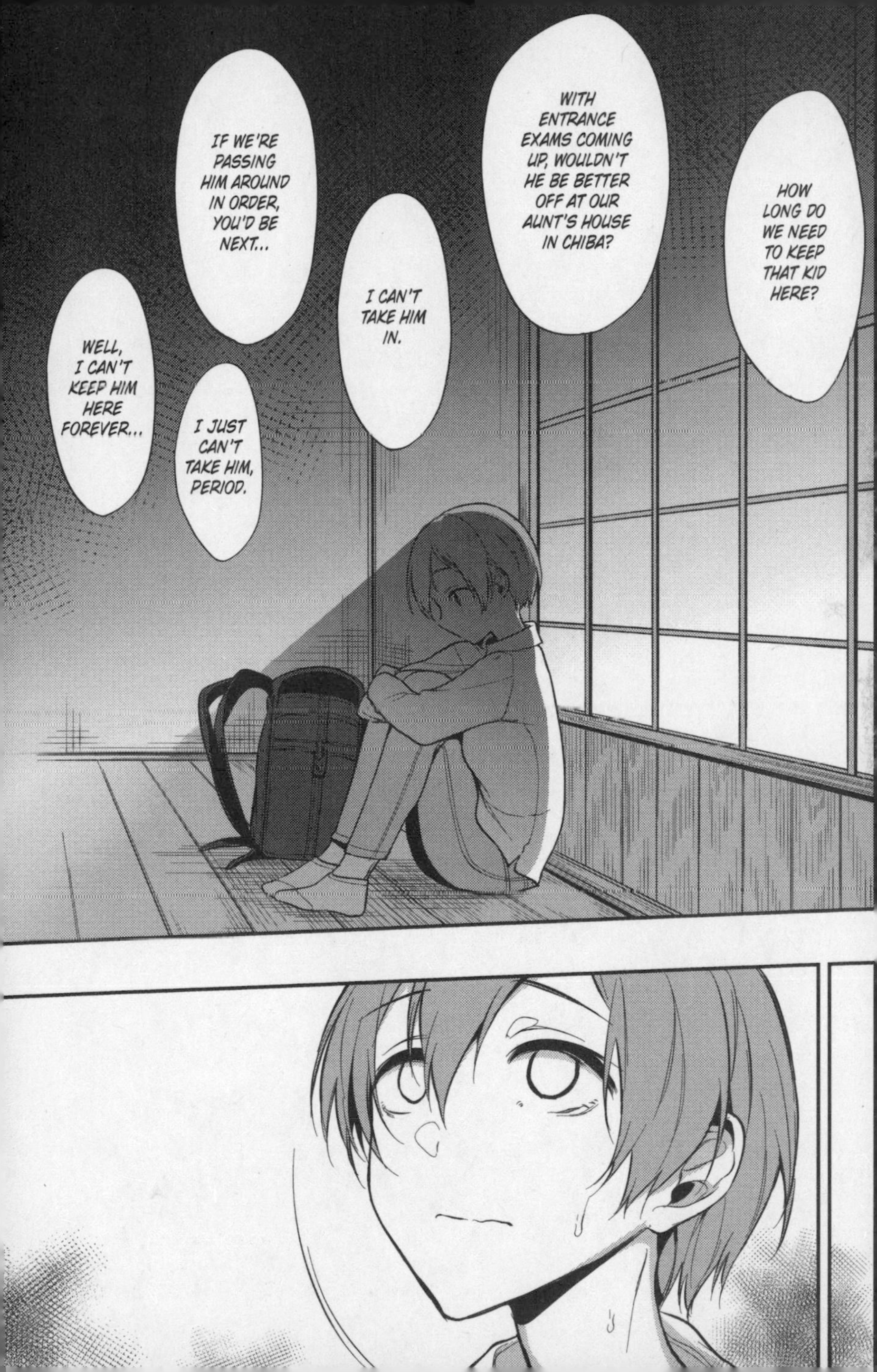
HOW LONG DO WE NEED TO KEEP THAT KID HERE?
WITH ENTRANCE EXAMS COMING UP, WOULDN'T HE BE BETTER OFF AT OUR AUNT'S HOUSE IN CHIBA?
IF WE'RE PASSING HIM AROUND IN ORDER, YOU'D BE NEXT...
I CAN'T TAKE HIM IN.
WELL, I CAN'T KEEP HIM HERE FOREVER...
I JUST CAN'T TAKE HIM, PERIOD.

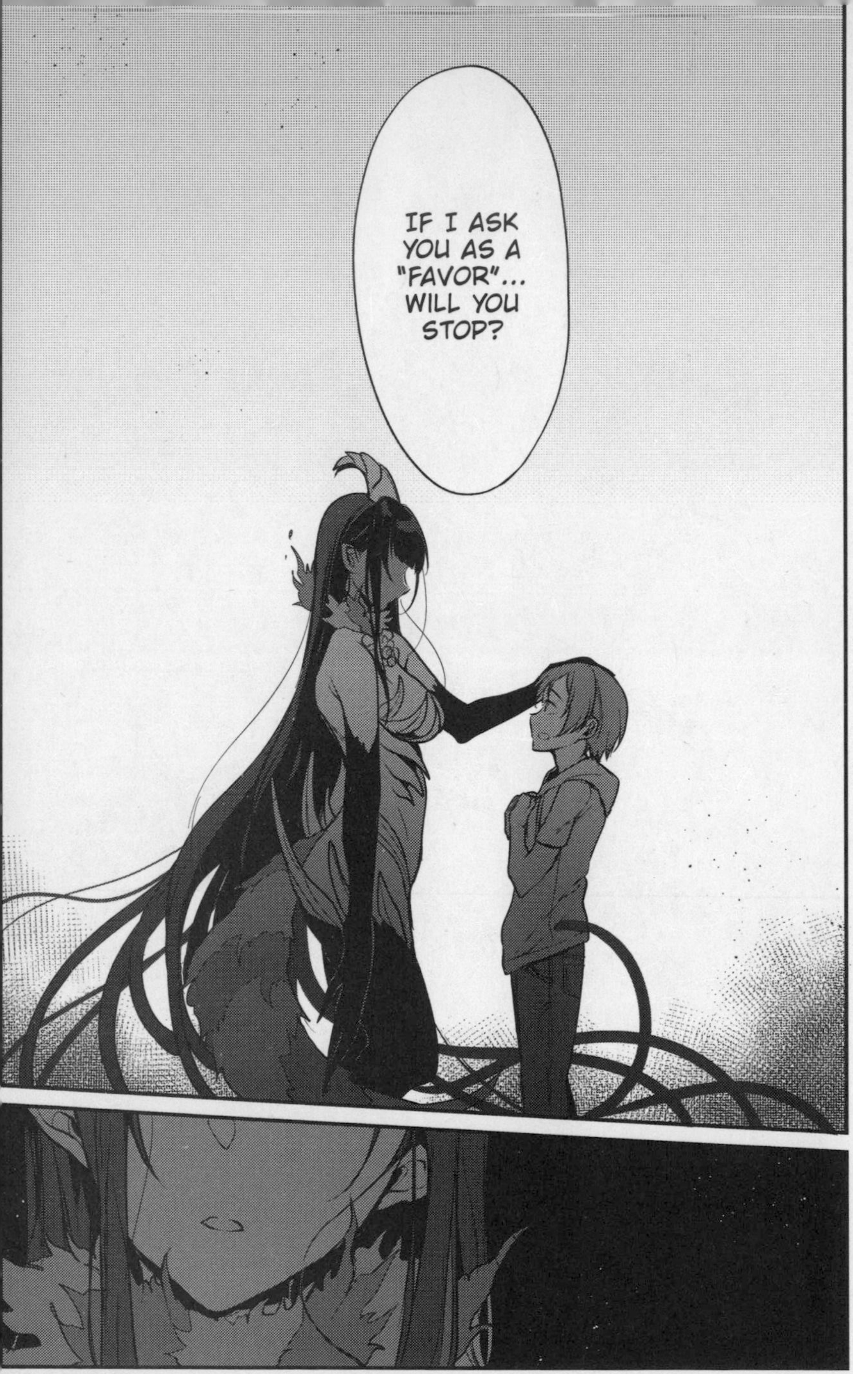
IF I ASK YOU AS A "FAVOR"... WILL YOU STOP?

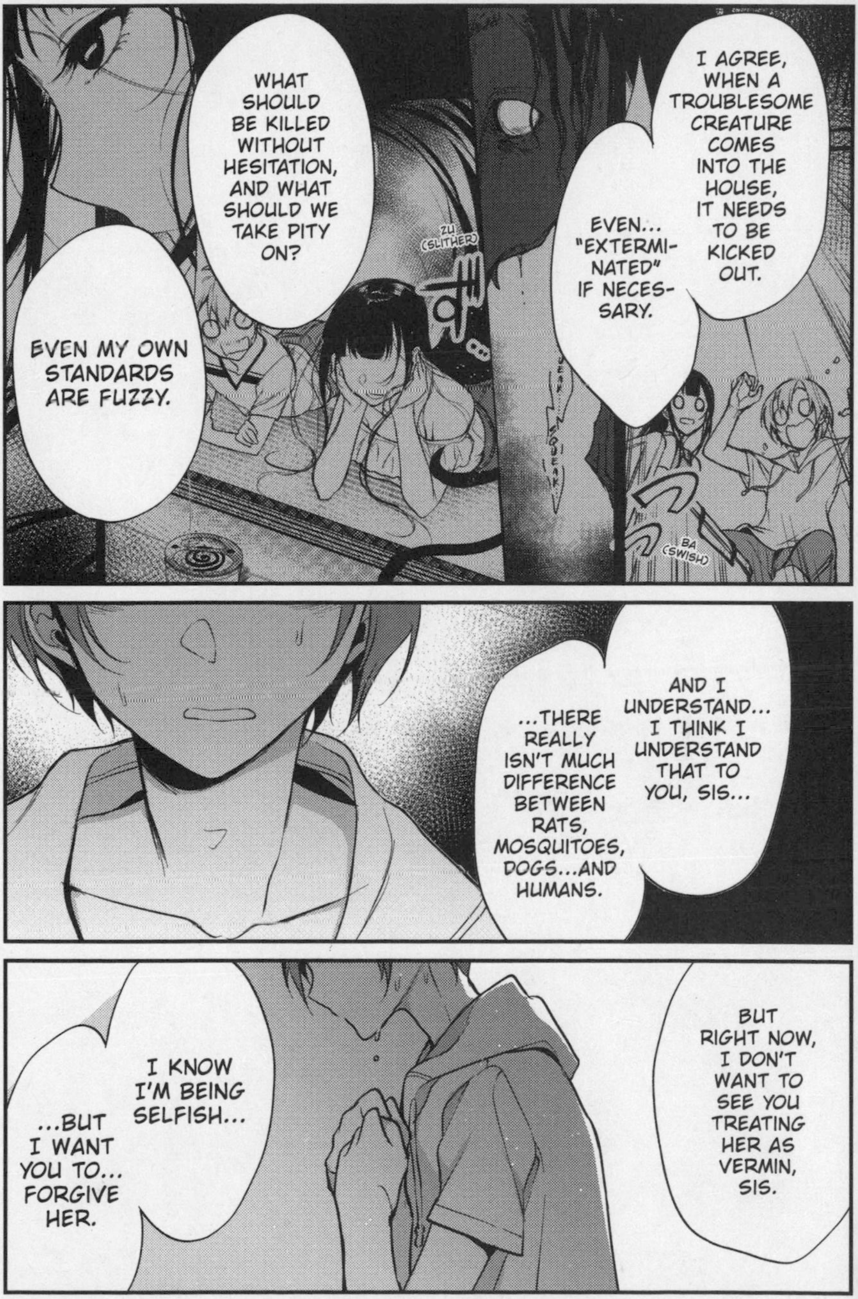
I AGREE, WHEN A TROUBLESOME CREATURE COMES INTO THE HOUSE, IT NEEDS TO BE KICKED OUT.
EVEN... "EXTERMINATED" IF NECESSARY.
BA (SWISH)
ZU (SLITHER)
WHAT SHOULD BE KILLED WITHOUT HESITATION, AND WHAT SHOULD WE TAKE PITY ON?
EVEN MY OWN STANDARDS ARE FUZZY.
AND I UNDERSTAND... I THINK I UNDERSTAND THAT TO YOU, SIS...
...THERE REALLY ISN'T MUCH DIFFERENCE BETWEEN RATS, MOSQUITOES, DOGS...AND HUMANS.
BUT RIGHT NOW, I DON'T WANT TO SEE YOU TREATING HER AS VERMIN, SIS.
I KNOW I'M BEING SELFISH...
...BUT I WANT YOU TO... FORGIVE HER.

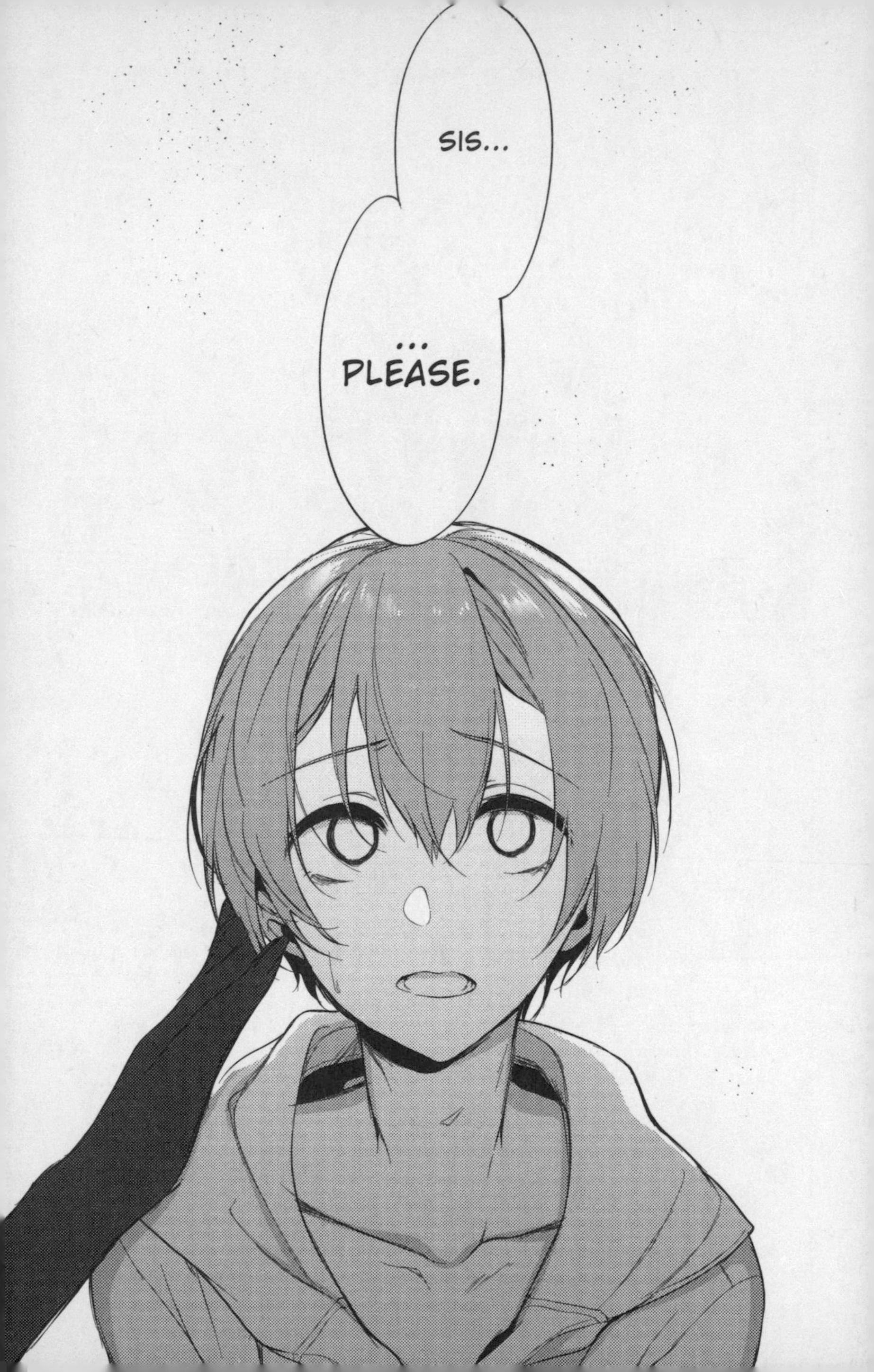
SIS...
... PLEASE.

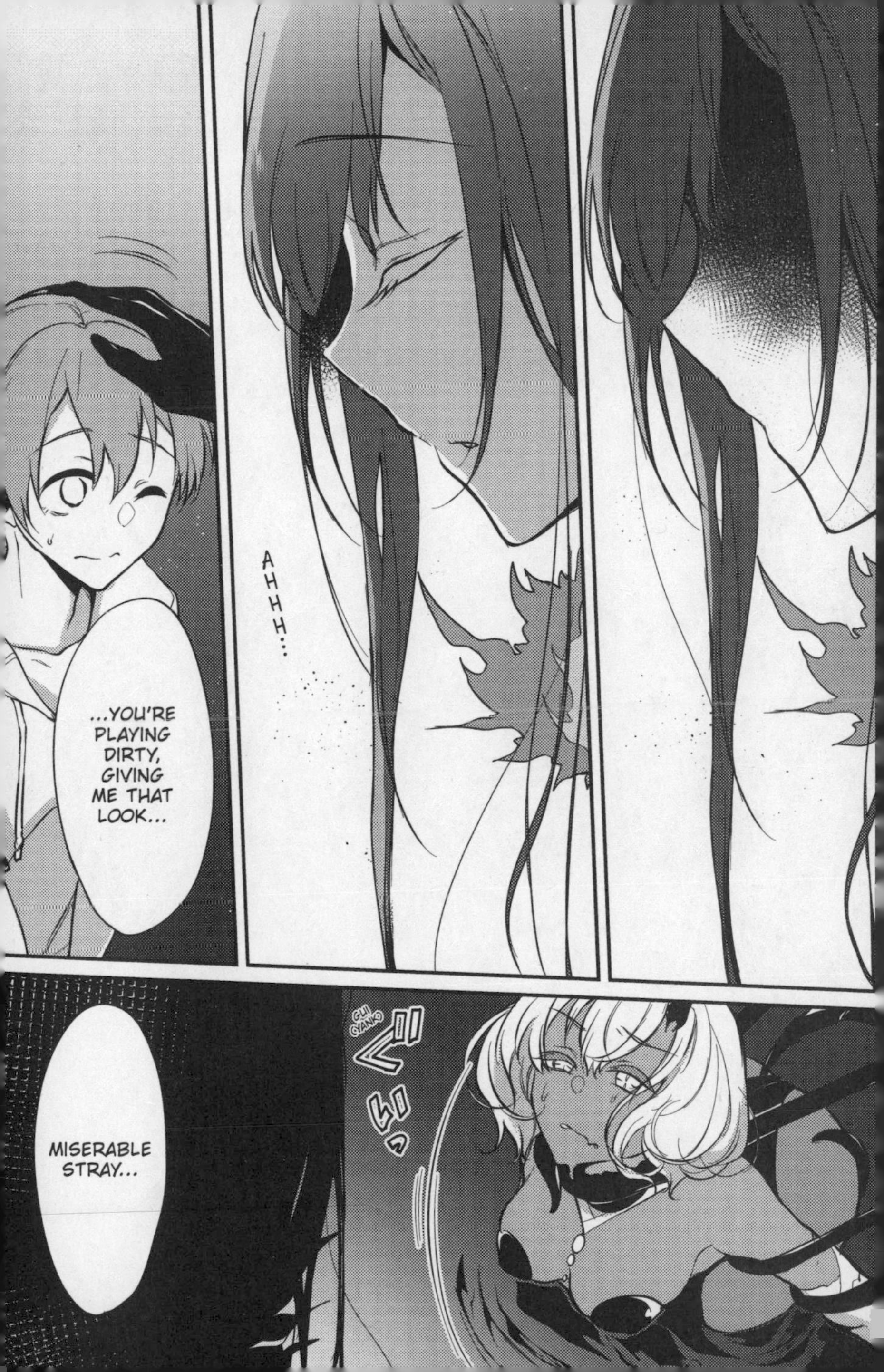
AHHH...
...YOU'RE PLAYING DIRTY, GIVING ME THAT LOOK...
GUI GYANK
MISERABLE STRAY...

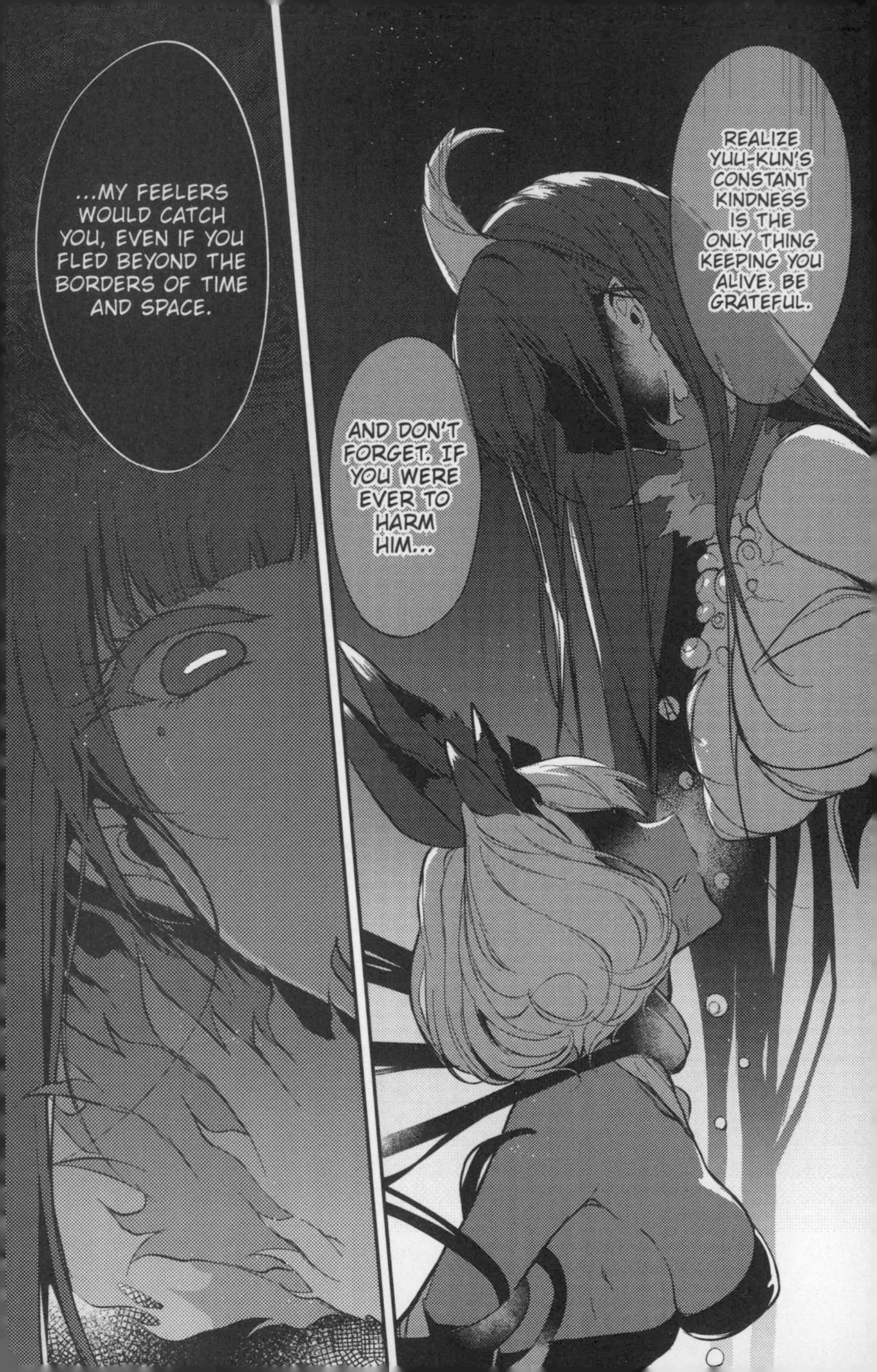
REALIZE YUU-KUN'S CONSTANT KINDNESS IS THE ONLY THING KEEPING YOU ALIVE. BE GRATEFUL.
AND DON'T FORGET. IF YOU WERE EVER TO HARM HIM...
...MY FEELERS WOULD CATCH YOU, EVEN IF YOU FLED BEYOND THE BORDERS OF TIME AND SPACE.

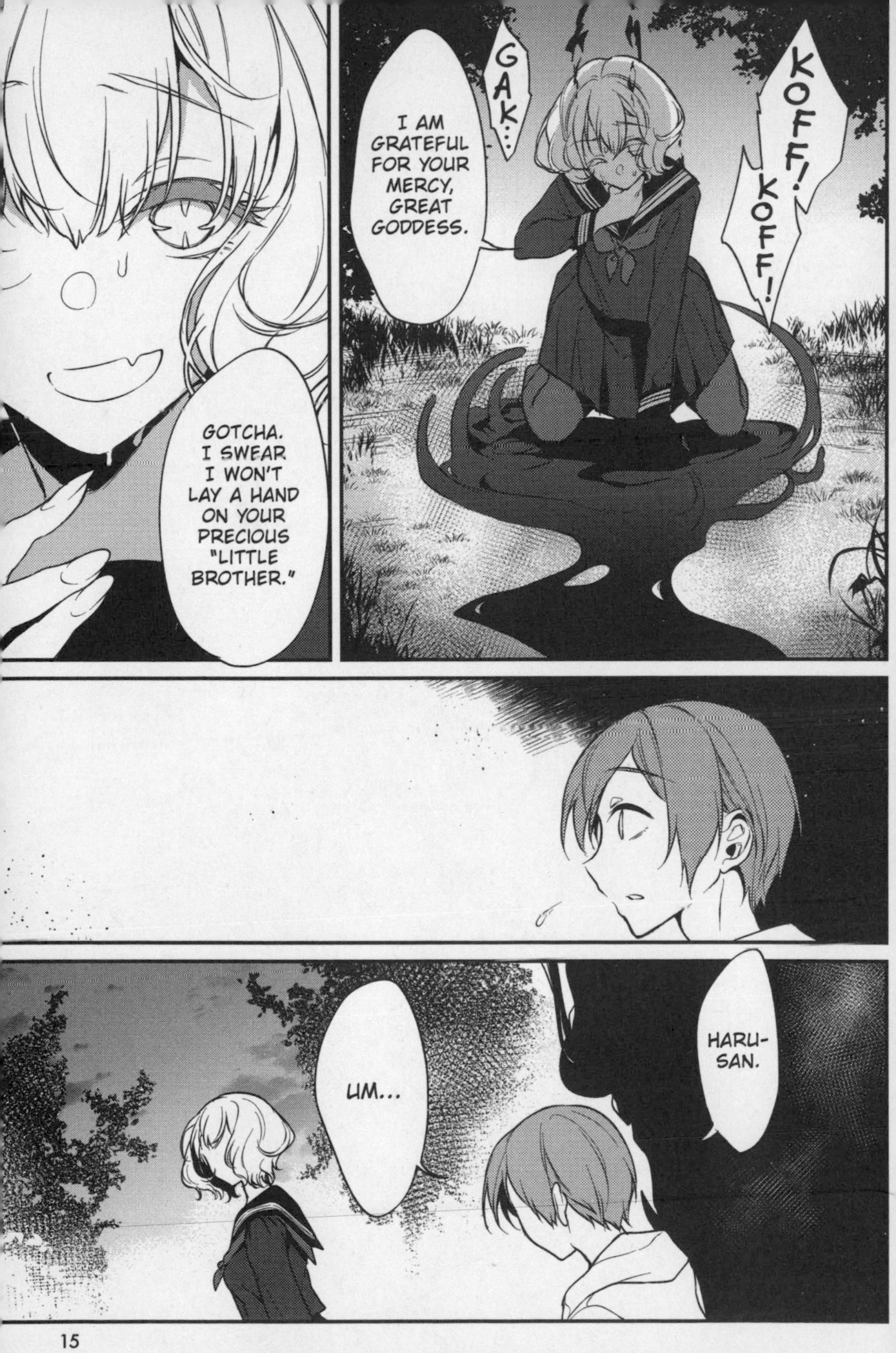
KOFF! KOFF!
GAK...
I AM GRATEFUL FOR YOUR MERCY, GREAT GODDESS.
GOTCHA. I SWEAR I WON'T LAY A HAND ON YOUR PRECIOUS "LITTLE BROTHER."
HARU-SAN.
UM...

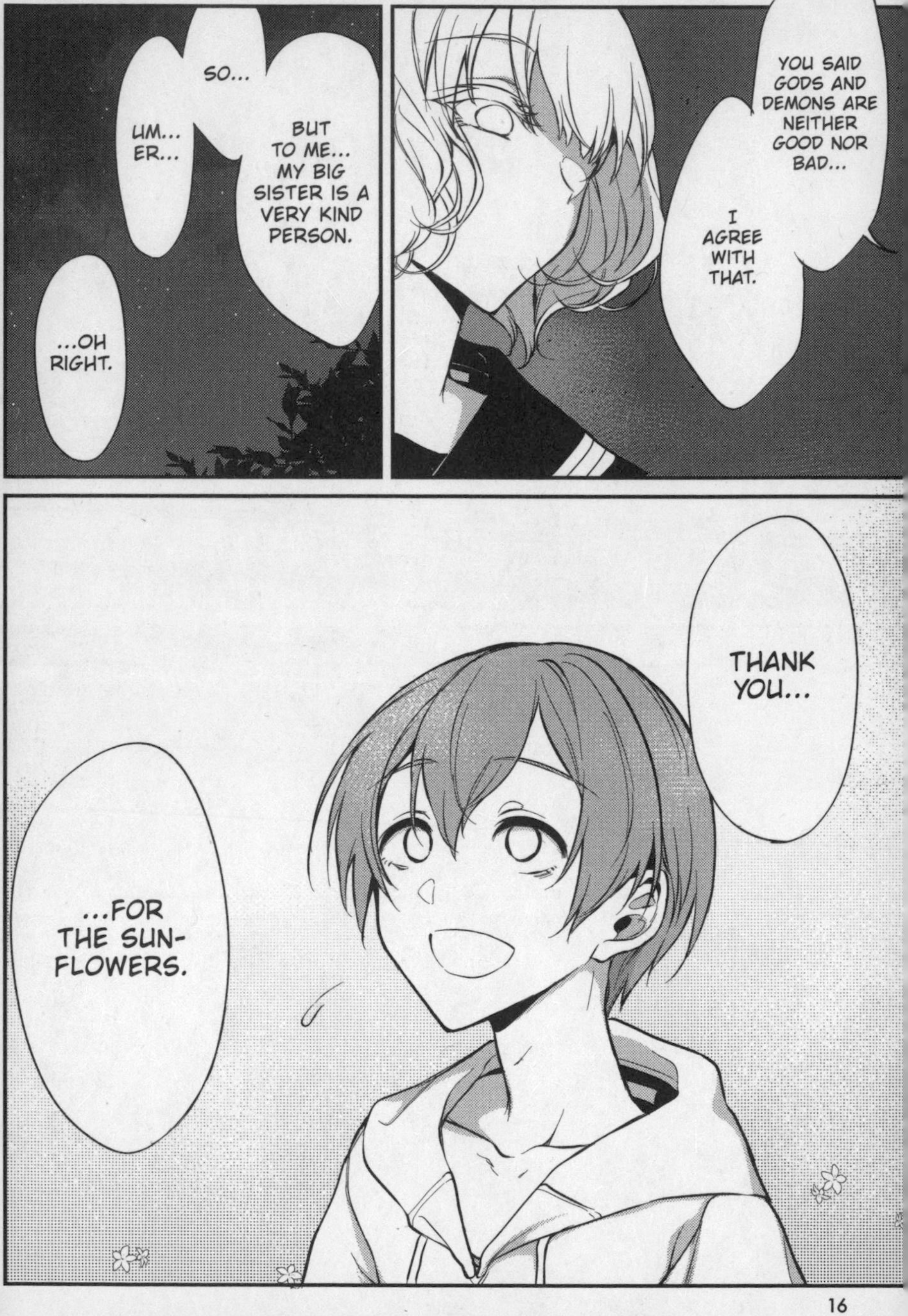
YOU SAID GODS AND DEMONS ARE NEITHER GOOD NOR BAD...
I AGREE WITH THAT.
SO...
BUT TO ME... MY BIG SISTER IS A VERY KIND PERSON.
UM... ER...
...OH RIGHT.
THANK YOU...
...FOR THE SUN-FLOWERS.

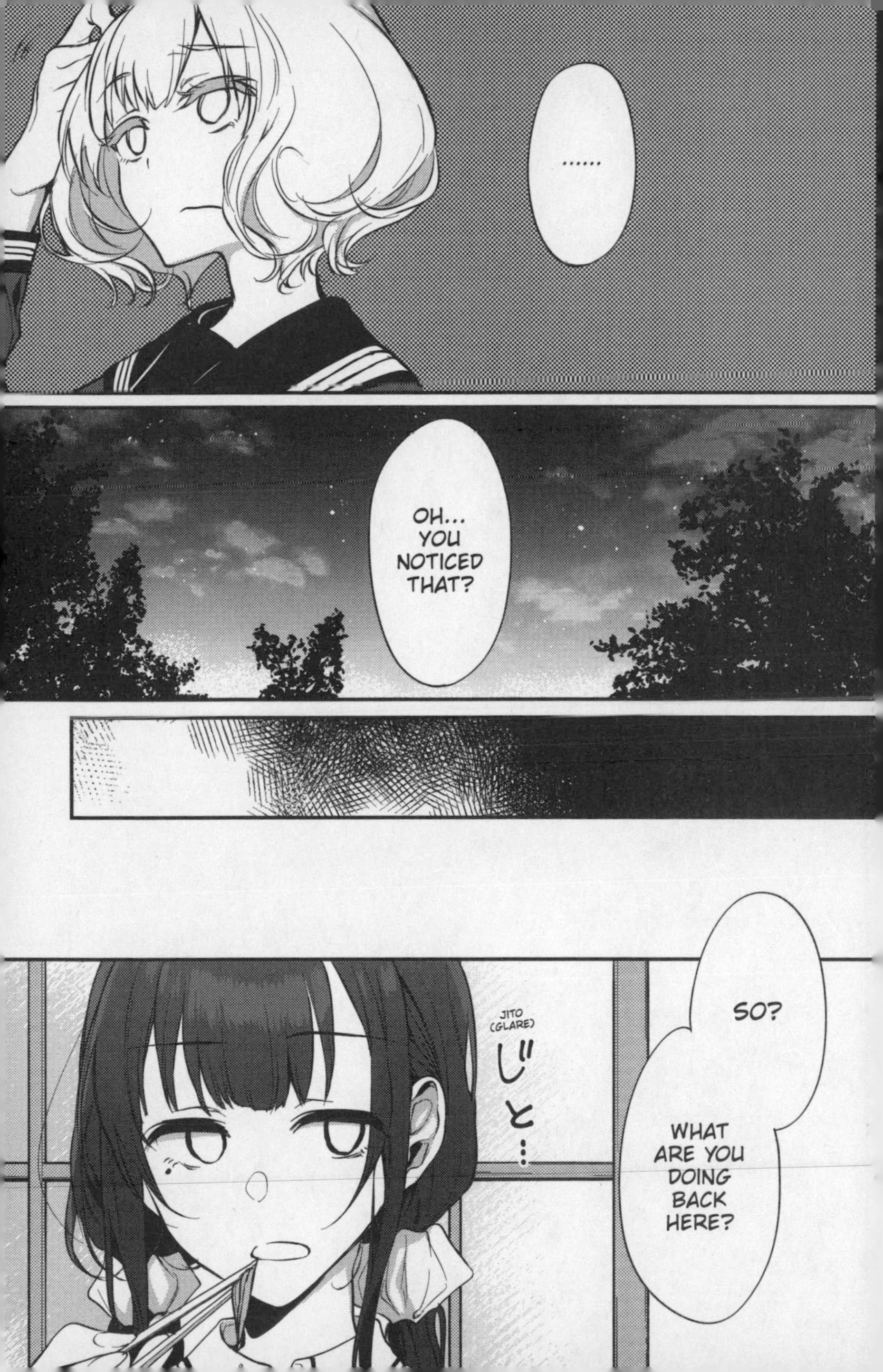
......
OH... YOU NOTICED THAT?
SO?
WHAT ARE YOU DOING BACK HERE?
JITO (GLARE)
じっと…

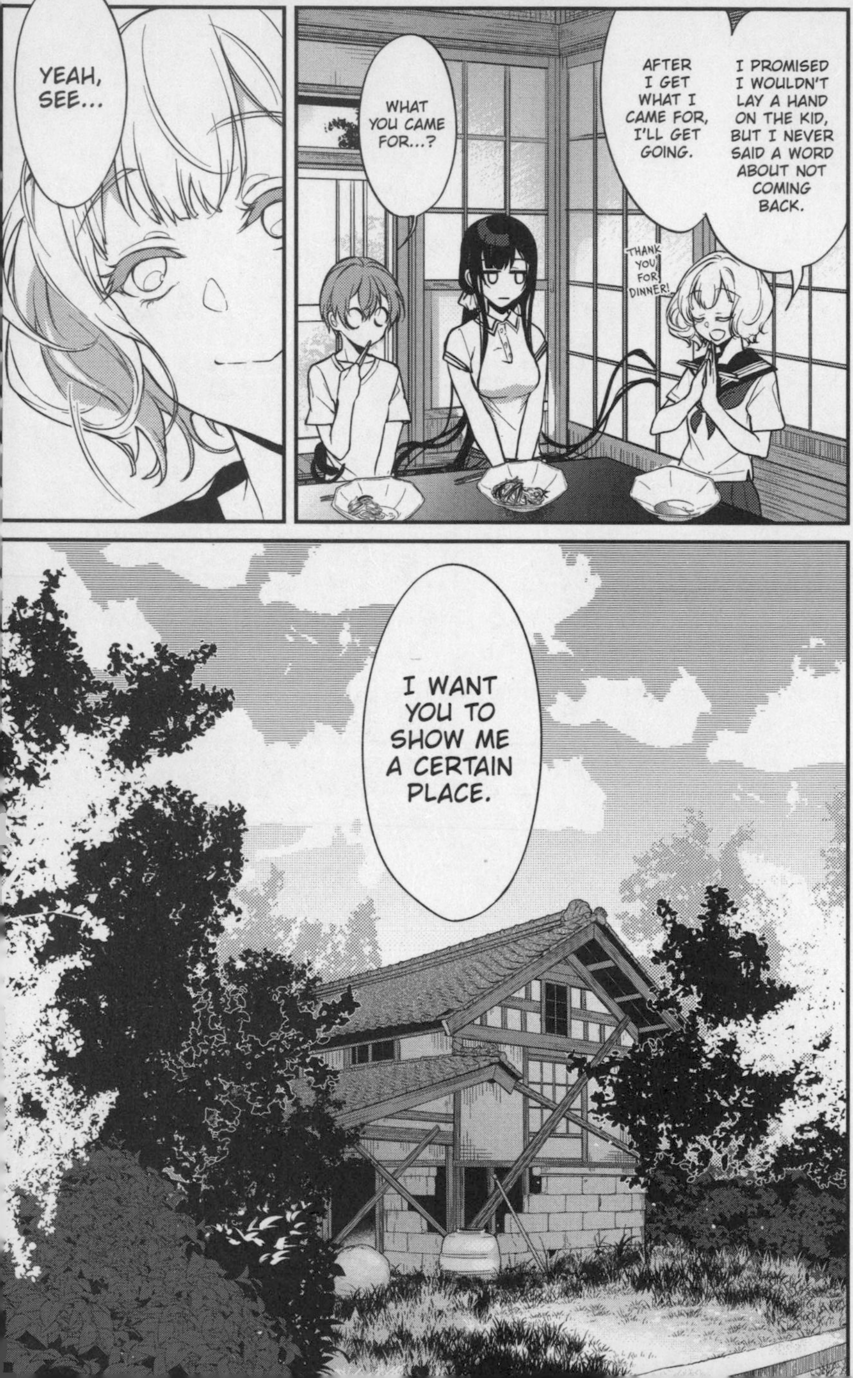
I PROMISED I WOULDN'T LAY A HAND ON THE KID, BUT I NEVER SAID A WORD ABOUT NOT COMING BACK.
AFTER I GET WHAT I CAME FOR, I'LL GET GOING.
THANK YOU FOR DINNER!
WHAT YOU CAME FOR...?
YEAH, SEE...
I WANT YOU TO SHOW ME A CERTAIN PLACE.

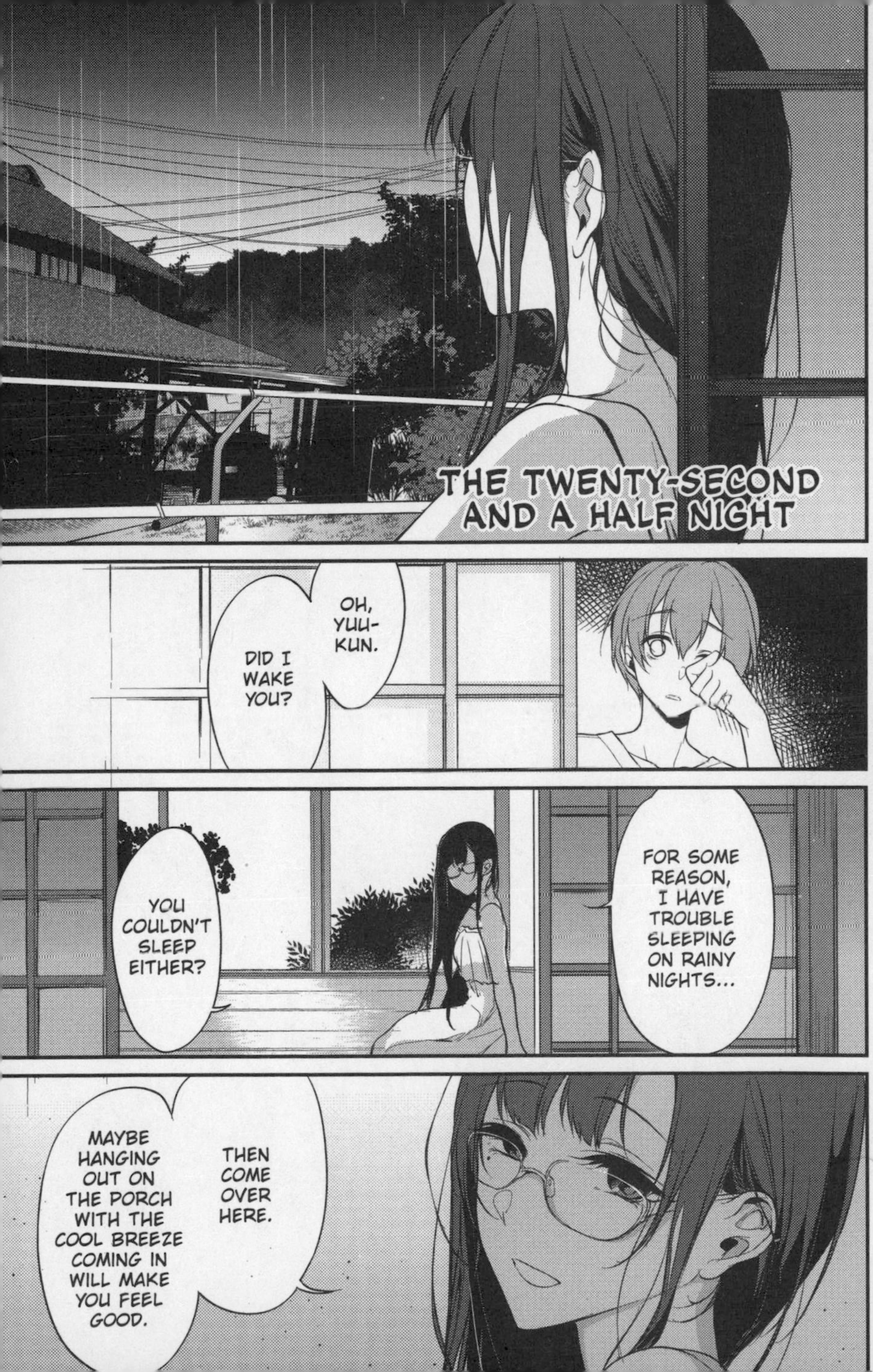
THE TWENTY-SECOND AND A HALF NIGHT
OH, YUU-KUN. DID I WAKE YOU?
FOR SOME REASON, I HAVE TROUBLE SLEEPING ON RAINY NIGHTS...
YOU COULDN'T SLEEP EITHER?
THEN COME OVER HERE.
MAYBE HANGING OUT ON THE PORCH WITH THE COOL BREEZE COMING IN WILL MAKE YOU FEEL GOOD.

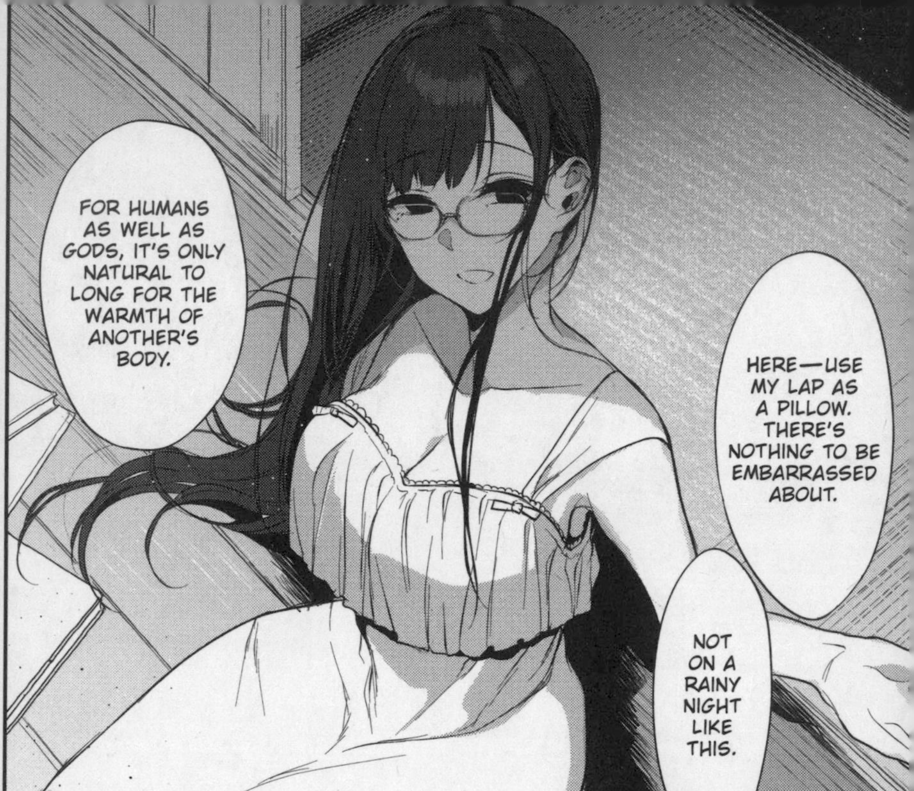
HERE—USE MY LAP AS A PILLOW. THERE'S NOTHING TO BE EMBARRASSED ABOUT.
NOT ON A RAINY NIGHT LIKE THIS.
FOR HUMANS AS WELL AS GODS, IT'S ONLY NATURAL TO LONG FOR THE WARMTH OF ANOTHER'S BODY.
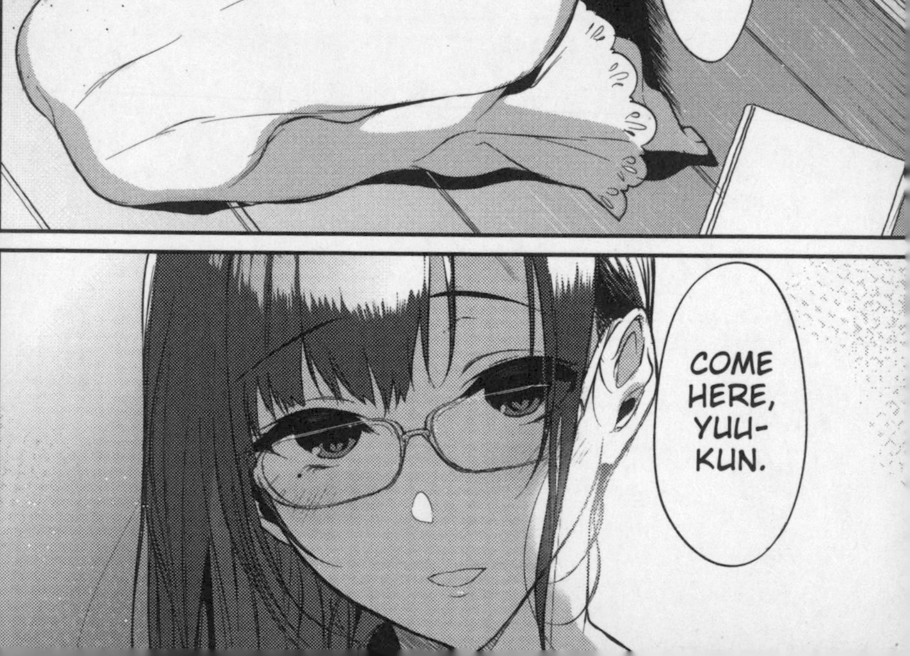
COME HERE, YUU-KUN.

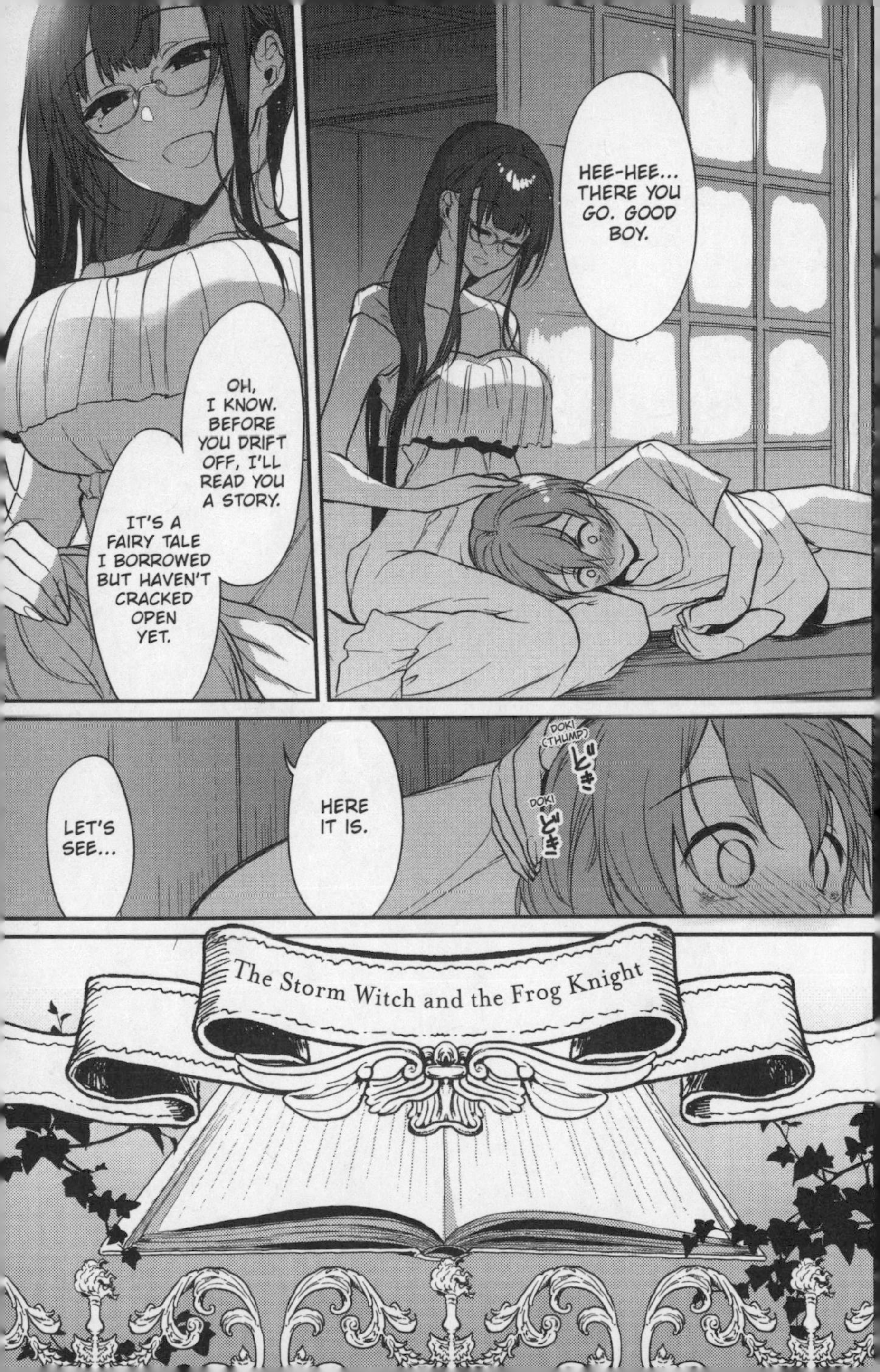
HEE-HEE... THERE YOU GO. GOOD BOY.
OH, I KNOW. BEFORE YOU DRIFT OFF, I'LL READ YOU A STORY.
IT'S A FAIRY TALE I BORROWED BUT HAVEN'T CRACKED OPEN YET.
DOKI (THUMP) どき
DOKI どき
HERE IT IS.
LET'S SEE...
The Storm Witch and the Frog Knight

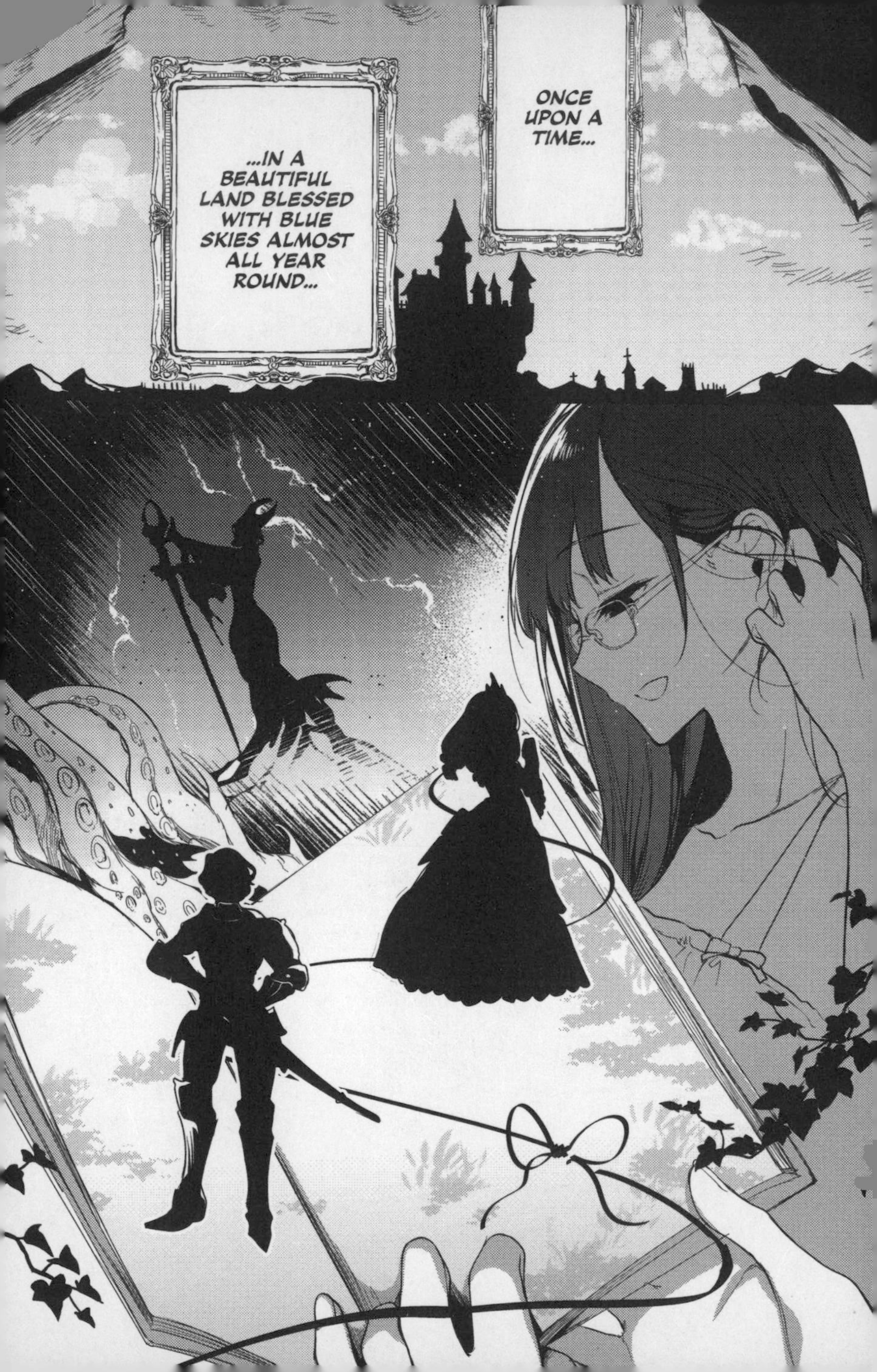
ONCE UPON A TIME...
...IN A BEAUTIFUL LAND BLESSED WITH BLUE SKIES ALMOST ALL YEAR ROUND...

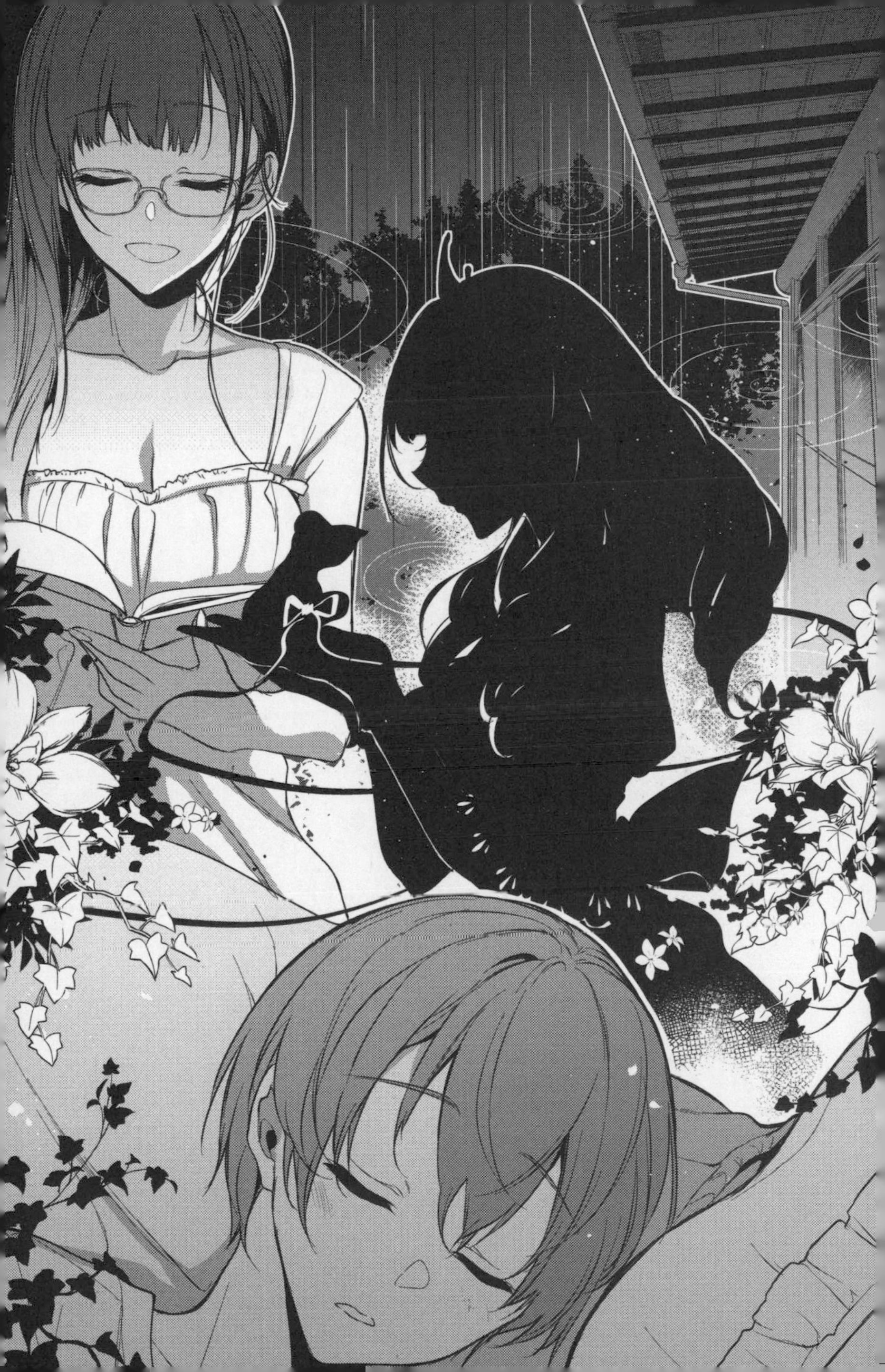

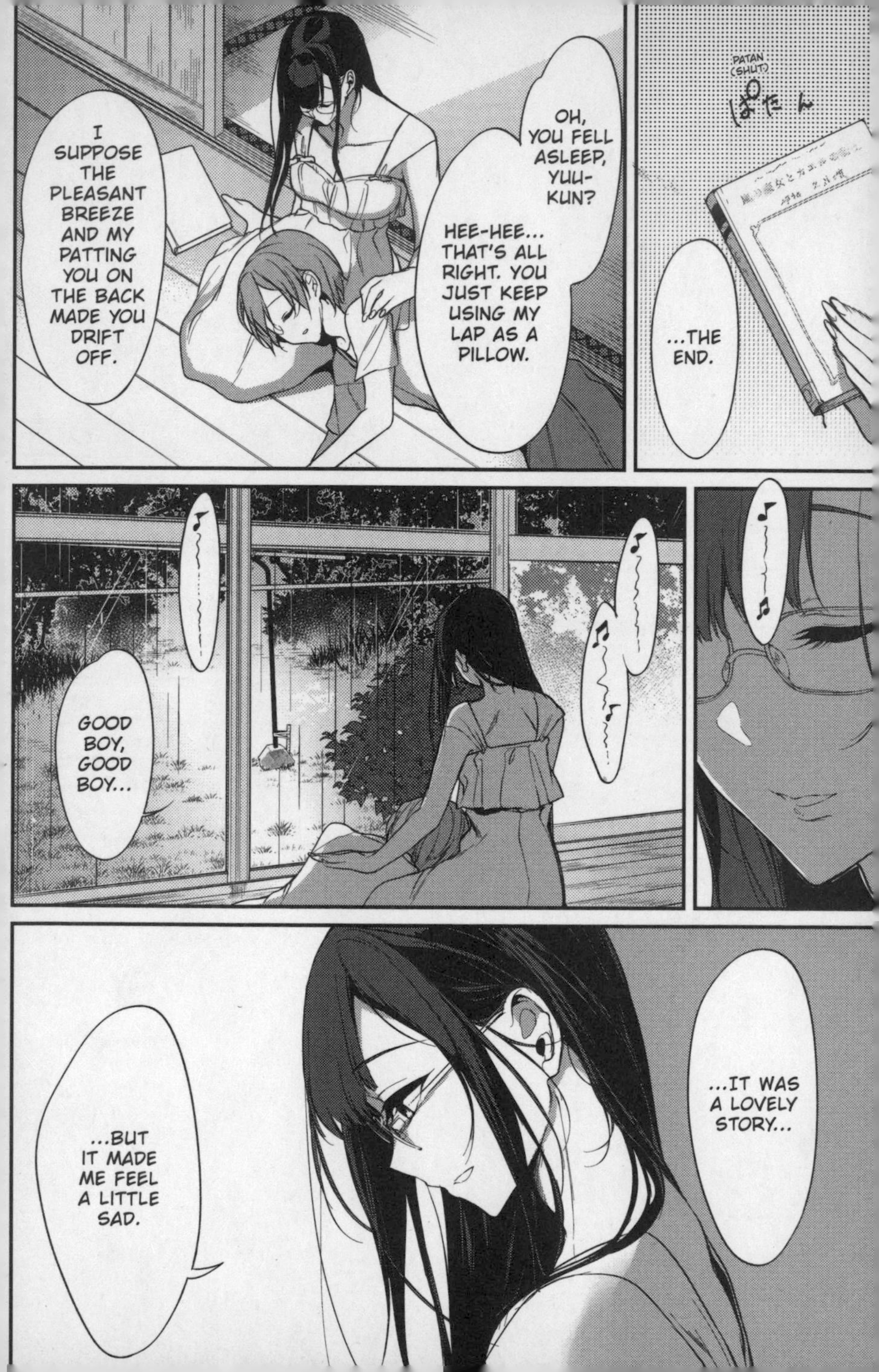
PATAN (SHUT)
ぱたん
...THE END.
OH, YOU FELL ASLEEP, YUU-KUN?
HEE-HEE... THAT'S ALL RIGHT. YOU JUST KEEP USING MY LAP AS A PILLOW.
I SUPPOSE THE PLEASANT BREEZE AND MY PATTING YOU ON THE BACK MADE YOU DRIFT OFF.
♪~~~♪
♪~~~
♪~~~
♪~~~
GOOD BOY, GOOD BOY...
...IT WAS A LOVELY STORY...
...BUT IT MADE ME FEEL A LITTLE SAD.

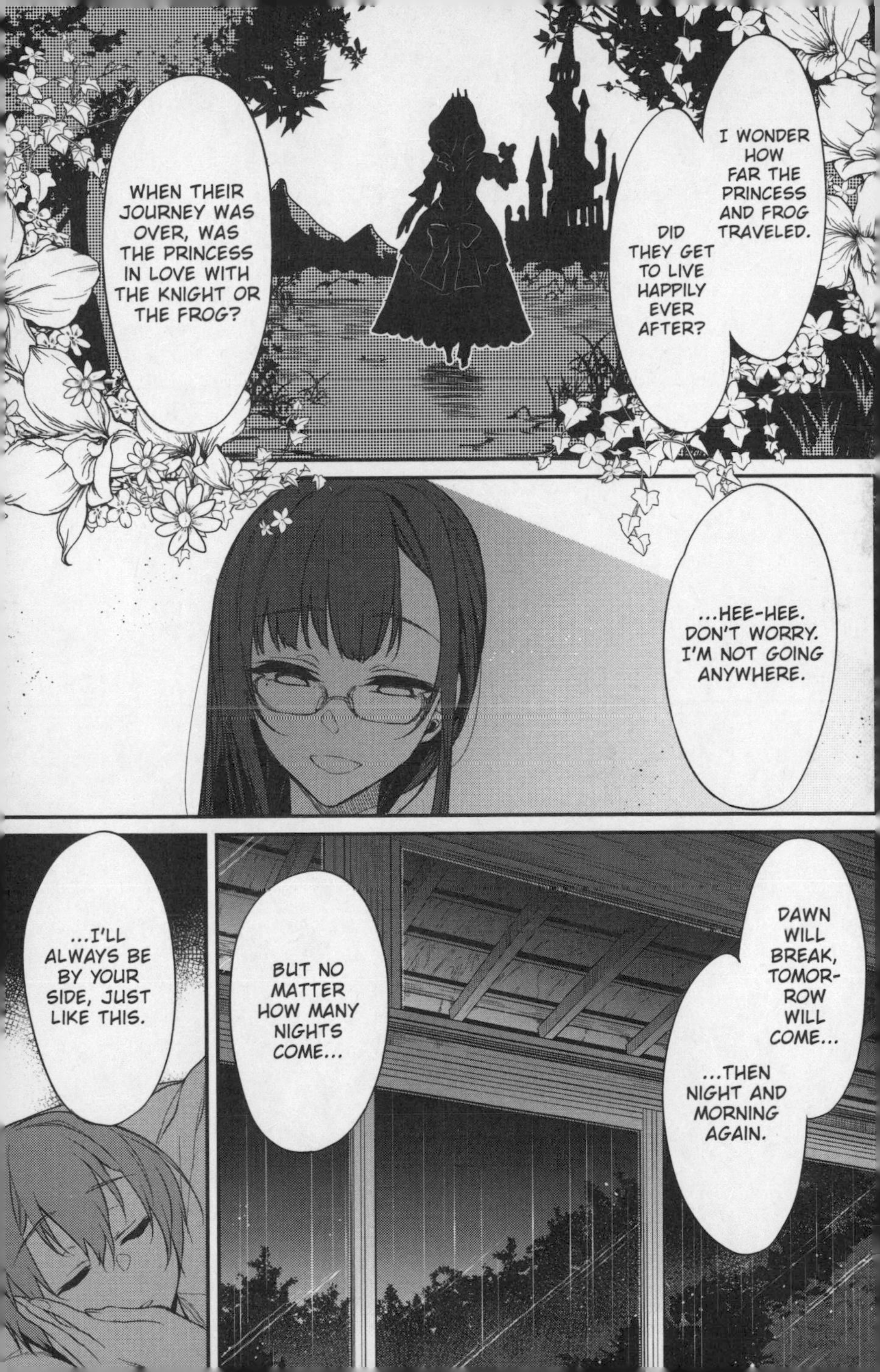
I WONDER HOW FAR THE PRINCESS AND FROG TRAVELED.
DID THEY GET TO LIVE HAPPILY EVER AFTER?
WHEN THEIR JOURNEY WAS OVER, WAS THE PRINCESS IN LOVE WITH THE KNIGHT OR THE FROG?
...HEE-HEE. DON'T WORRY. I'M NOT GOING ANYWHERE.
DAWN WILL BREAK, TOMORROW WILL COME...
...THEN NIGHT AND MORNING AGAIN.
BUT NO MATTER HOW MANY NIGHTS COME...
...I'LL ALWAYS BE BY YOUR SIDE, JUST LIKE THIS.

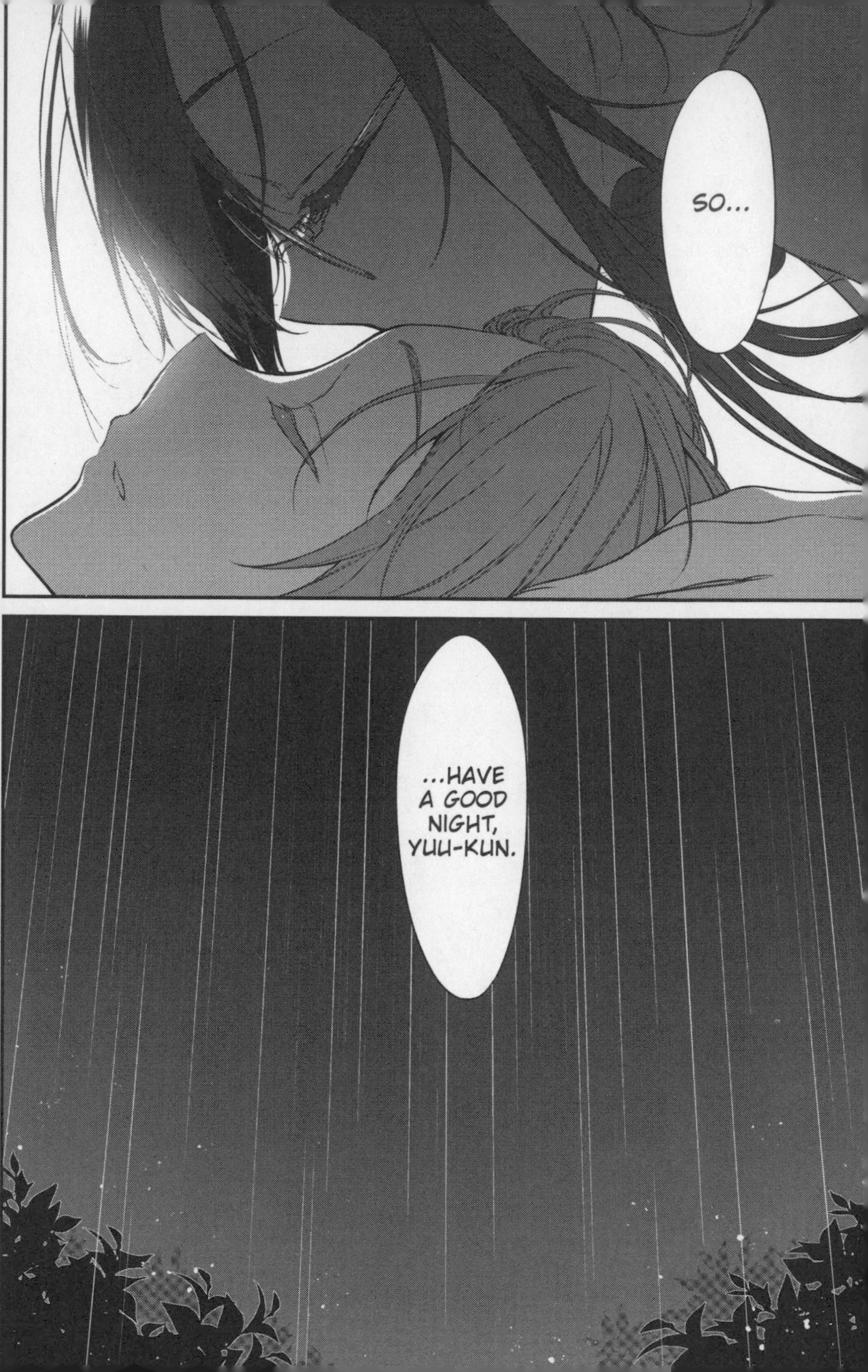
SO...
...HAVE A GOOD NIGHT, YUU-KUN.

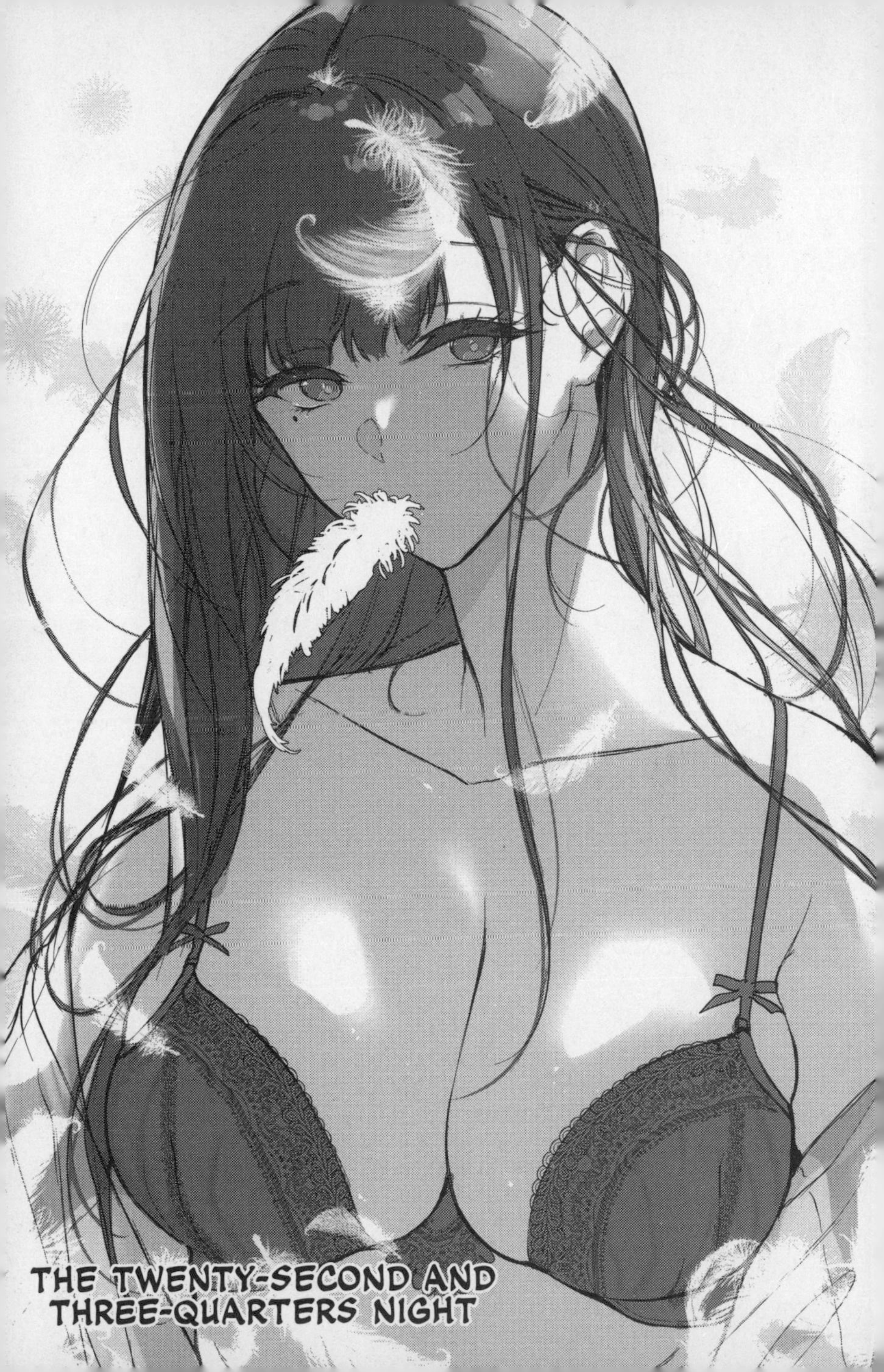

THE TWENTY-SECOND AND THREE-QUARTERS NIGHT

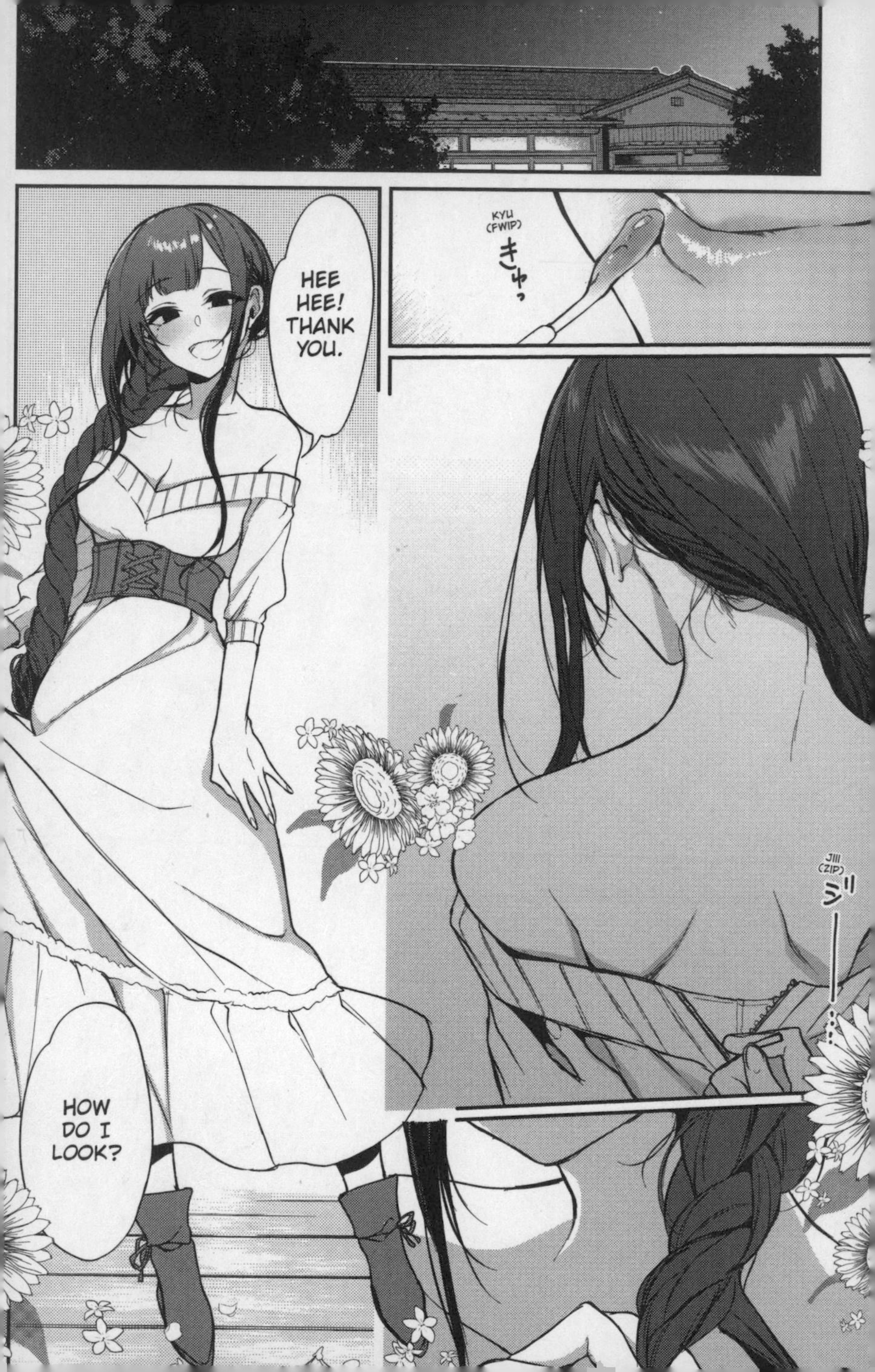
KYU (FWIP)
きゅっ
JIII (ZIP)
ジー……
HEE HEE! THANK YOU.
HOW DO I LOOK?

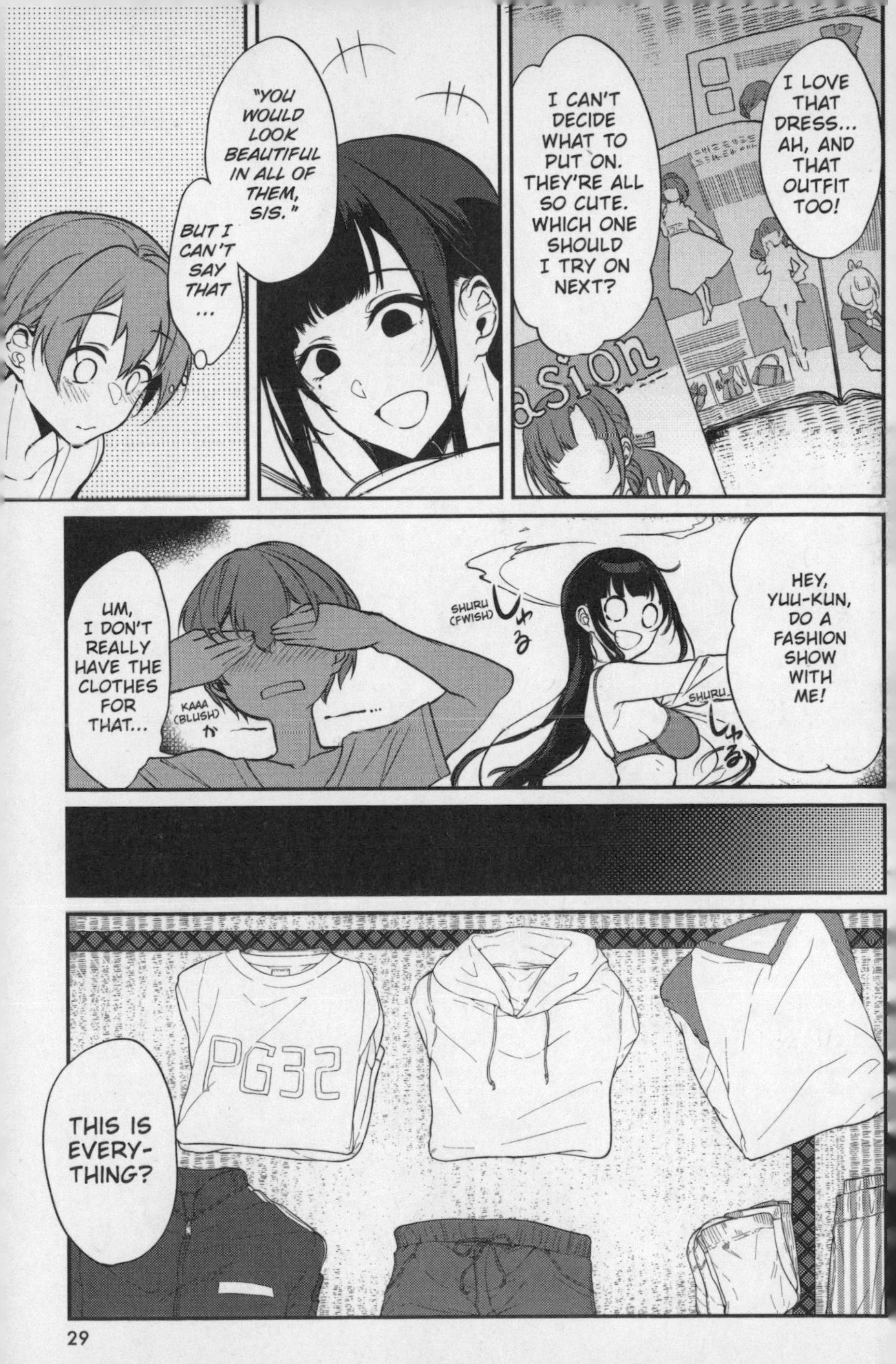
I LOVE THAT DRESS... AH, AND THAT OUTFIT TOO!
I CAN'T DECIDE WHAT TO PUT ON. THEY'RE ALL SO CUTE. WHICH ONE SHOULD I TRY ON NEXT?
"YOU WOULD LOOK BEAUTIFUL IN ALL OF THEM, SIS."
BUT I CAN'T SAY THAT ...
HEY, YUU-KUN, DO A FASHION SHOW WITH ME!
SHURU しゅる
SHURU (FWISH) しゅる
KAAA (BLUSH) か
UM, I DON'T REALLY HAVE THE CLOTHES FOR THAT...
PG32
THIS IS EVERY-THING?

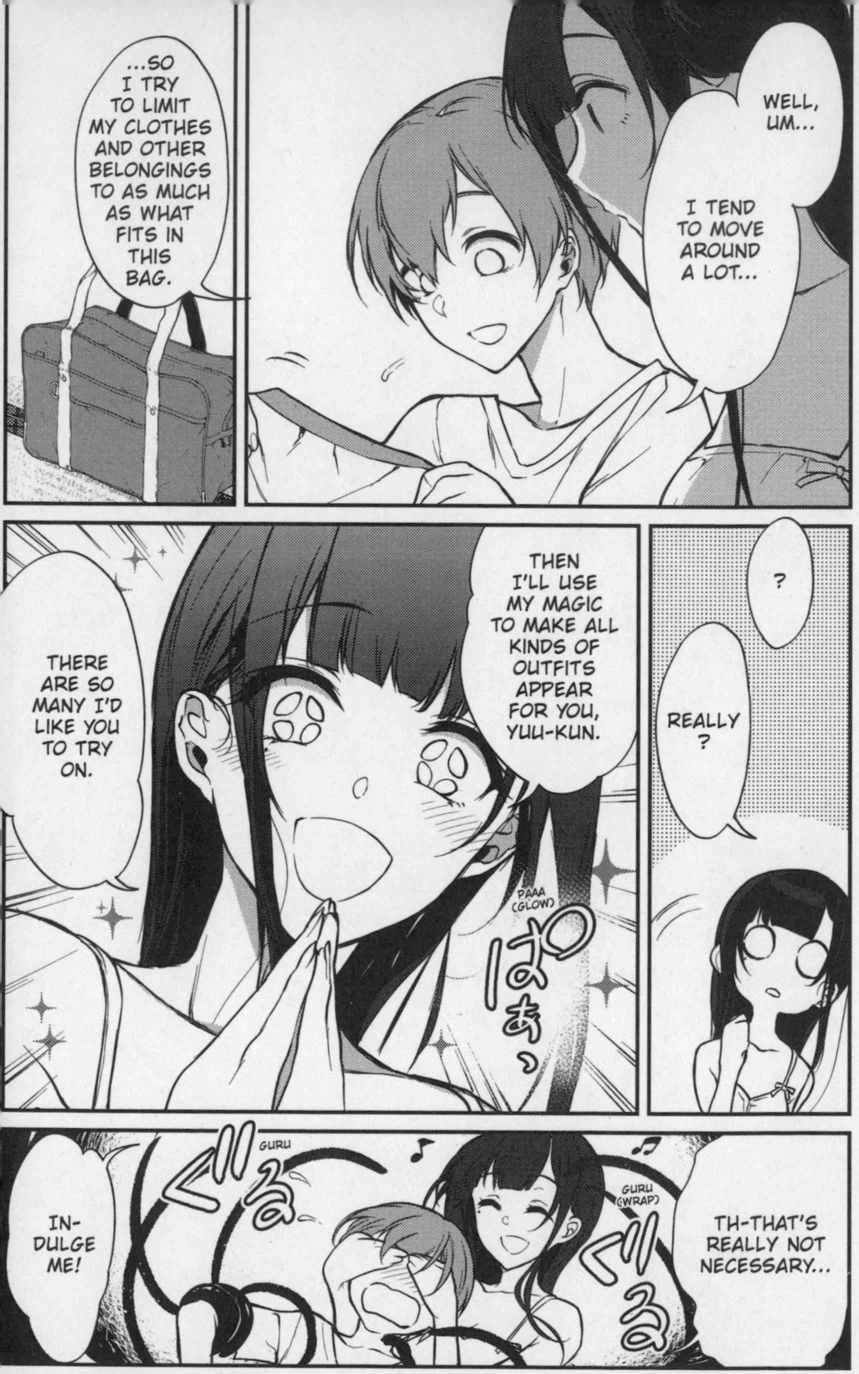
WELL, UM...
I TEND TO MOVE AROUND A LOT...
...SO I TRY TO LIMIT MY CLOTHES AND OTHER BELONGINGS TO AS MUCH AS WHAT FITS IN THIS BAG.
?
REALLY ?
THEN I'LL USE MY MAGIC TO MAKE ALL KINDS OF OUTFITS APPEAR FOR YOU, YUU-KUN.
THERE ARE SO MANY I'D LIKE YOU TO TRY ON.
PAAA (GLOW)
ぱぁっ
TH-THAT'S REALLY NOT NECESSARY...
GURU (WRAP)
GURU
IN-DULGE ME!

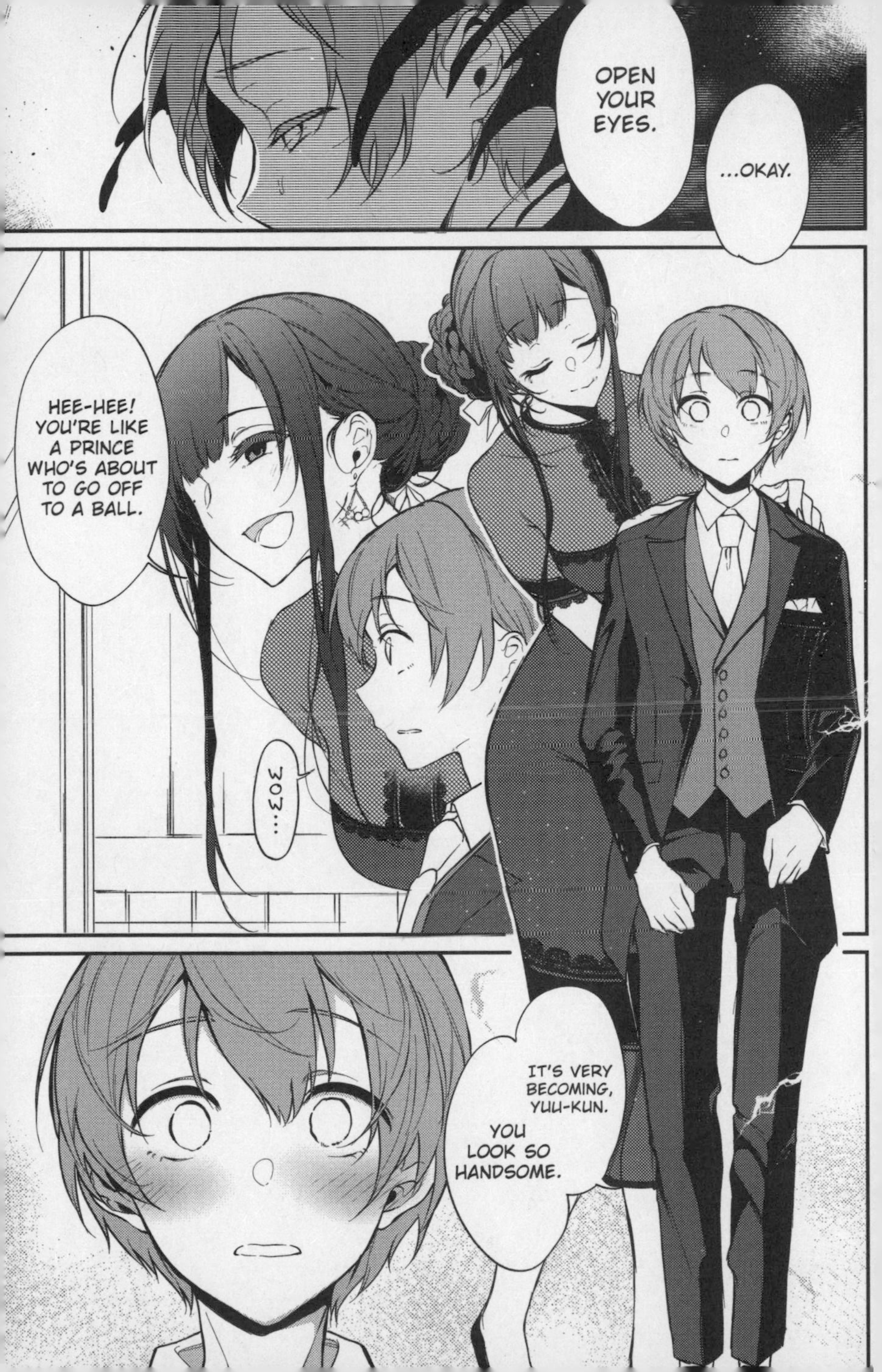
OPEN YOUR EYES.
...OKAY.
WOW...
HEE-HEE! YOU'RE LIKE A PRINCE WHO'S ABOUT TO GO OFF TO A BALL.
IT'S VERY BECOMING, YUU-KUN.
YOU LOOK SO HANDSOME.

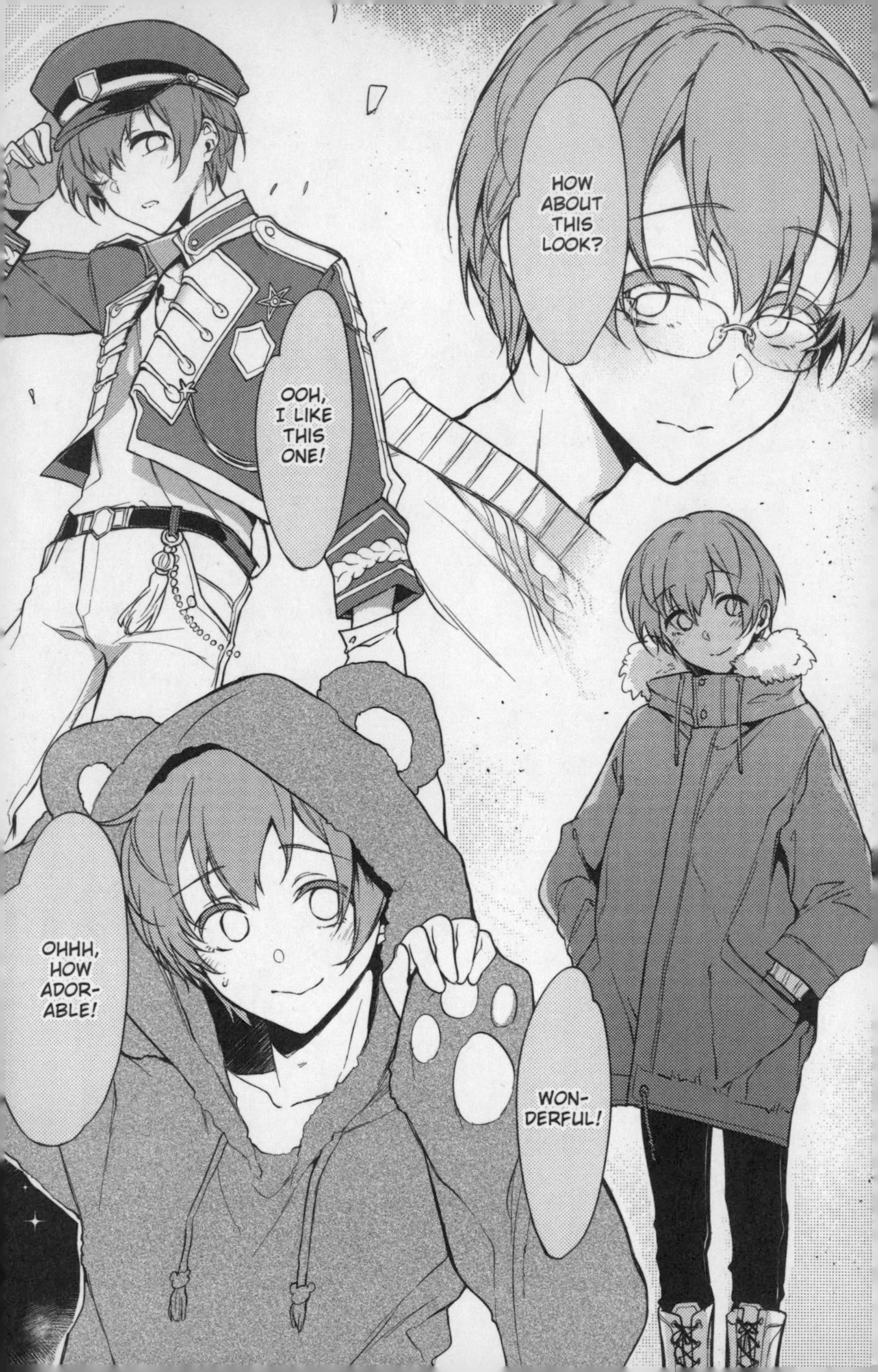
HOW ABOUT THIS LOOK?
OOH, I LIKE THIS ONE!
WON-DERFUL!
OHHH, HOW ADOR-ABLE!

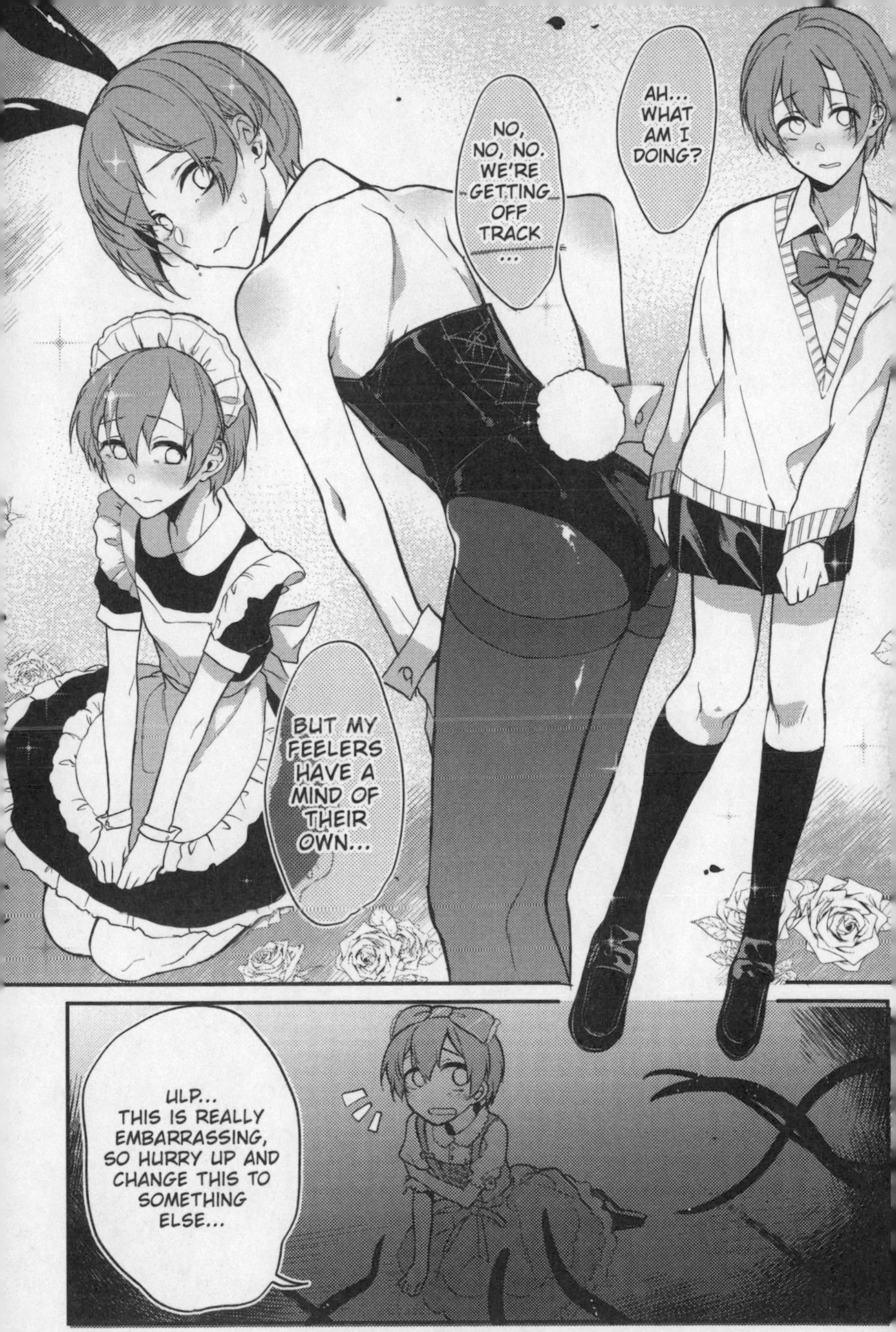
AH... WHAT AM I DOING?
NO, NO, NO. WE'RE GETTING OFF TRACK ...
BUT MY FEELERS HAVE A MIND OF THEIR OWN...
ULP... THIS IS REALLY EMBARRASSING, SO HURRY UP AND CHANGE THIS TO SOMETHING ELSE...

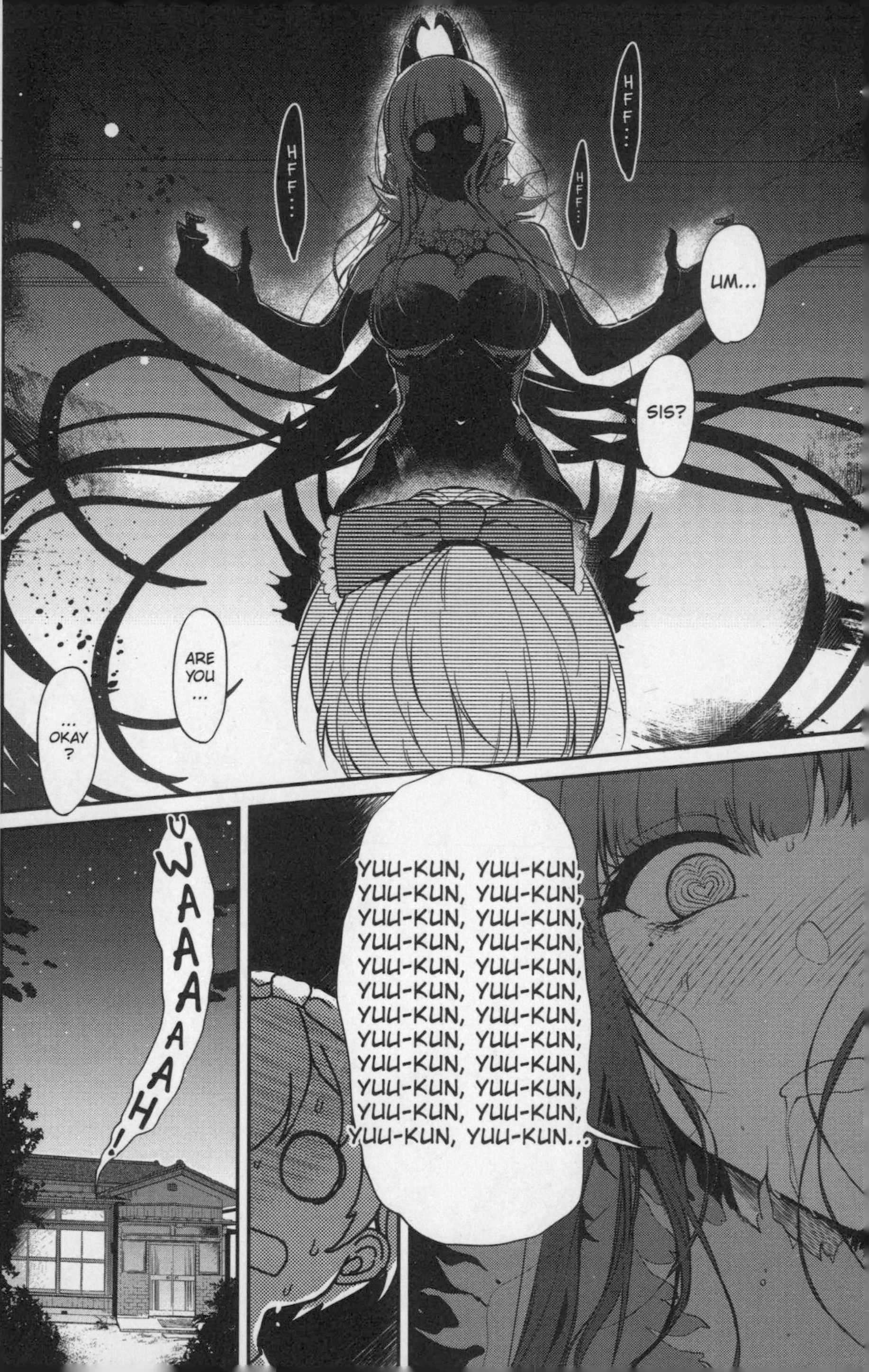
HFF...
HFF...
HFF...
UM...
SIS?
ARE YOU...
...OKAY?
YUU-KUN, YUU-KUN..
UWAAAAAH!

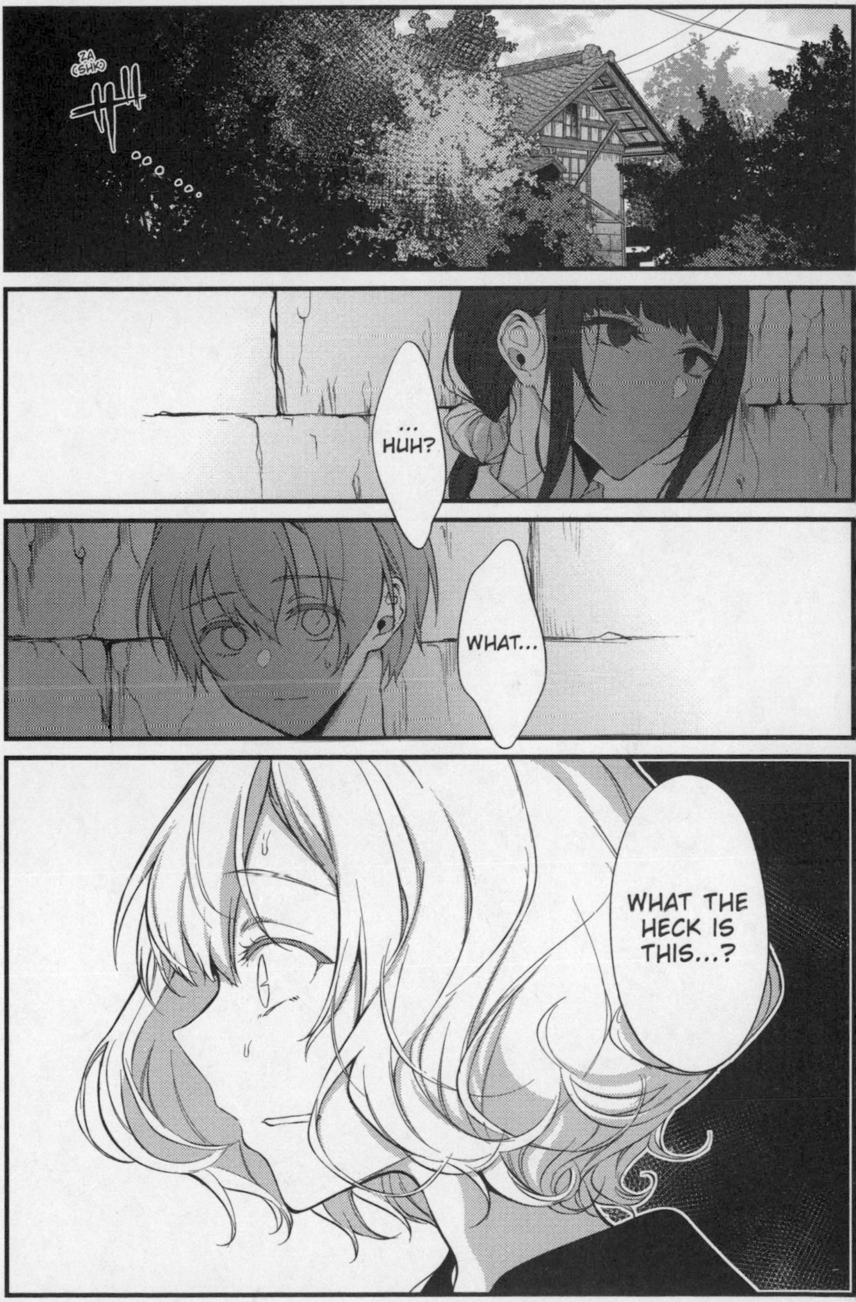
ZA (SHK)
... HUH?
WHAT...
WHAT THE HECK IS THIS...?

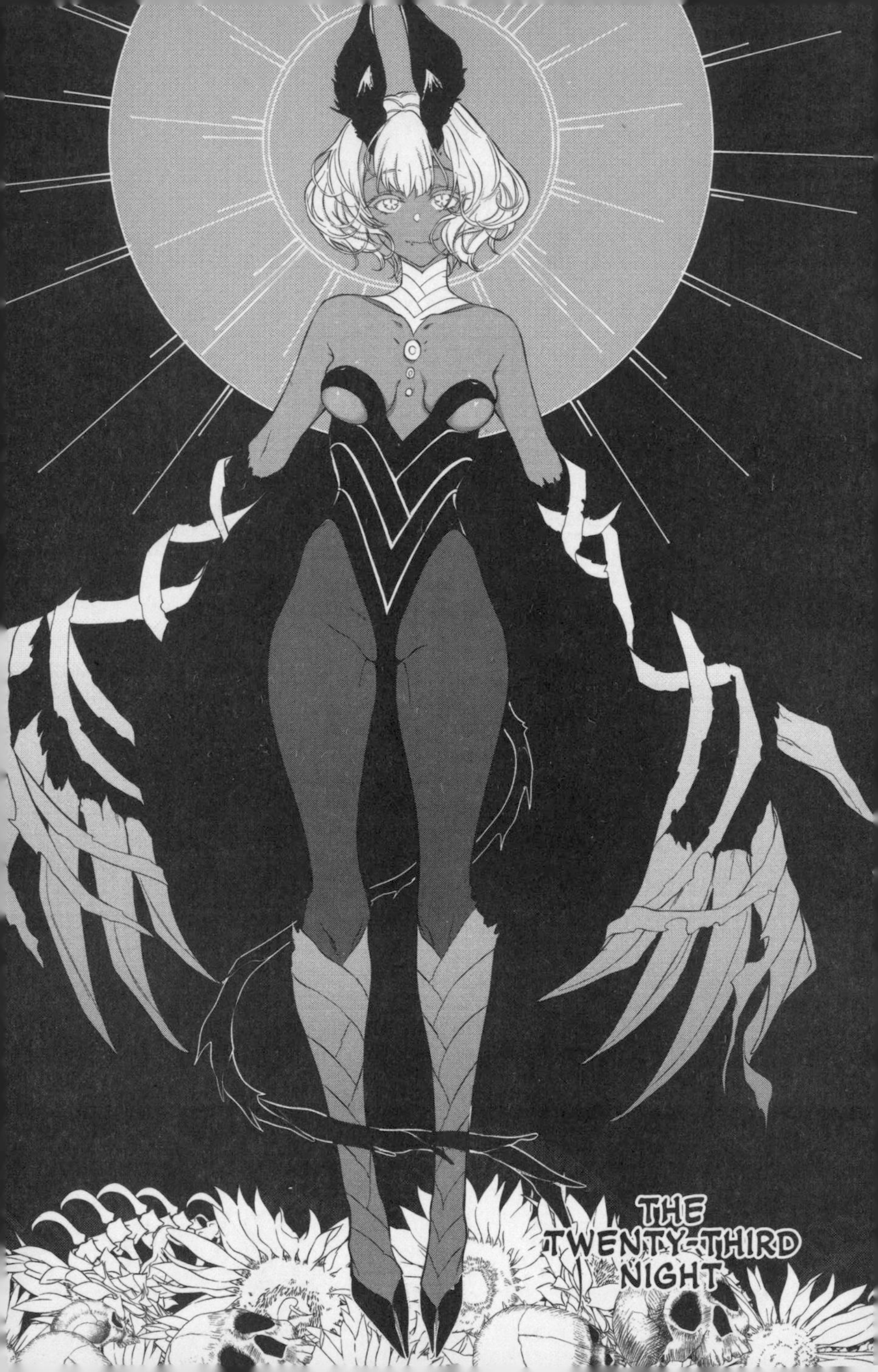
THE
TWENTY-THIRD
NIGHT

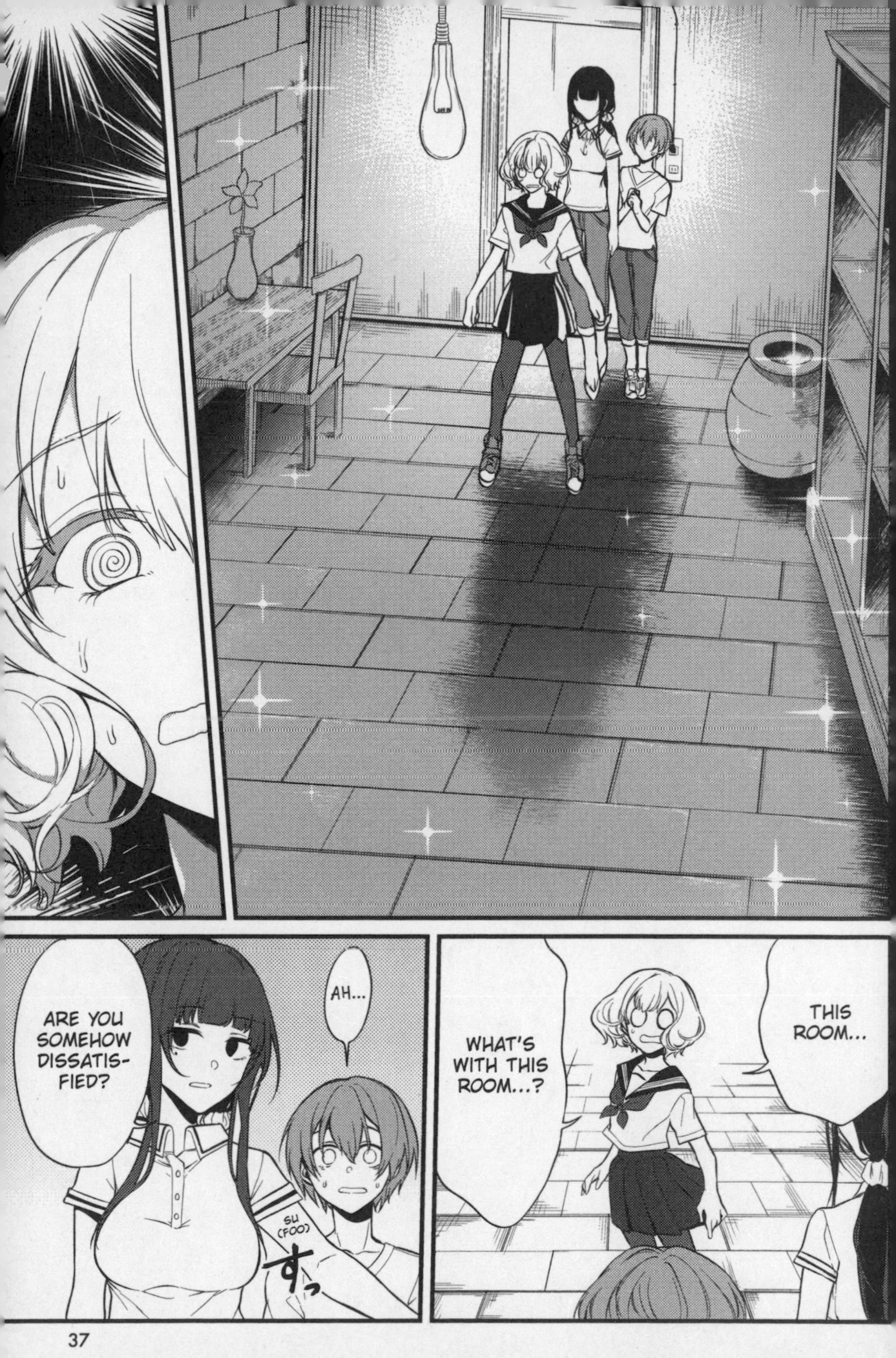
THIS ROOM...
WHAT'S WITH THIS ROOM...?
AH...
ARE YOU SOMEHOW DISSATIS-FIED?
SU (FOO)

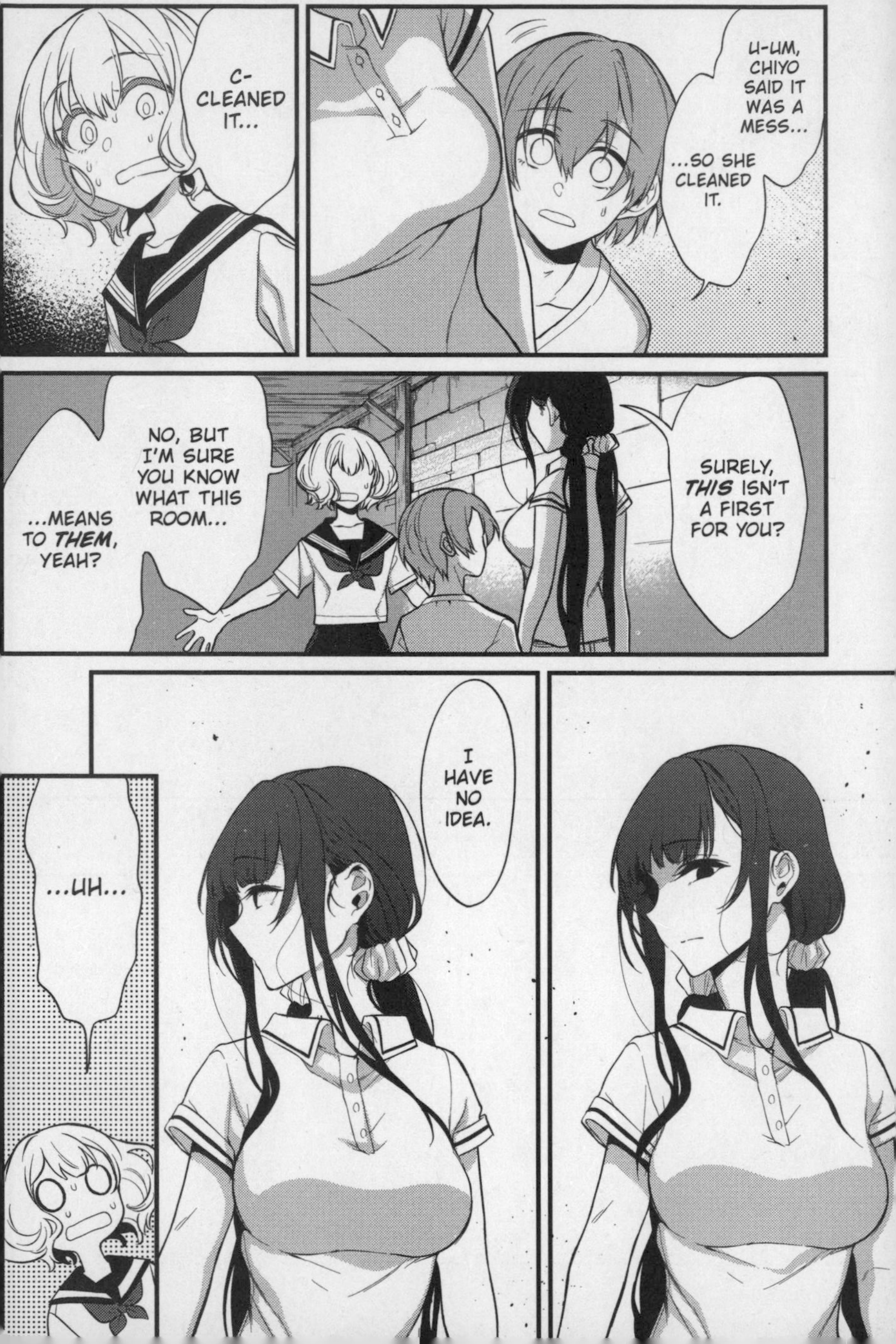
U-UM, CHIYO SAID IT WAS A MESS...
...SO SHE CLEANED IT.
C-CLEANED IT...
SURELY, ***THIS*** ISN'T A FIRST FOR YOU?
NO, BUT I'M SURE YOU KNOW WHAT THIS ROOM...
...MEANS TO ***THEM***, YEAH?
I HAVE NO IDEA.
...UH...

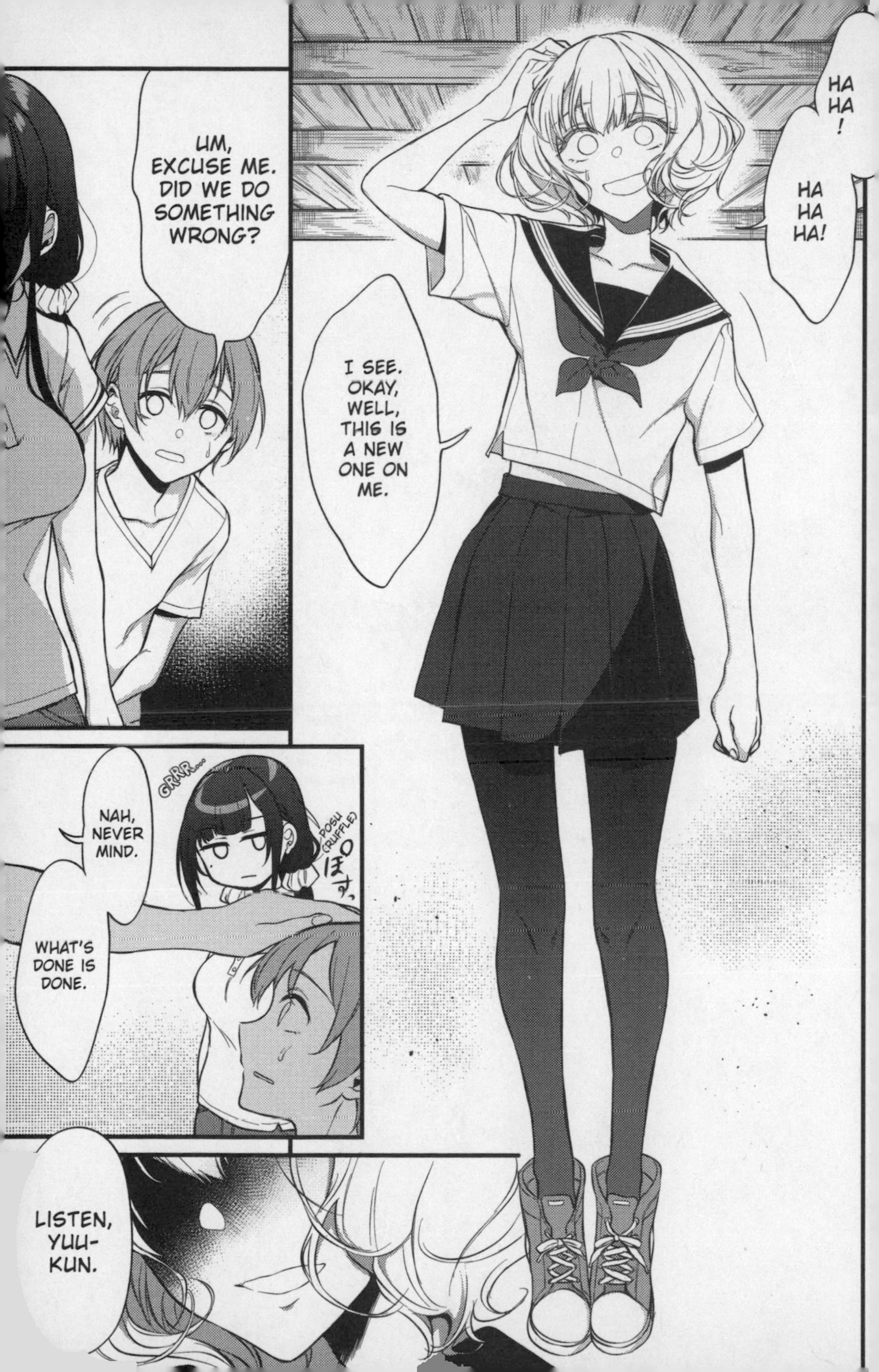
HA HA!
HA HA HA!
I SEE. OKAY, WELL, THIS IS A NEW ONE ON ME.
UM, EXCUSE ME. DID WE DO SOMETHING WRONG?
GRRR...
POSU (RUFFLE)
ぽす
NAH, NEVER MIND.
WHAT'S DONE IS DONE.
LISTEN, YUU-KUN.

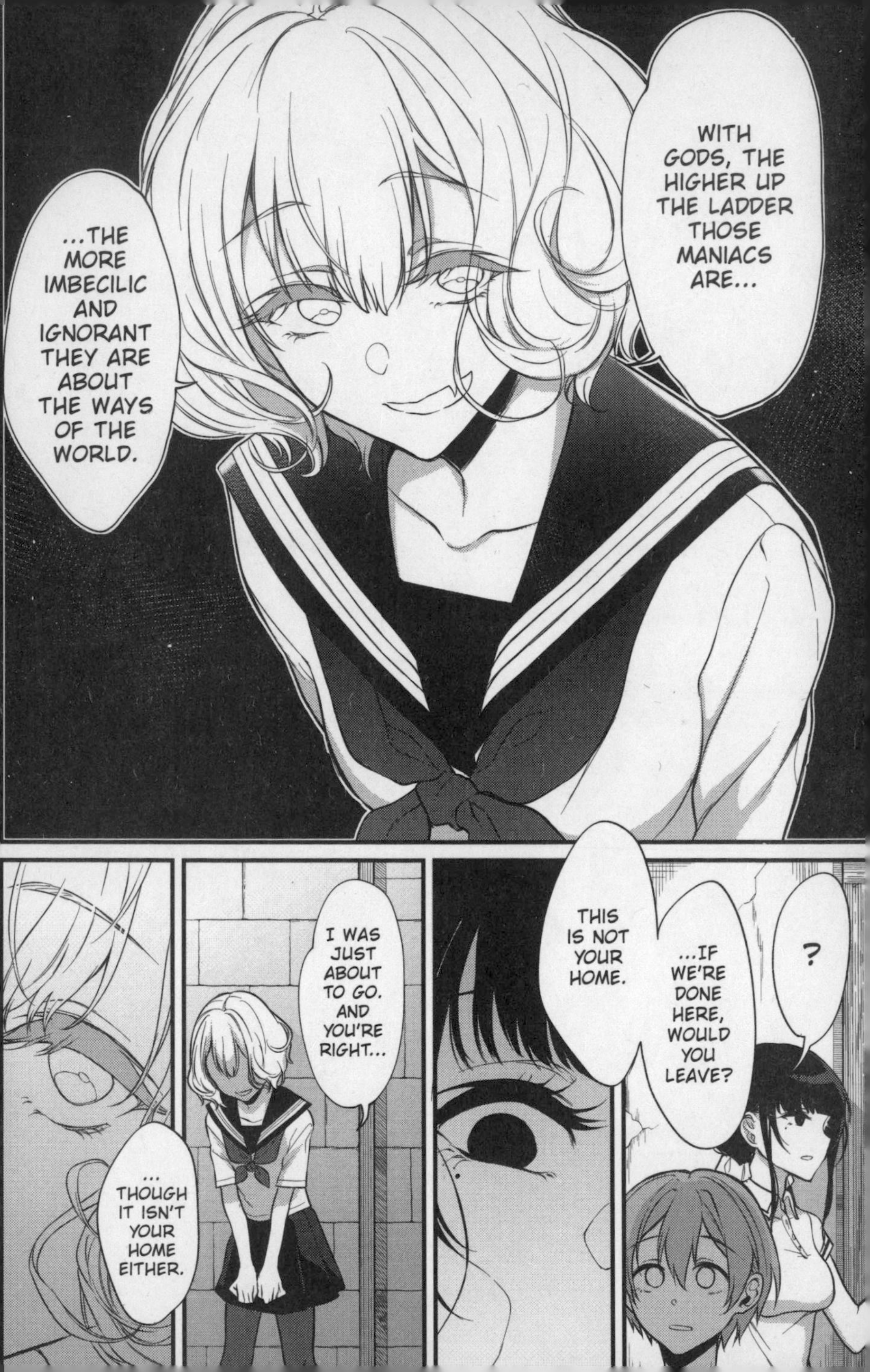
WITH GODS, THE HIGHER UP THE LADDER THOSE MANIACS ARE...
...THE MORE IMBECILIC AND IGNORANT THEY ARE ABOUT THE WAYS OF THE WORLD.
?
...IF WE'RE DONE HERE, WOULD YOU LEAVE?
THIS IS NOT YOUR HOME.
I WAS JUST ABOUT TO GO. AND YOU'RE RIGHT...
...THOUGH IT ISN'T YOUR HOME EITHER.

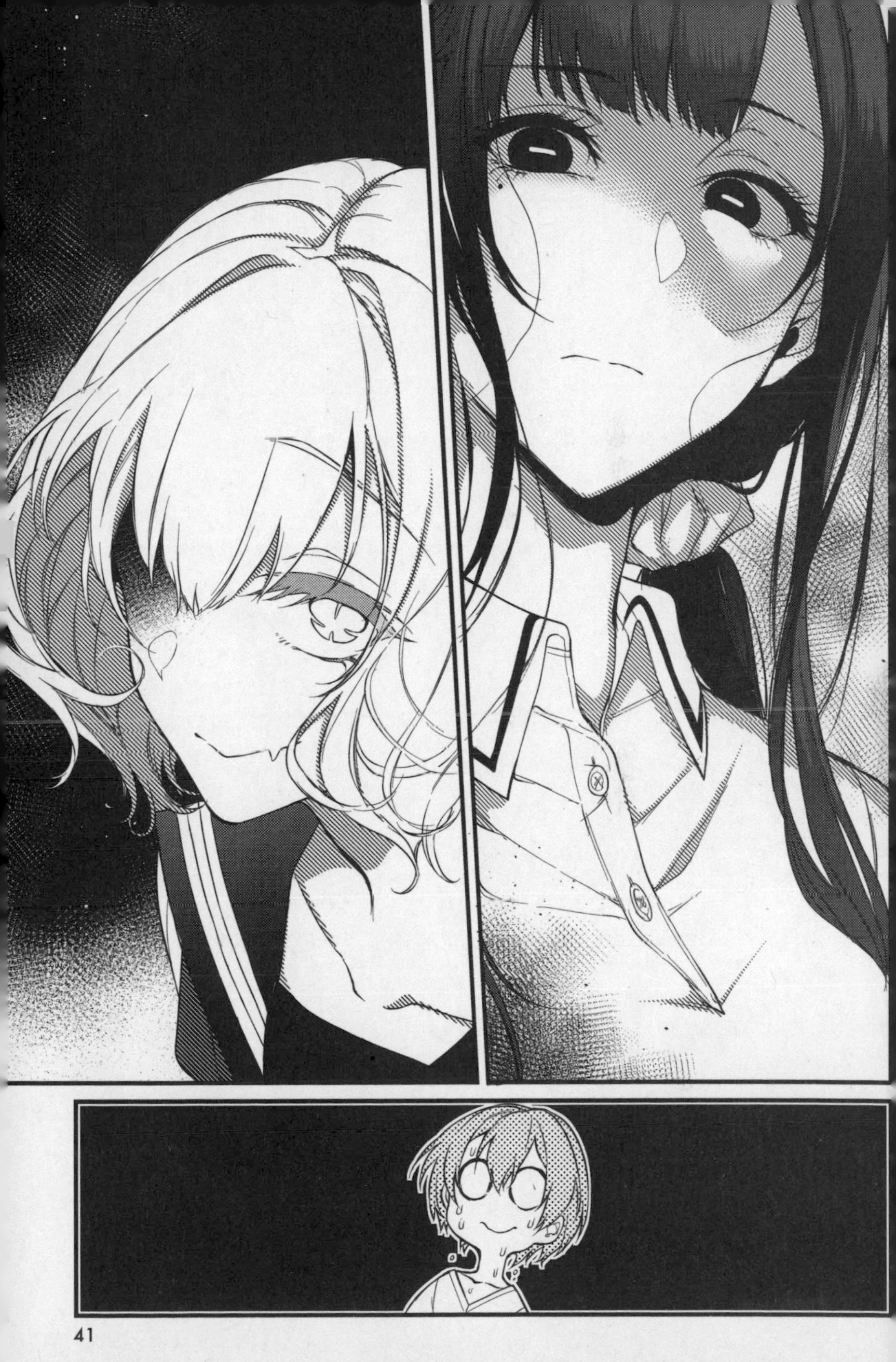

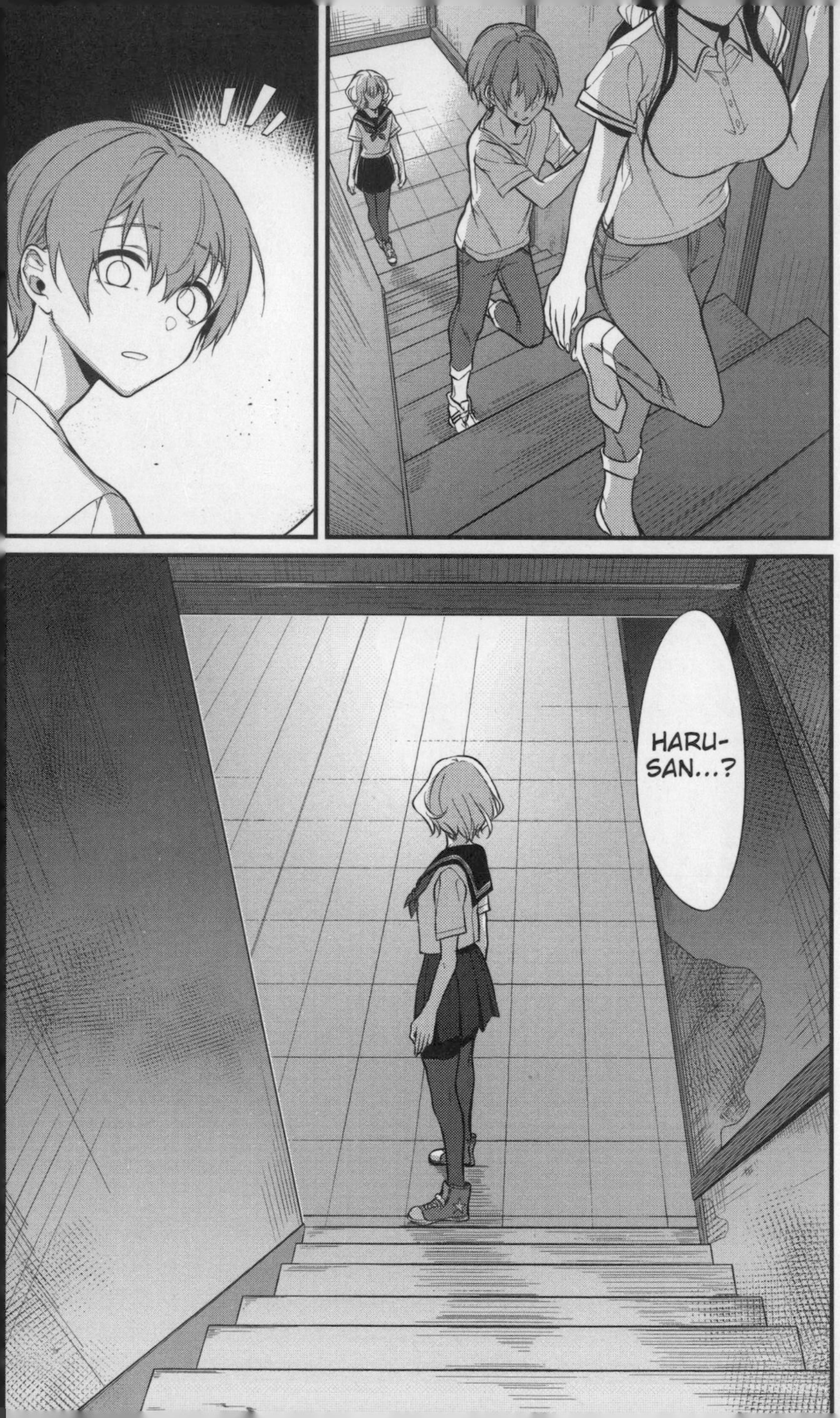
HARU-
SAN...?

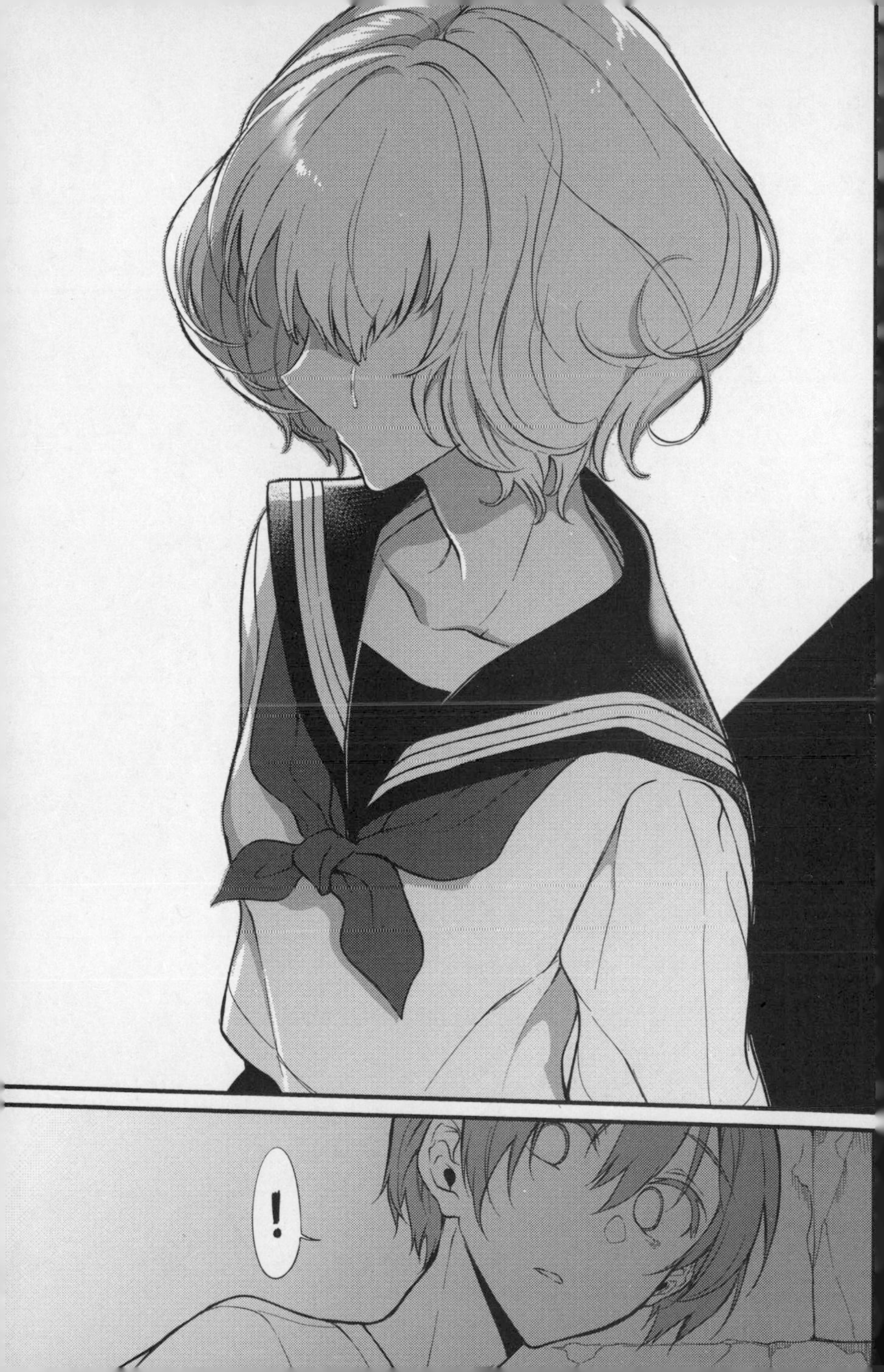
!

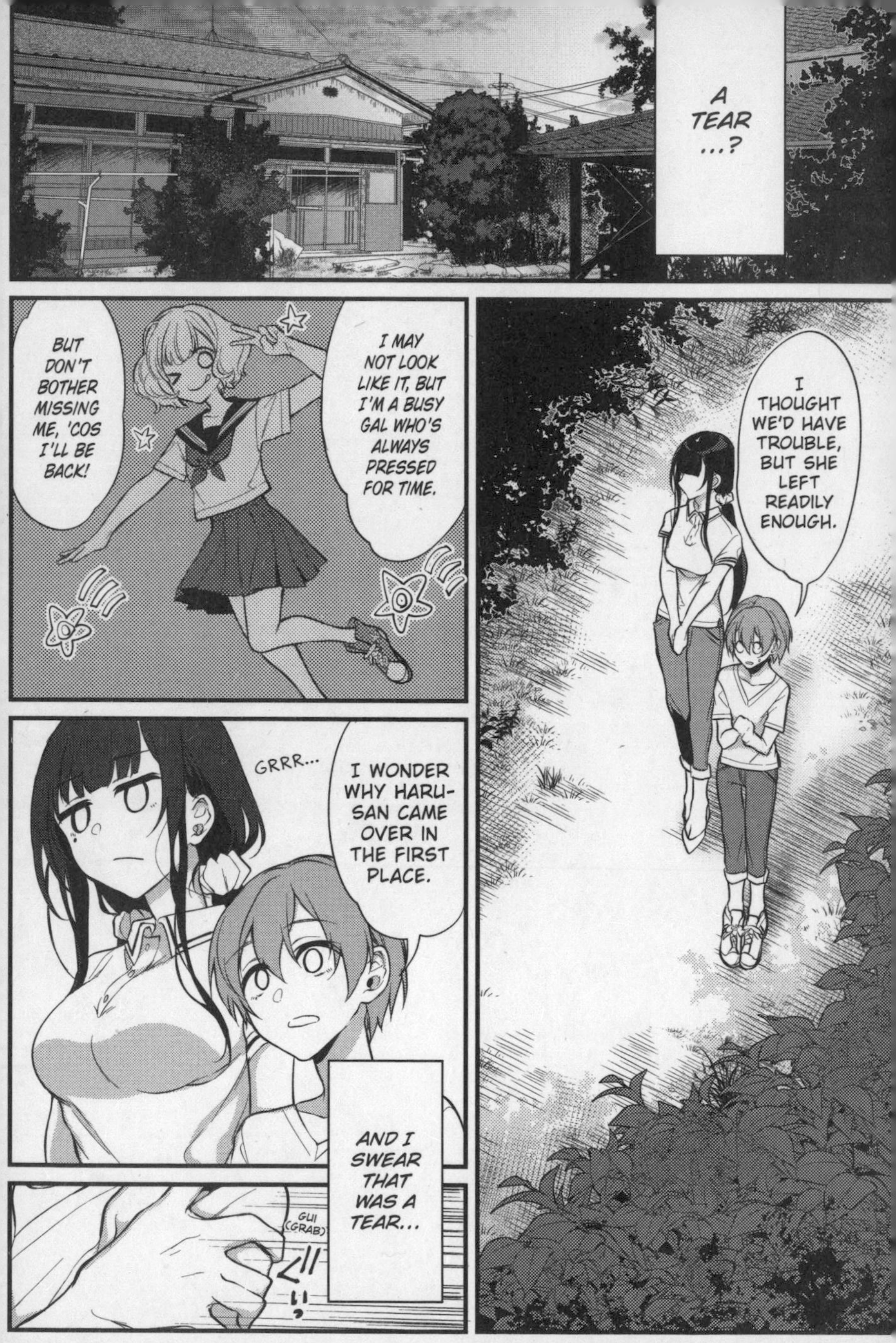
A TEAR ...?
I THOUGHT WE'D HAVE TROUBLE, BUT SHE LEFT READILY ENOUGH.
I MAY NOT LOOK LIKE IT, BUT I'M A BUSY GAL WHO'S ALWAYS PRESSED FOR TIME.
BUT DON'T BOTHER MISSING ME, 'COS I'LL BE BACK!
I WONDER WHY HARU-SAN CAME OVER IN THE FIRST PLACE.
GRRR...
AND I SWEAR THAT WAS A TEAR...
GUI (GRAB)

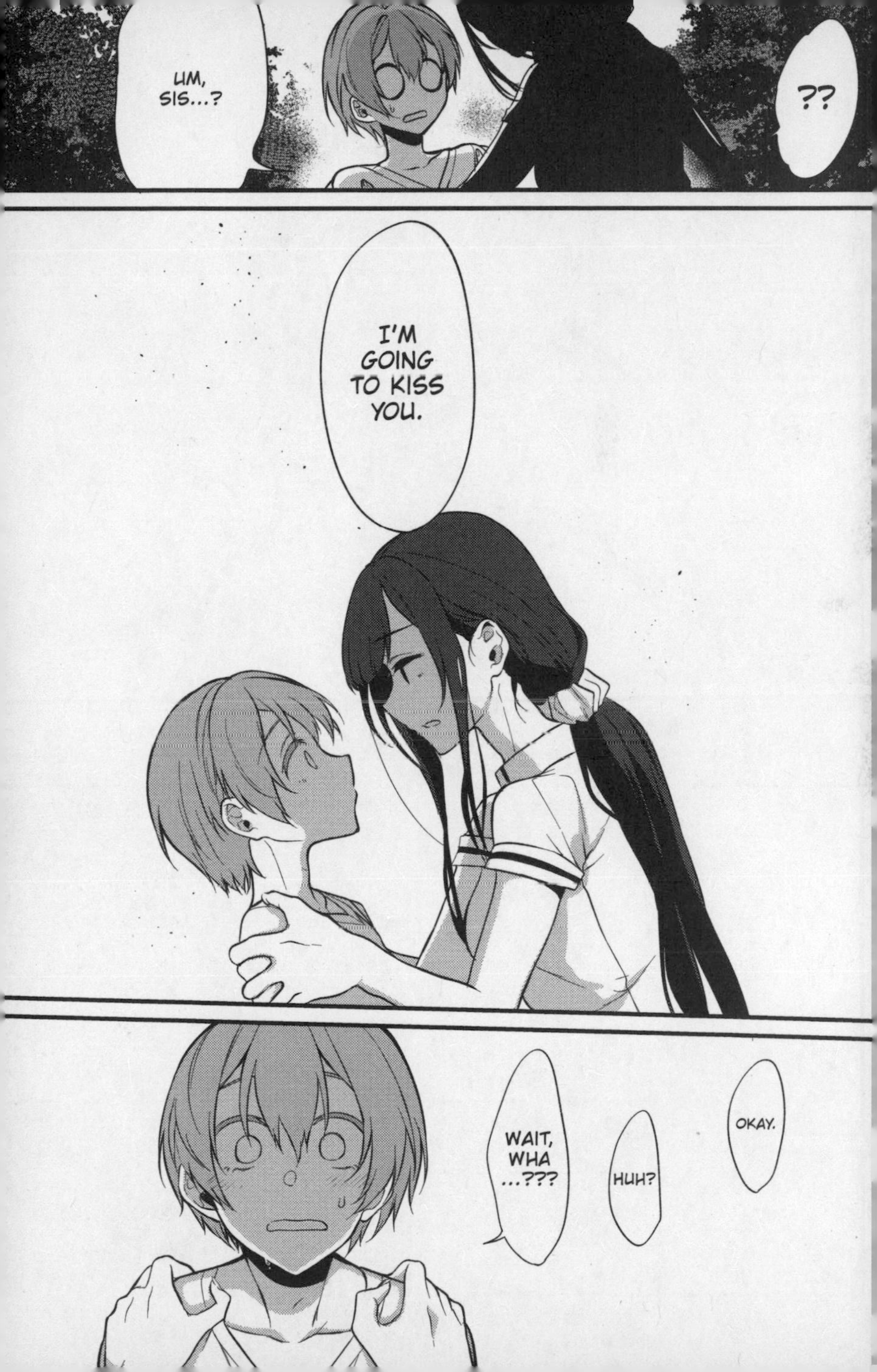
??
UM, SIS...?
I'M GOING TO KISS YOU.
OKAY.
HUH?
WAIT, WHA ...???

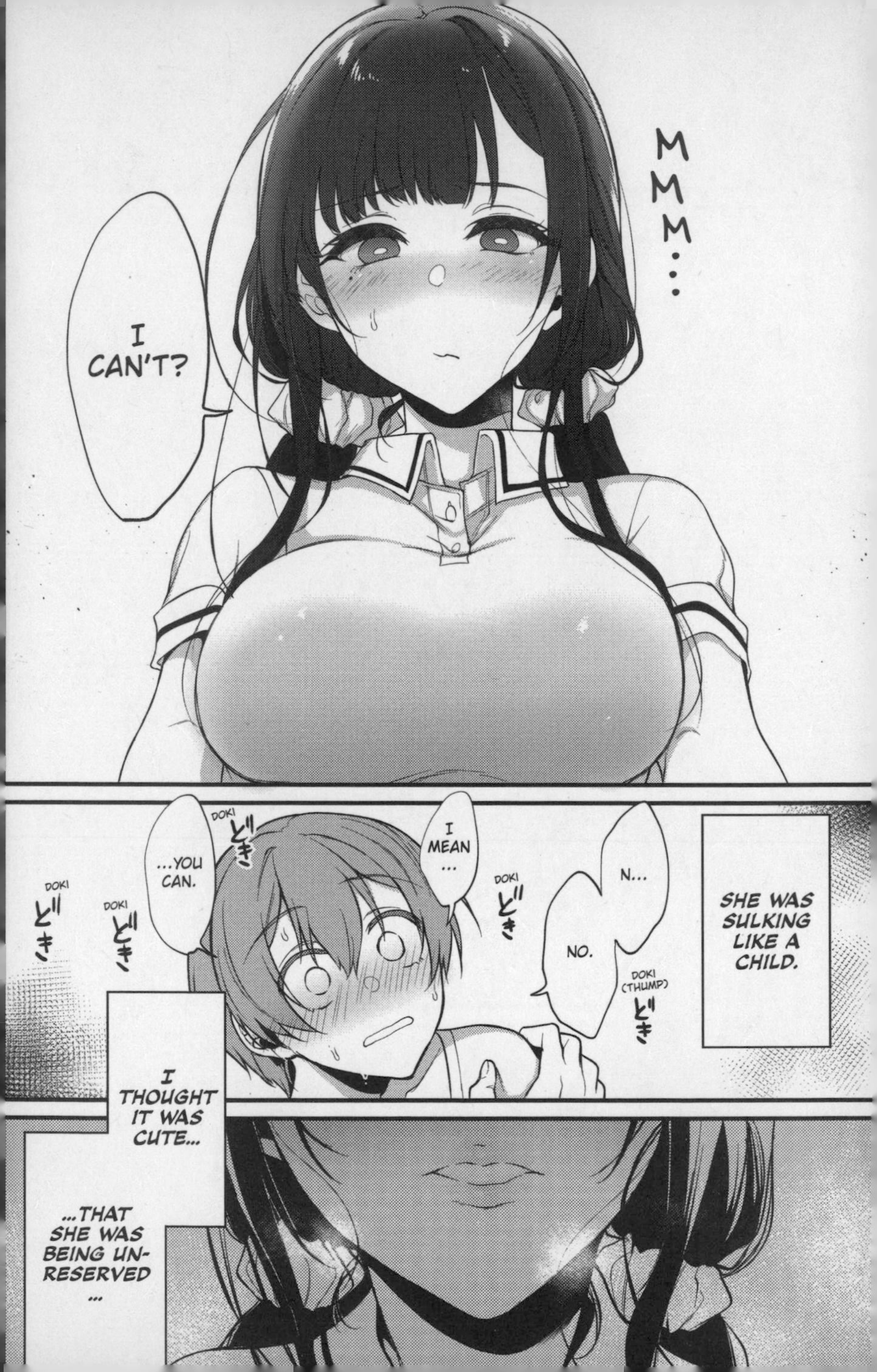
MMM...
I CAN'T?
SHE WAS SULKING LIKE A CHILD.
N... NO.
DOKI (THUMP) どき
DOKI どき
I MEAN ...
...YOU CAN.
DOKI どき
DOKI どき
DOKI どき
I THOUGHT IT WAS CUTE...
...THAT SHE WAS BEING UN-RESERVED ...

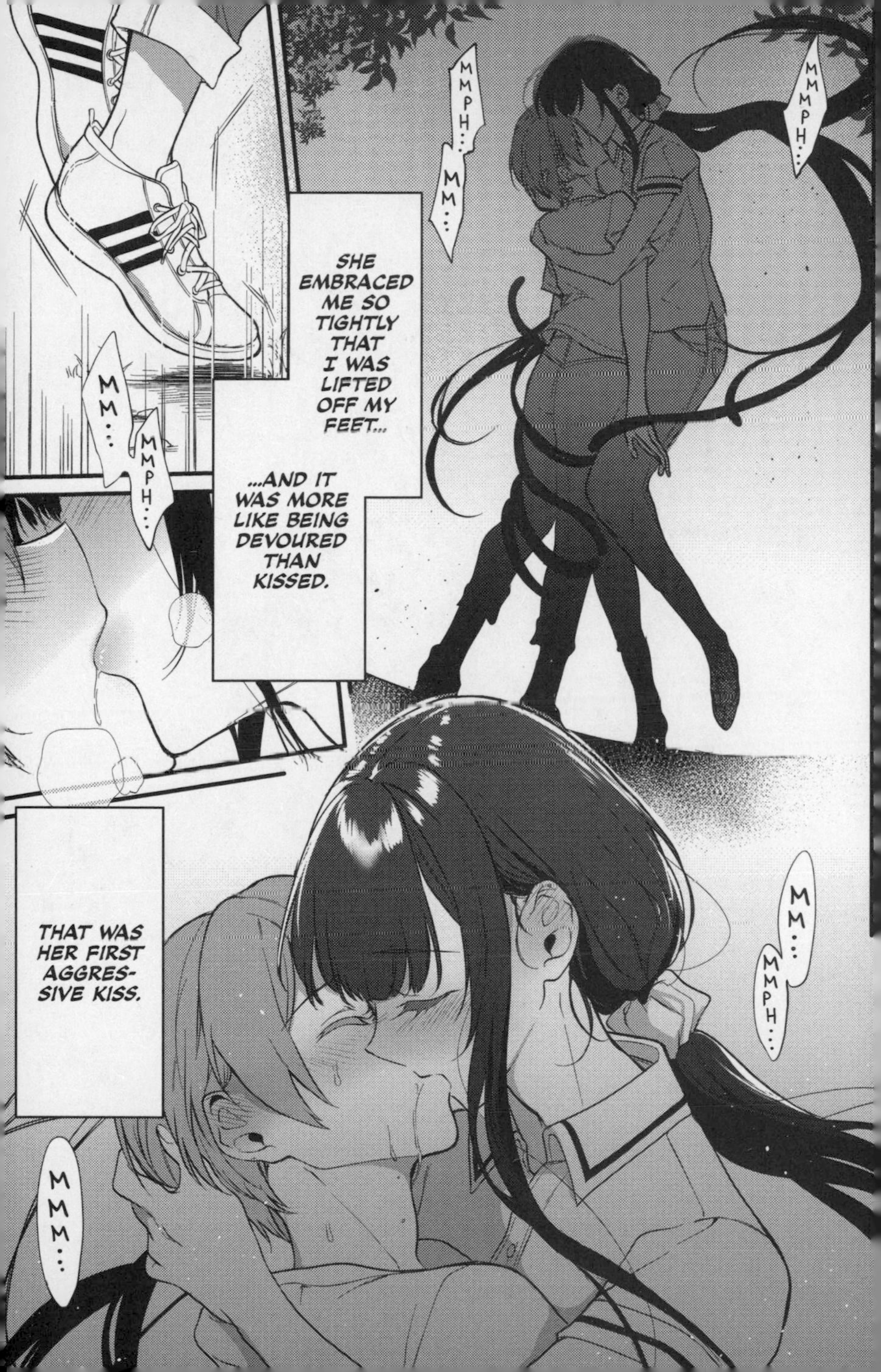
MMMPH...
MMPH...
MM...
SHE EMBRACED ME SO TIGHTLY THAT I WAS LIFTED OFF MY FEET...
...AND IT WAS MORE LIKE BEING DEVOURED THAN KISSED.
MM...
MMPH...
MM...
MMPH...
THAT WAS HER FIRST AGGRES-SIVE KISS.
MMM...

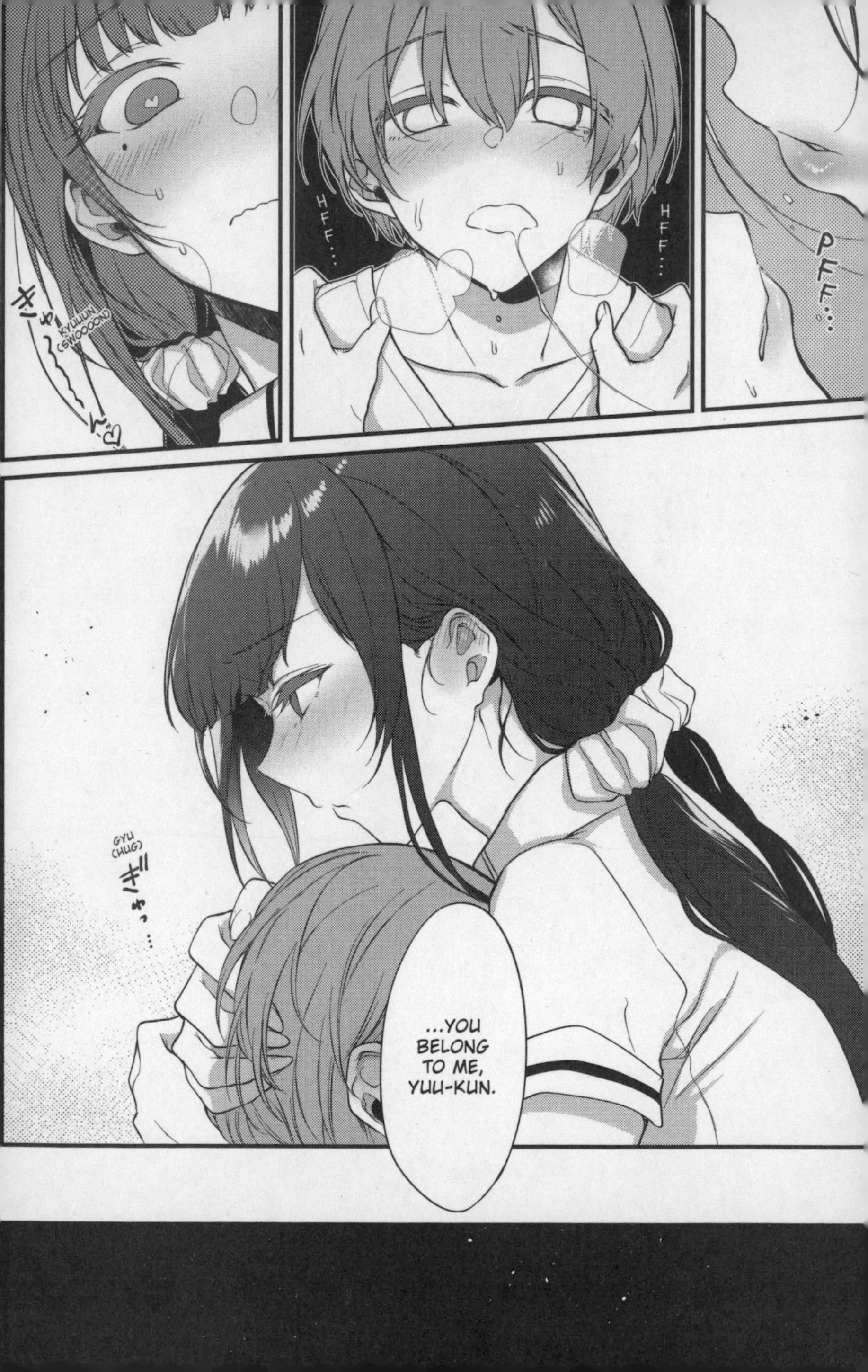
PFF...
HFF...
HFF...
きゅ〜〜〜ん♡
KYUUUN (SWOOOON)
...YOU BELONG TO ME, YUU-KUN.
ぎゅっ…
GYU (HUG)

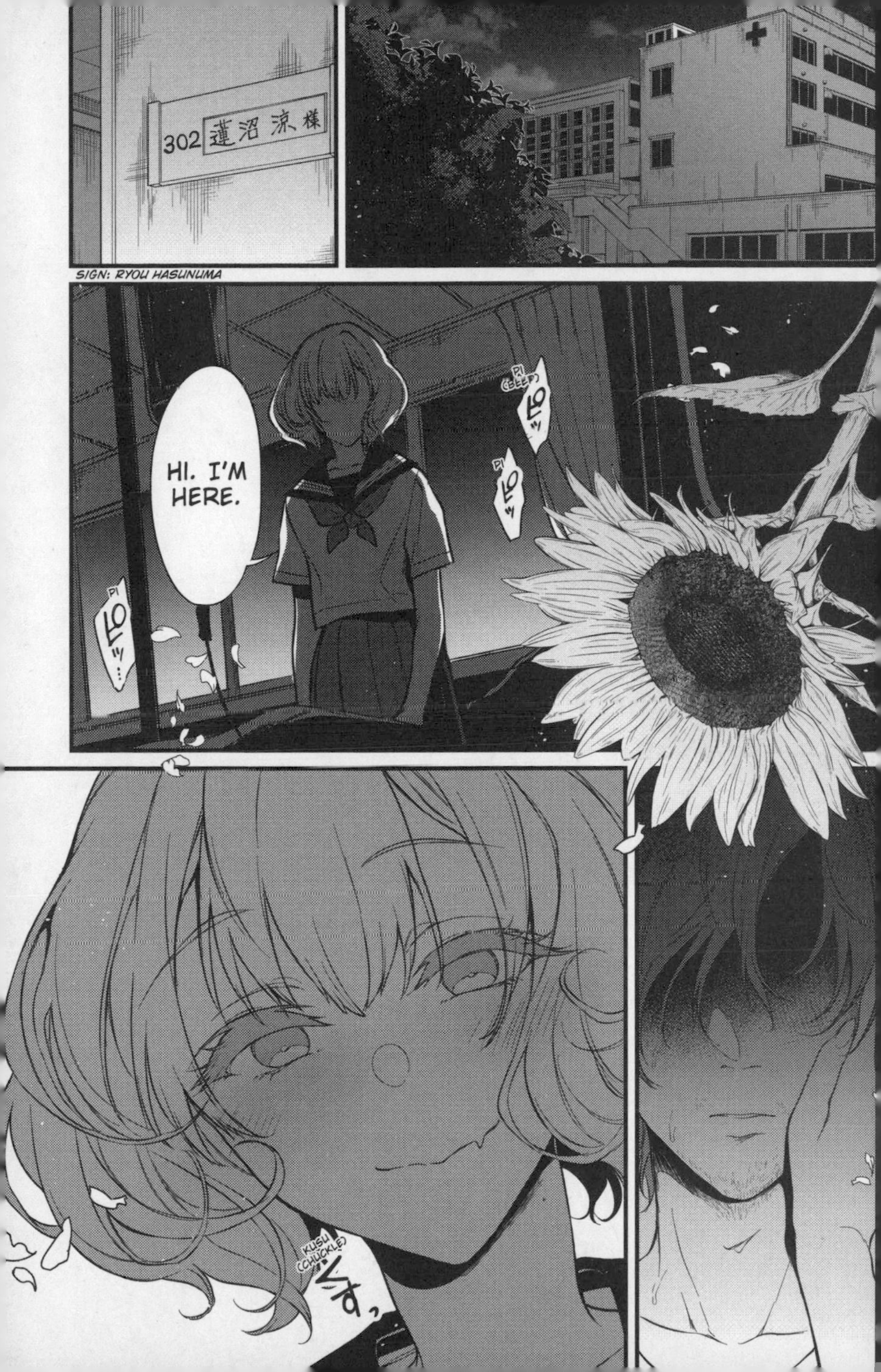
302 蓮沼涼様
SIGN: RYOU HASUNUMA
PI (BEEP) ピッ
PI ピッ
HI. I'M HERE.
PI ピッ…
KUSU (CHUCKLE) くすっ

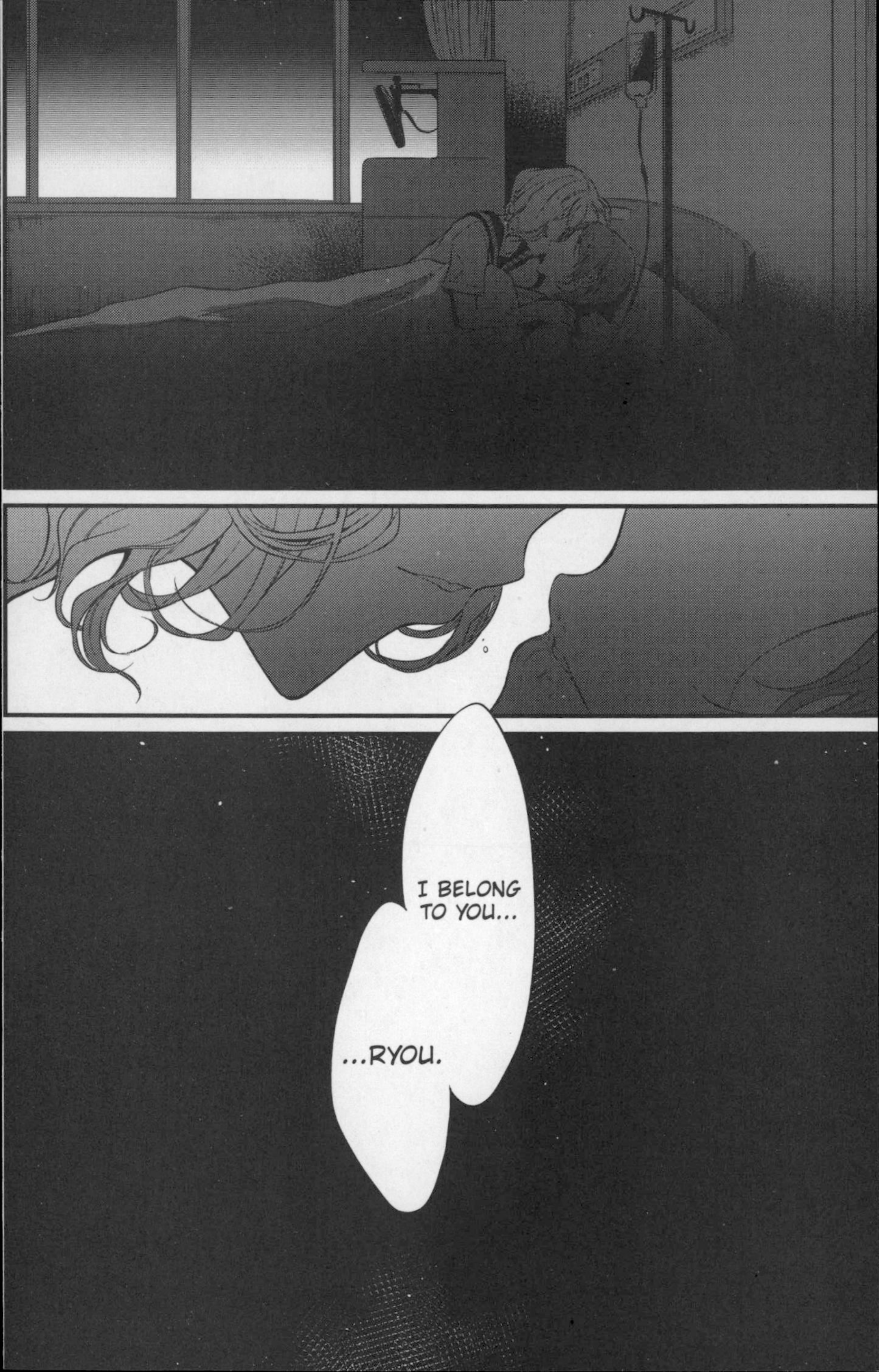
I BELONG TO YOU...
...RYOU.

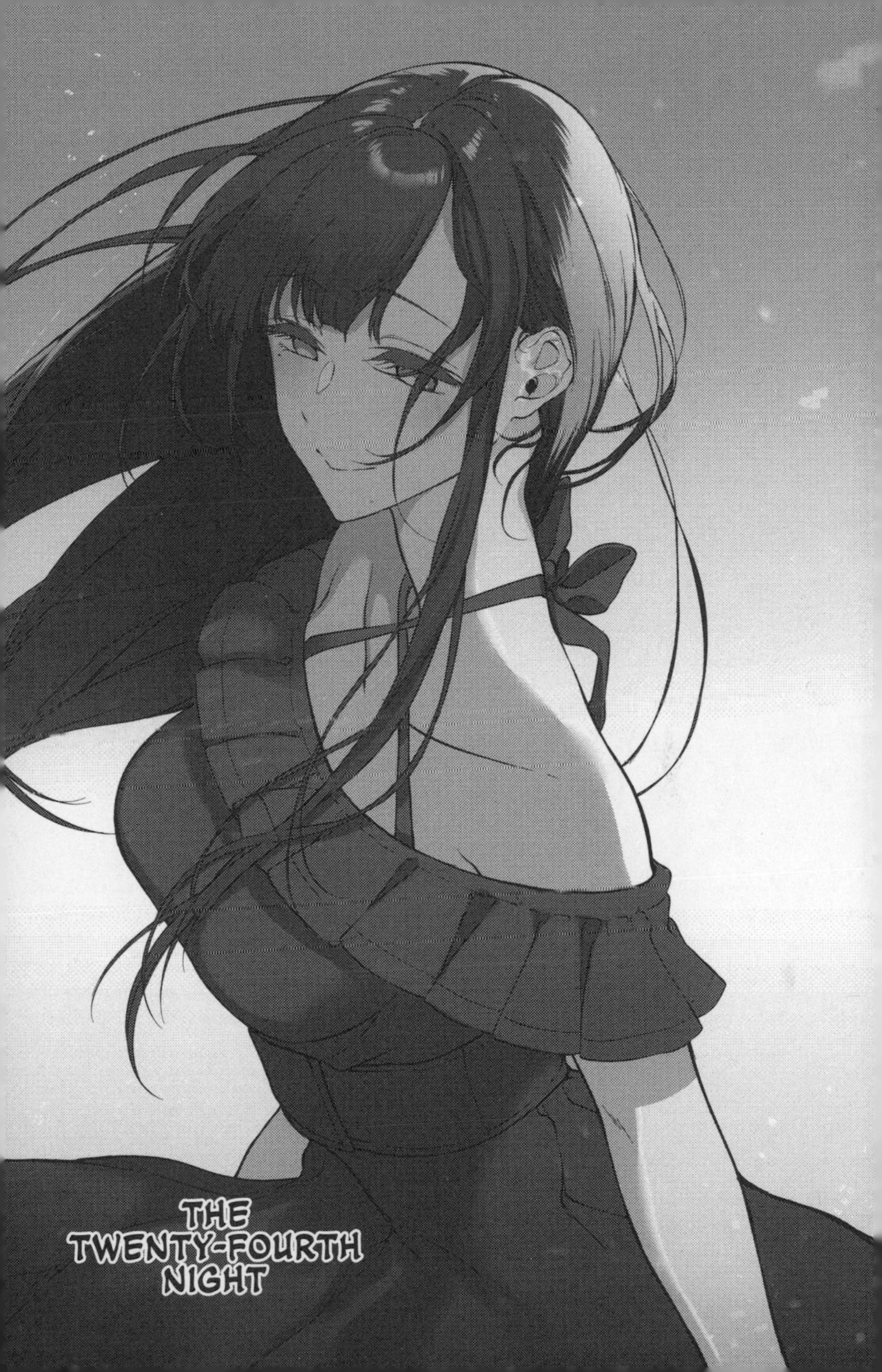
THE TWENTY-FOURTH NIGHT

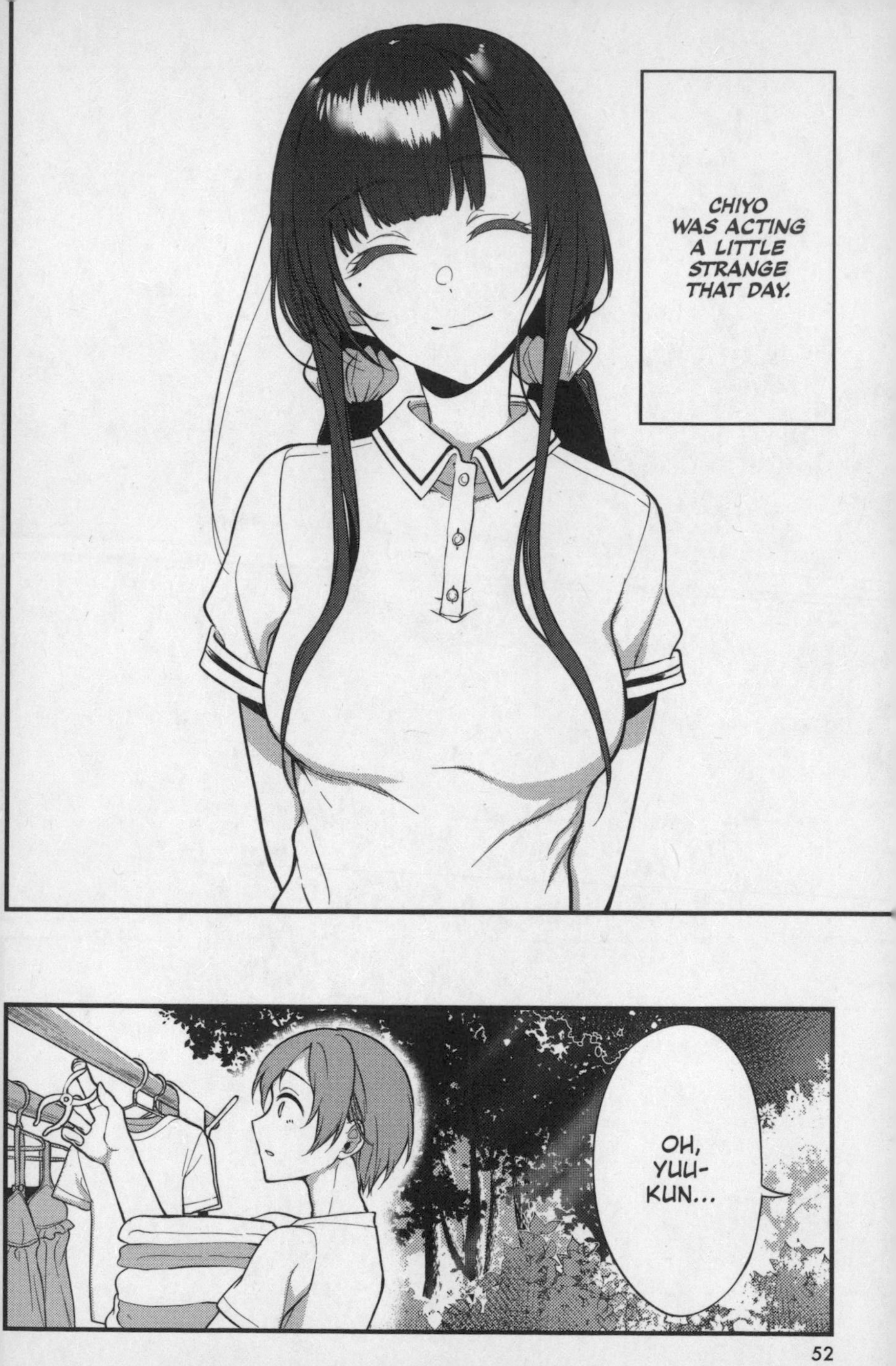
CHIYO WAS ACTING A LITTLE STRANGE THAT DAY.
OH, YUU-KUN...

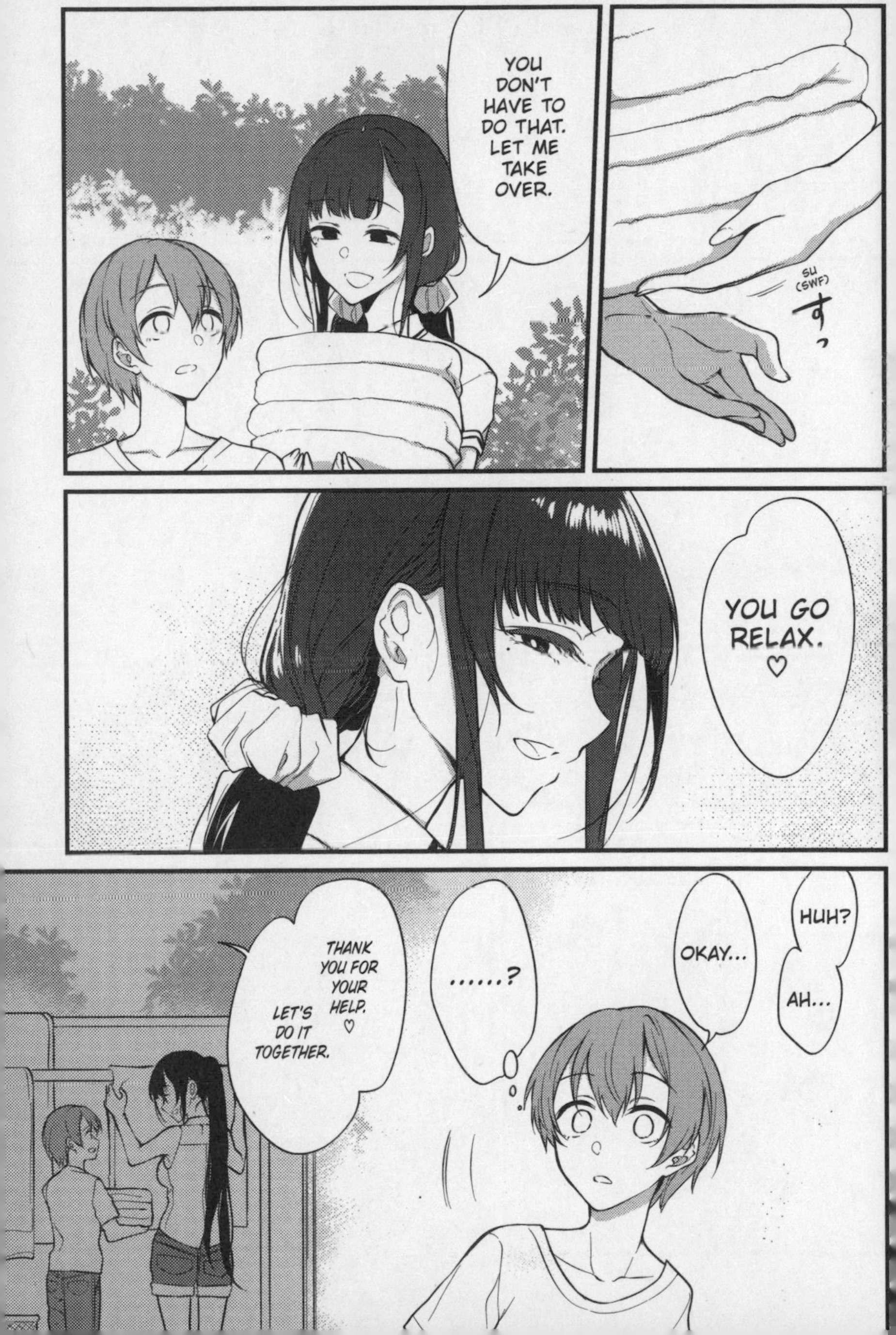
SU (SWF)
すっ
YOU DON'T HAVE TO DO THAT. LET ME TAKE OVER.
YOU GO RELAX. ♡
HUH?
AH...
OKAY...
......?
THANK YOU FOR YOUR HELP. ♡
LET'S DO IT TOGETHER.

?   ?

DON'T WORRY ABOUT THAT. JUST HAVE A SEAT, YUU-KUN.

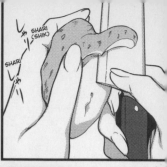

SHARI (SHIK)

SHARI

EAT UP! ♡

DINNER'S READY!

PATA (PAT)

PATA (PAT)

?

THANK YOU FOR THE...

SU (SHF)

SU SU す す す

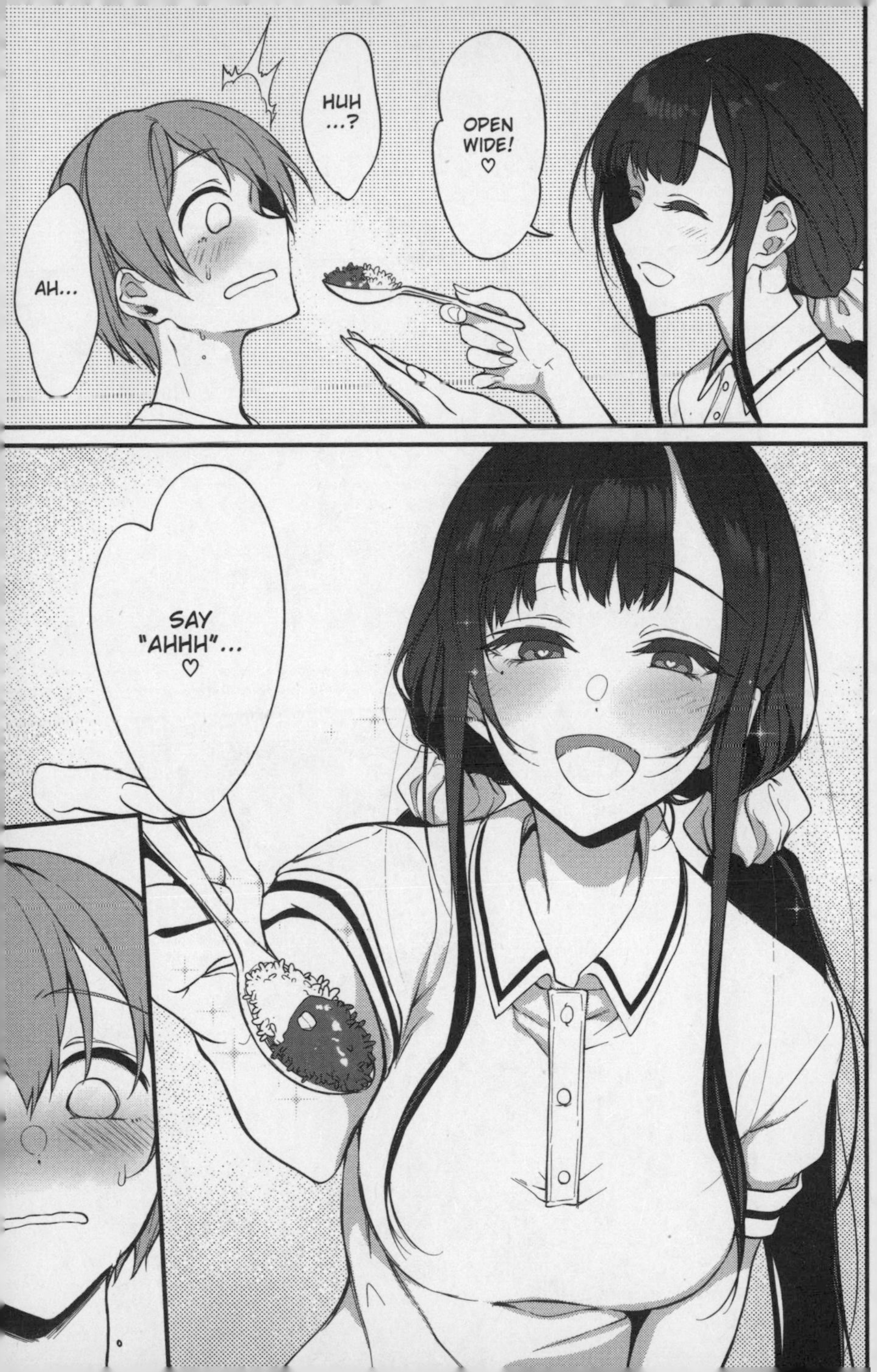
OPEN WIDE! ♡
HUH ...?
AH...
SAY "AHHH"... ♡

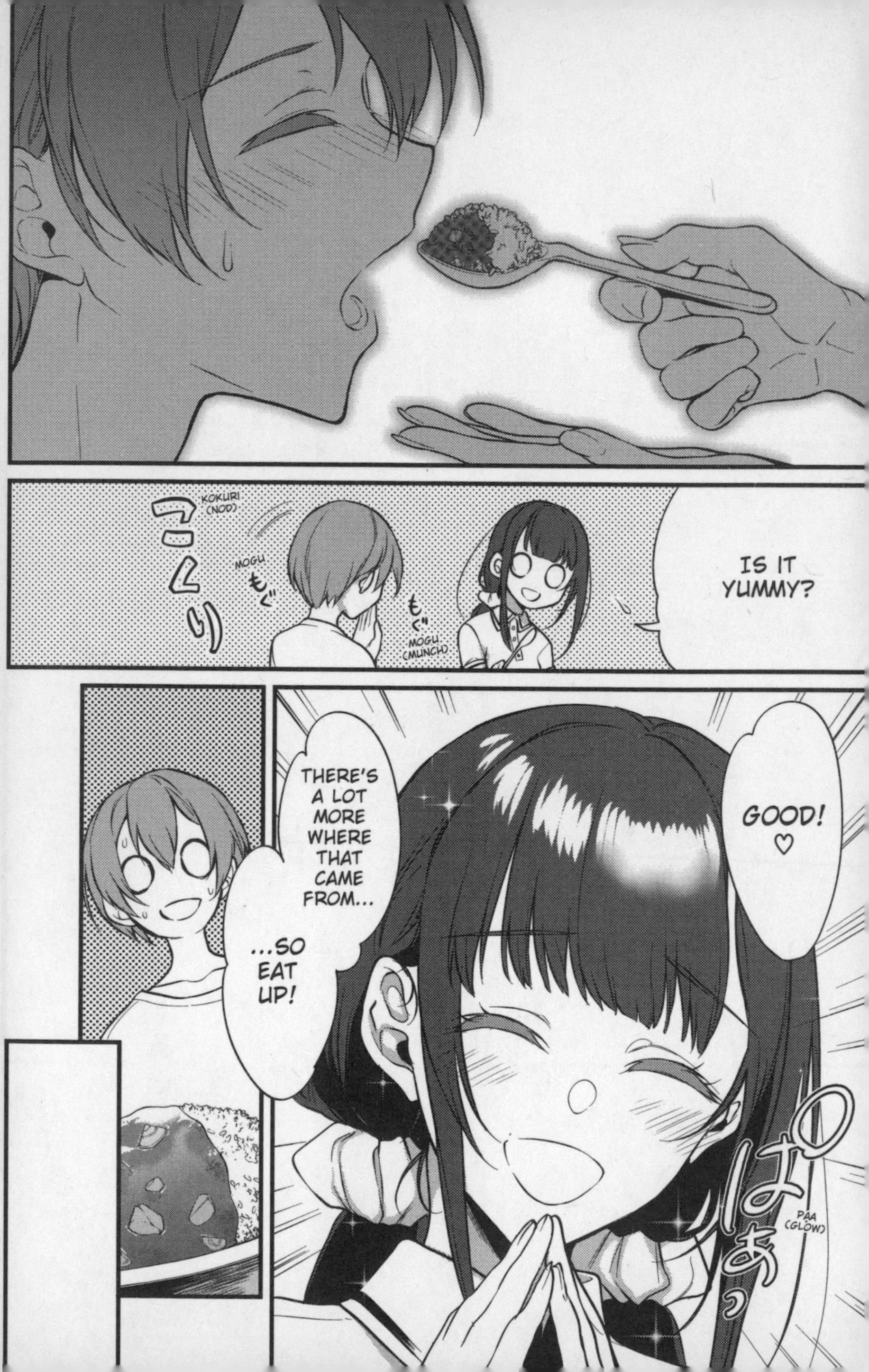
IS IT YUMMY?
もぐ MOGU (MUNCH)
MOGU もぐ
KOKURI (NOD) こくり
GOOD! ♡
THERE'S A LOT MORE WHERE THAT CAME FROM...
...SO EAT UP!
ぱあっ PAA (GLOW)

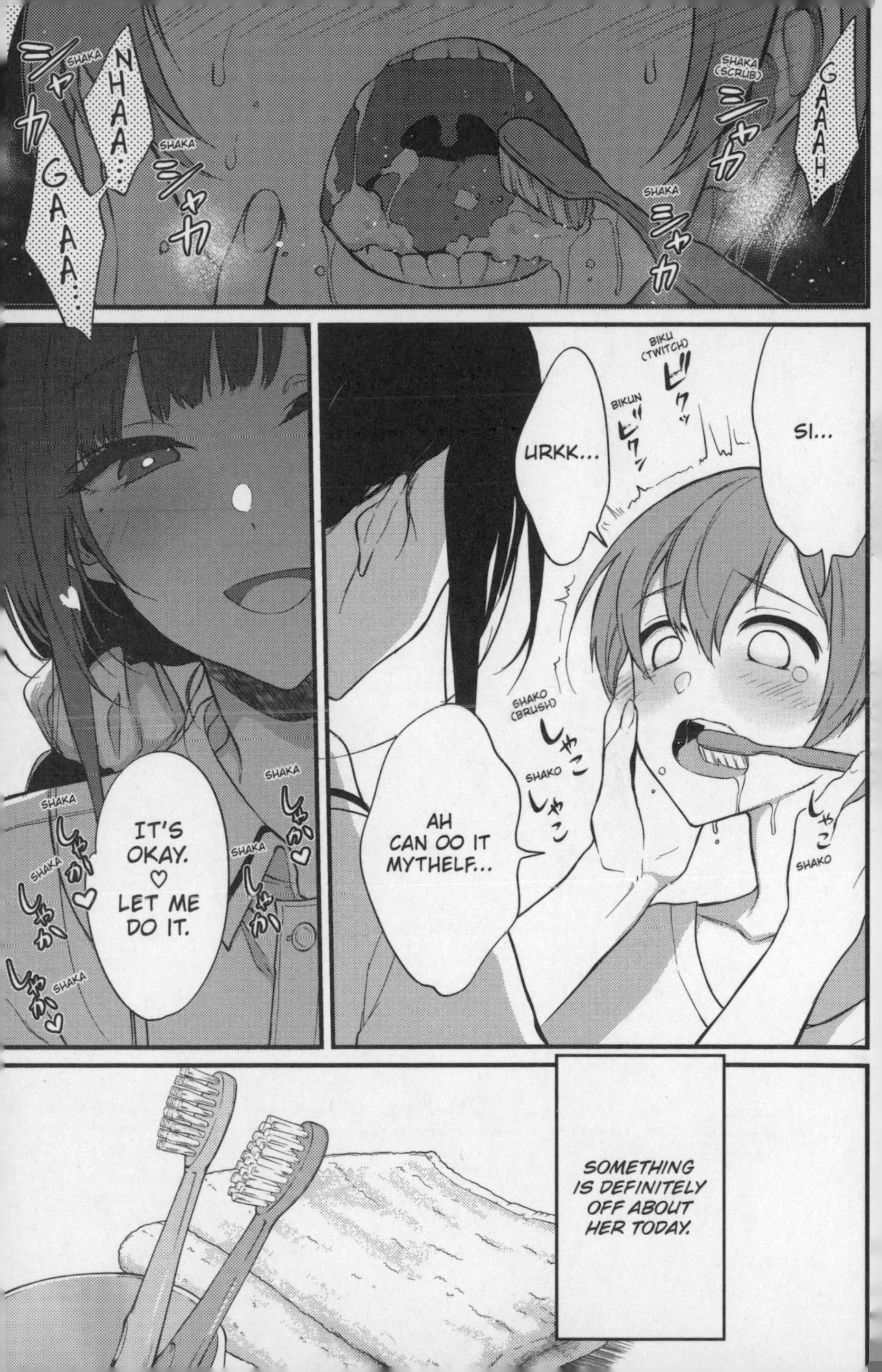
GAAAH
SHAKA (SCRUB)
シャカ
SHAKA
シャカ
SHAKA
シャカ
SHAKA
シャカ
NHAA...
GAAA...
SI...
BIKU (TWITCH)
ビクッ
BIKUN
ビクン
URKK...
SHAKO
しゃこ
SHAKO (BRUSH)
しゃこ
SHAKO
しゃこ
AH CAN OO IT MYTHELF...
SHAKA
しゃか♡
SHAKA
しゃか
IT'S OKAY. ♡ LET ME DO IT.
SHAKA
しゃか♡
SHAKA
しゃか
SHAKA
しゃか♡
SOMETHING IS DEFINITELY OFF ABOUT HER TODAY.

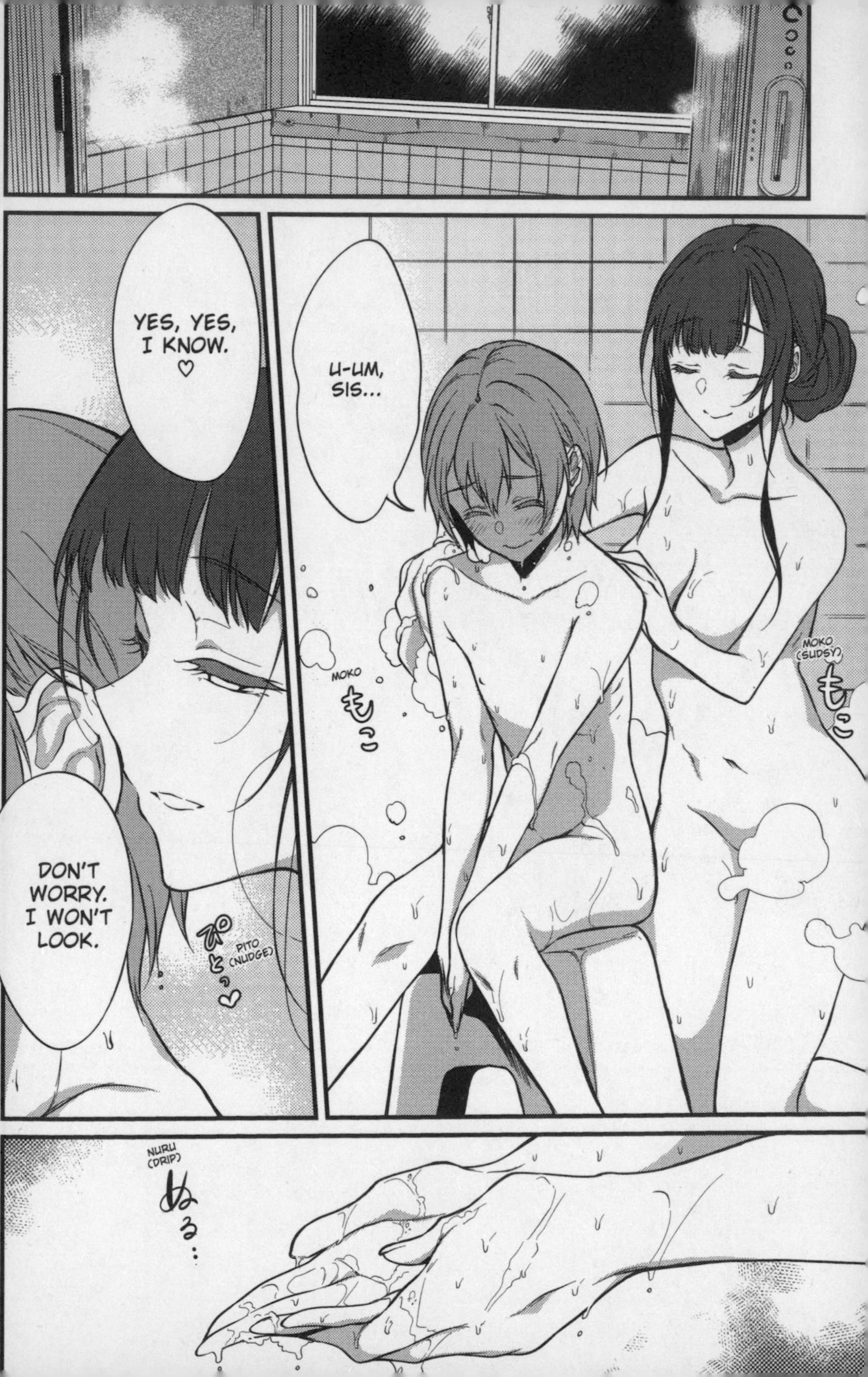
U-UM, SIS...
MOKO (SUDSY) もこ
MOKO もこ
YES, YES, I KNOW. ♡
DON'T WORRY. I WON'T LOOK.
ぴとっ PITO (NUDGE) ♡
NURU (DRIP) ぬる...

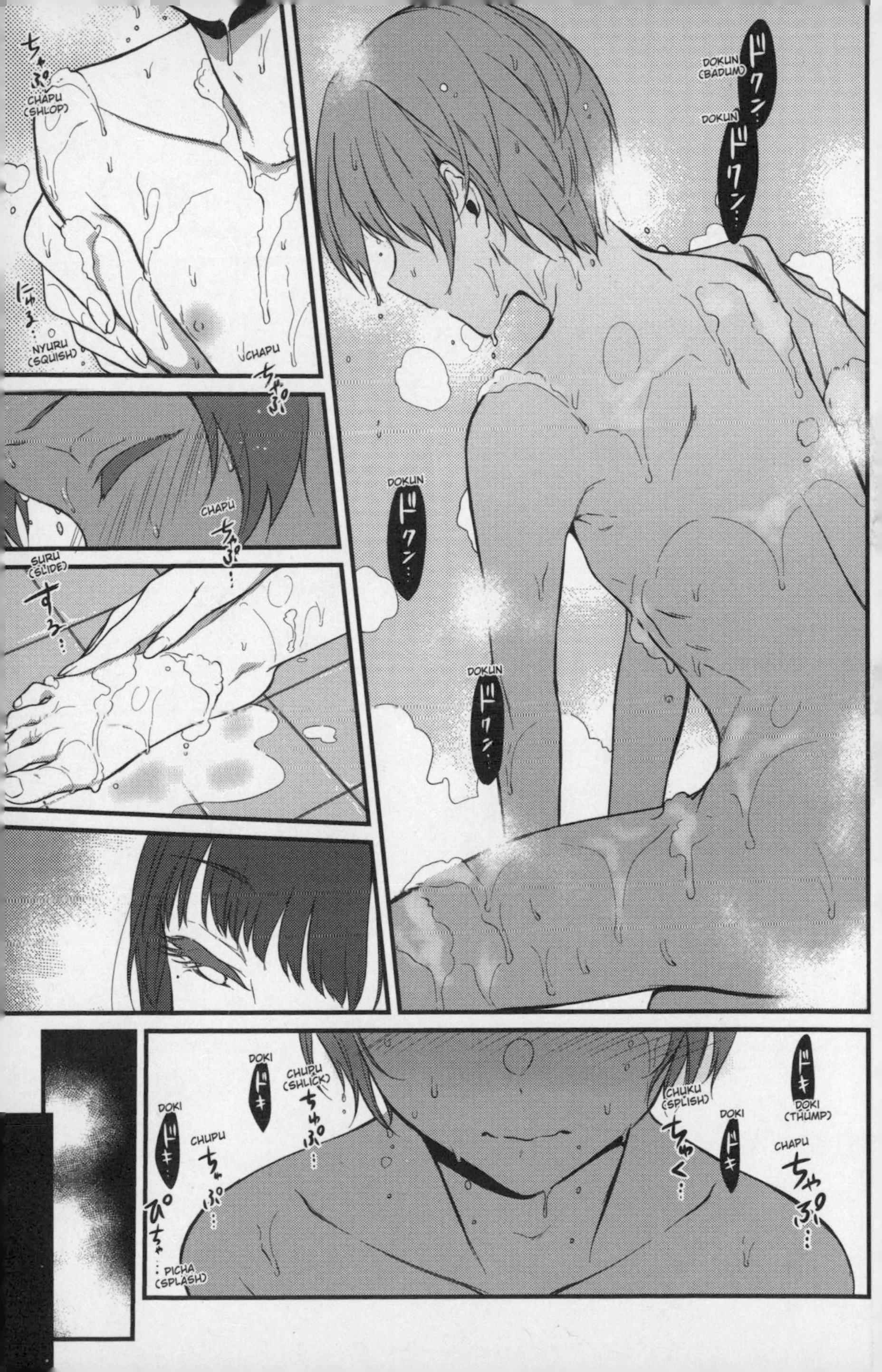
ドクン…
DOKUN (BADUM)
ドクン…
DOKUN
ドクン…
DOKUN
ドクン…
DOKUN
ちゃぷ
CHAPU (SHLOP)
にゅる…
NYURU (SQUISH)
ちゃぷ
CHAPU
ちゃぷ…
CHAPU
する…
SURU (SLIDE)
ドキ
DOKI (THUMP)
ちゃぷ…
CHAPU
ドキ
DOKI
ちゅく…
CHUKU (SPLISH)
ちゅぷ…
CHUPU (SHLICK)
ドキ
DOKI
ちゃぷ…
CHUPU
ドキ…
DOKI
ぴちゃ…
PICHA (SPLASH)

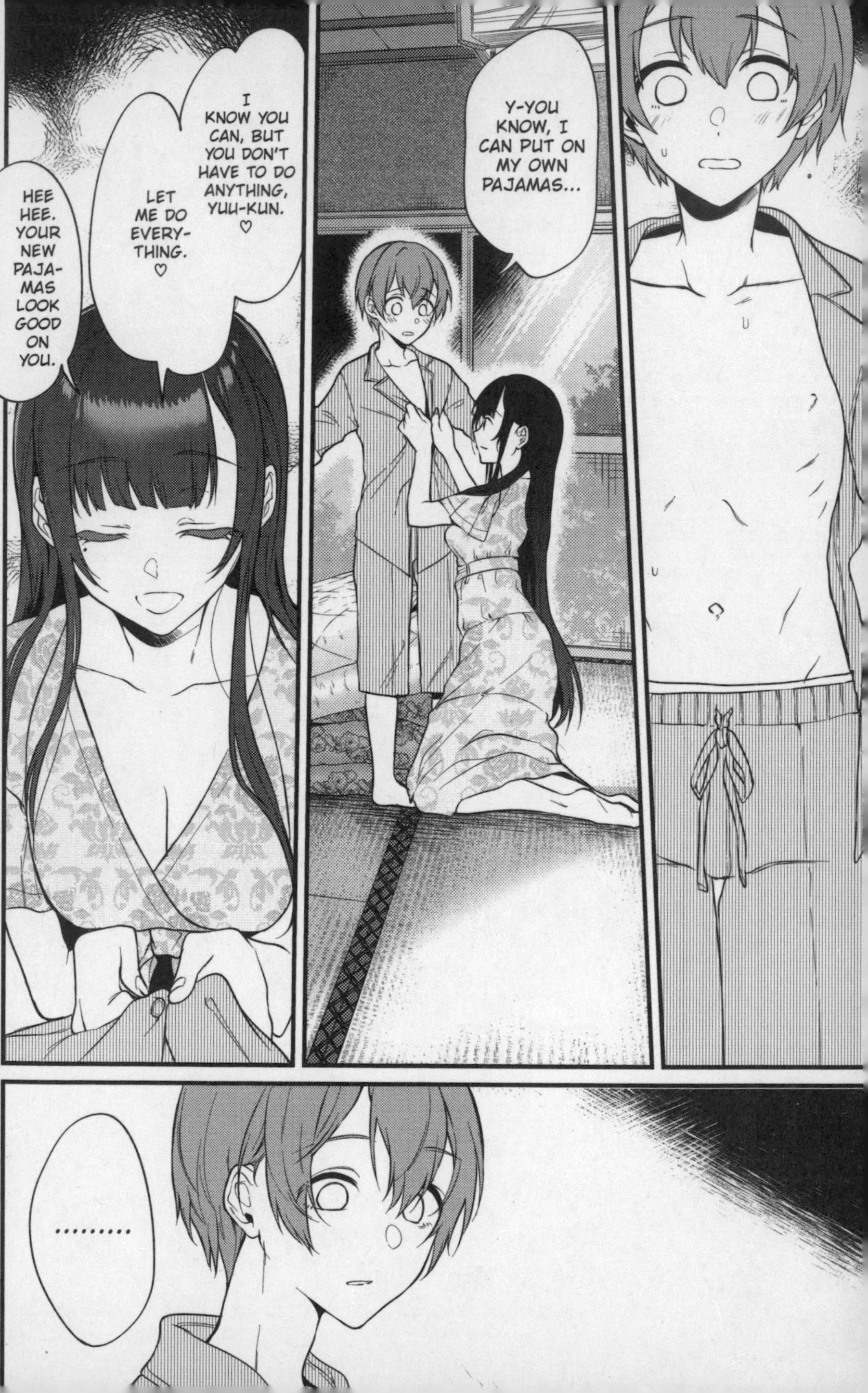
Y-YOU KNOW, I CAN PUT ON MY OWN PAJAMAS...
I KNOW YOU CAN, BUT YOU DON'T HAVE TO DO ANYTHING, YUU-KUN. ♡
LET ME DO EVERY-THING. ♡
HEE HEE. YOUR NEW PAJA-MAS LOOK GOOD ON YOU.
....

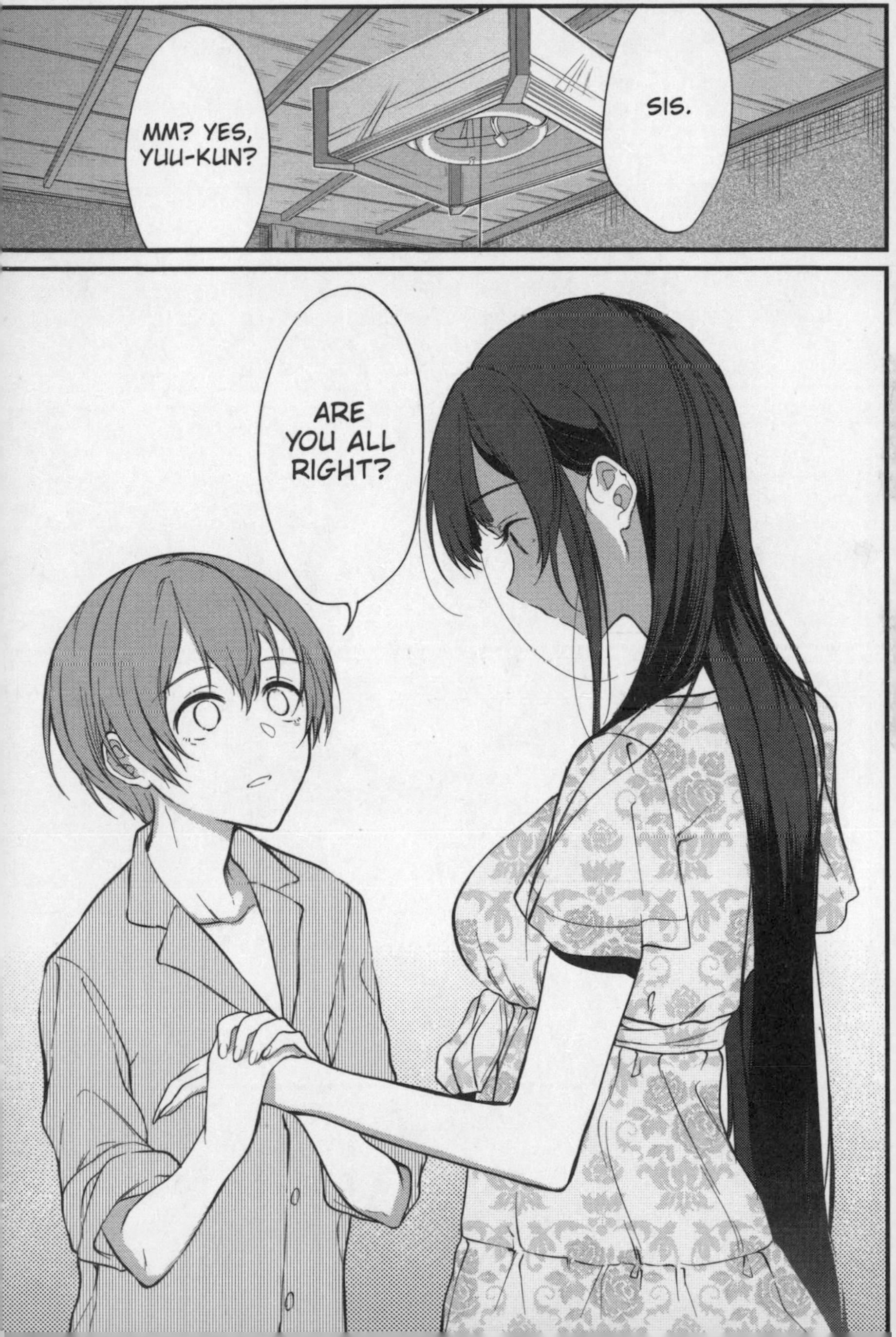
SIS.
MM? YES, YUU-KUN?
ARE YOU ALL RIGHT?

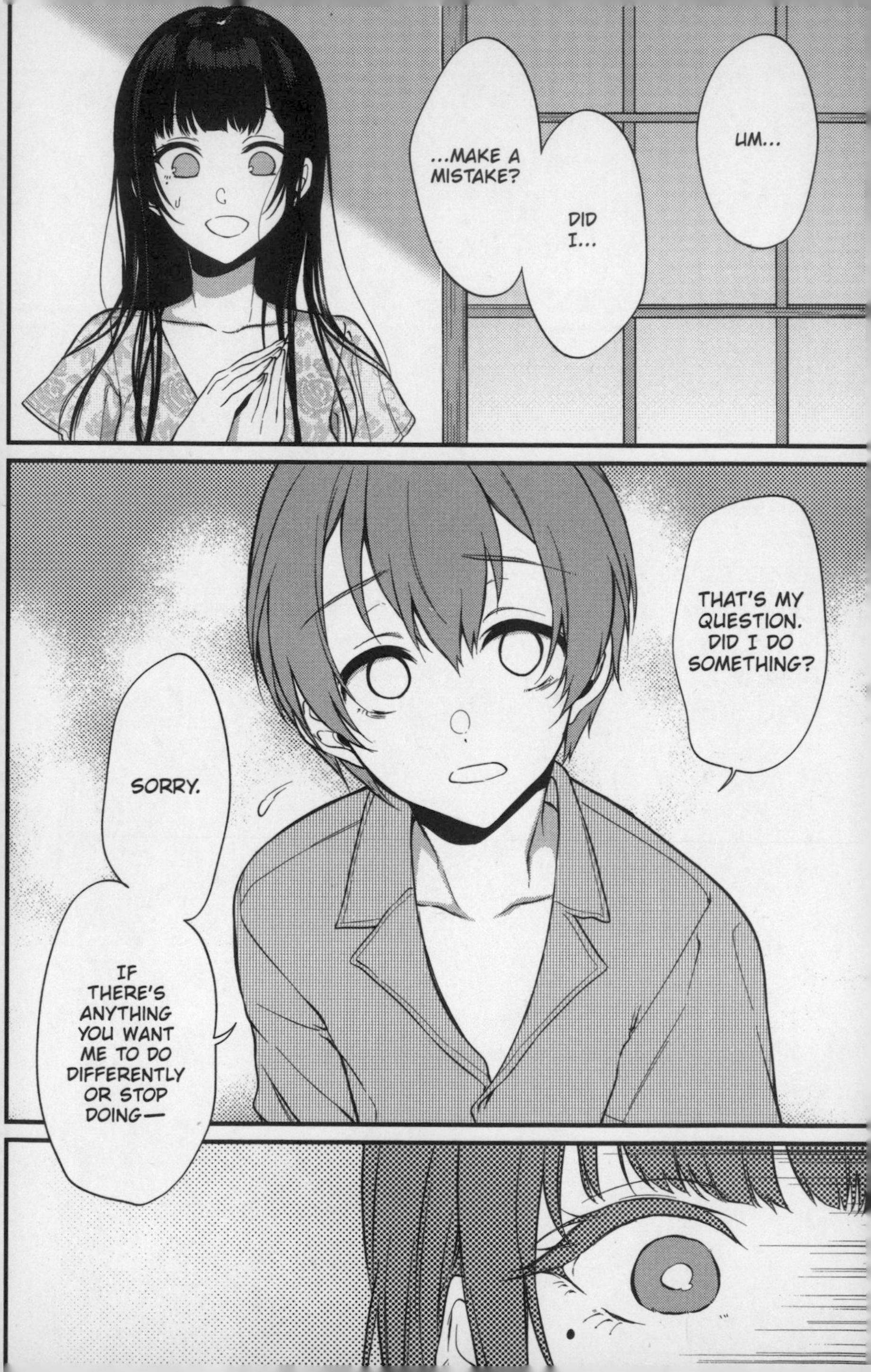
UM...
DID I...
...MAKE A MISTAKE?
THAT'S MY QUESTION. DID I DO SOMETHING?
SORRY.
IF THERE'S ANYTHING YOU WANT ME TO DO DIFFERENTLY OR STOP DOING—

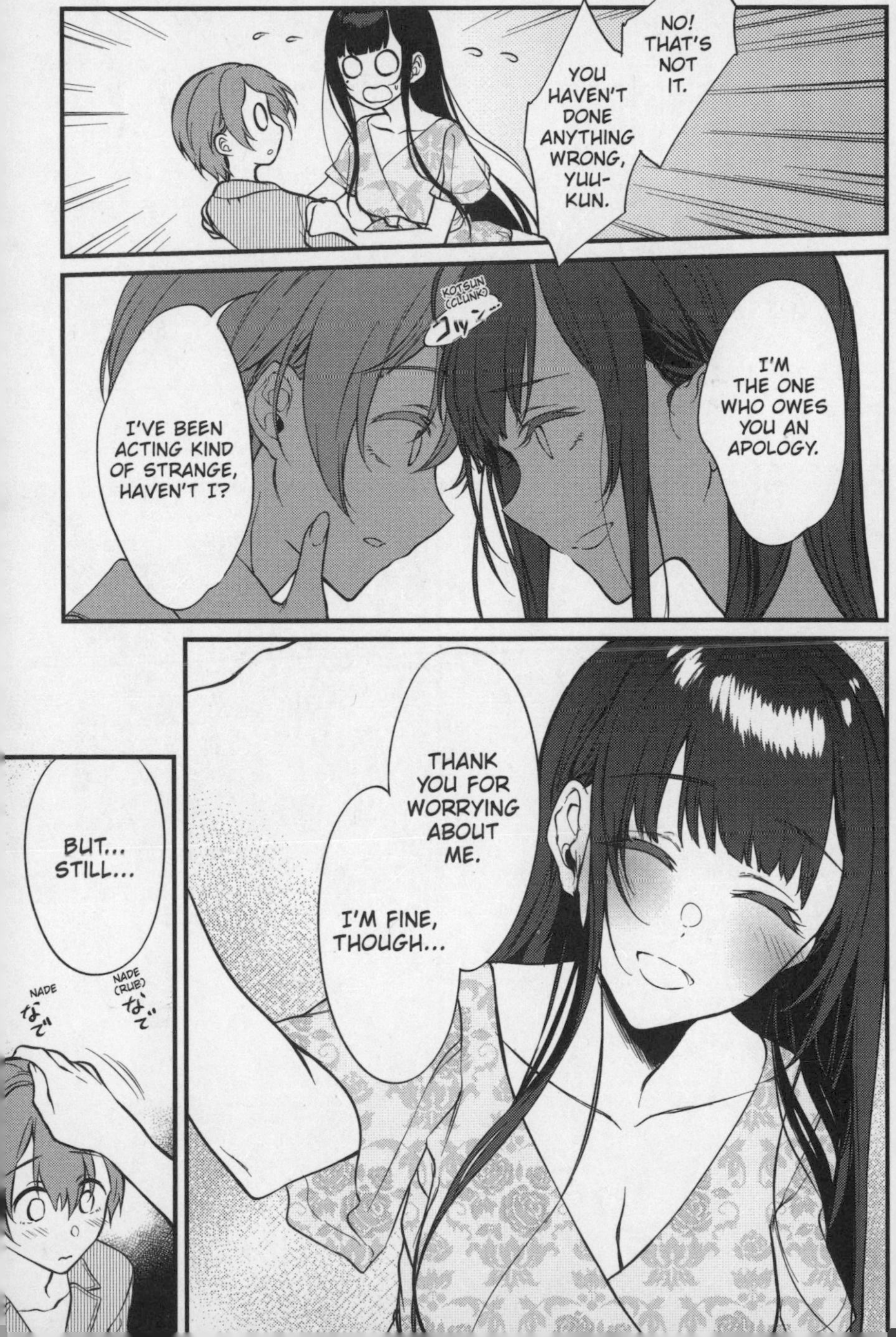
NO! THAT'S NOT IT.
YOU HAVEN'T DONE ANYTHING WRONG, YUU-KUN.
I'M THE ONE WHO OWES YOU AN APOLOGY.
KOTSUN (CLUNK)
I'VE BEEN ACTING KIND OF STRANGE, HAVEN'T I?
THANK YOU FOR WORRYING ABOUT ME.
I'M FINE, THOUGH...
BUT... STILL...
NADE (RUB)
なで
NADE
なで

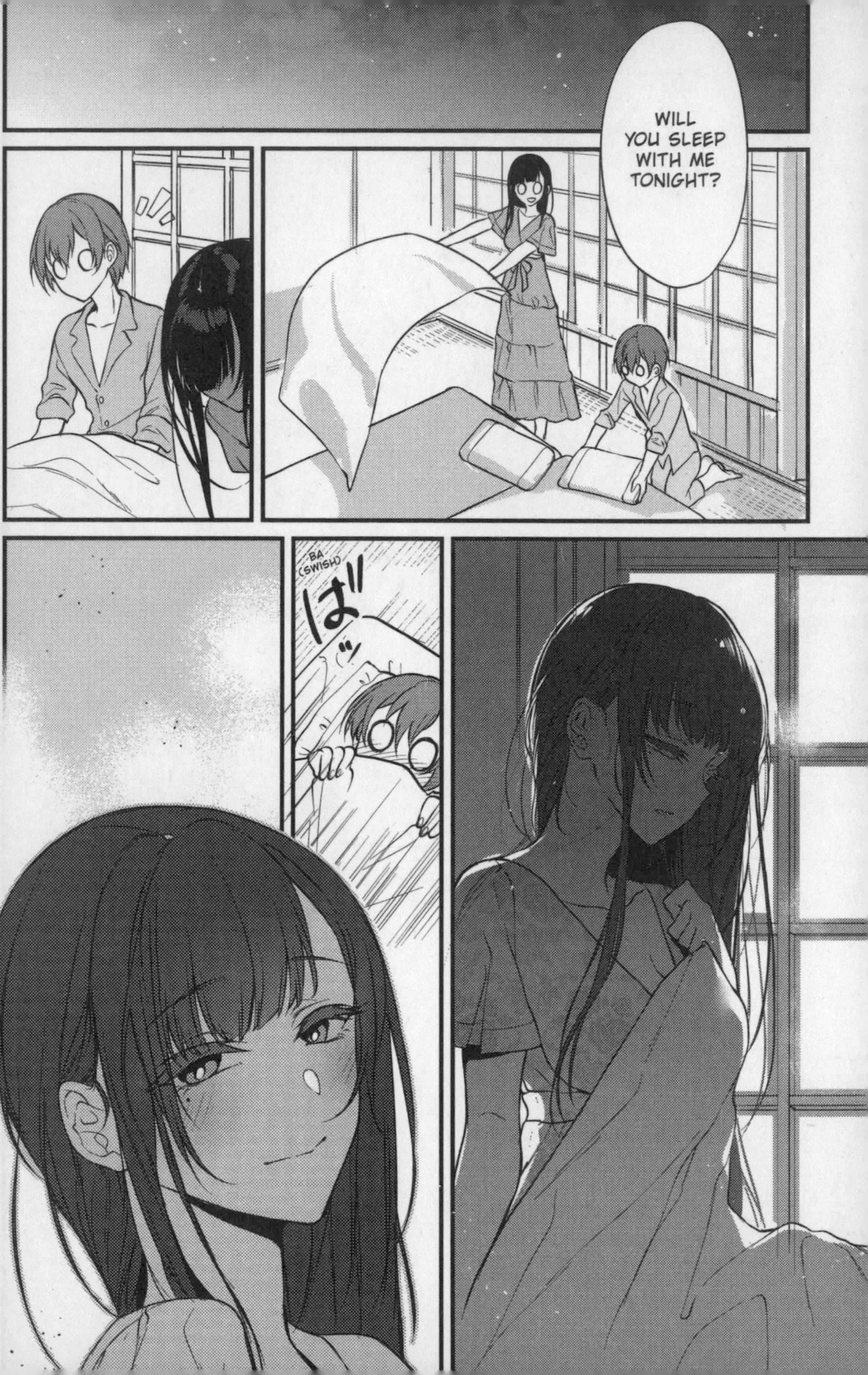
WILL YOU SLEEP WITH ME TONIGHT?
BA (SWISH)
ばっ

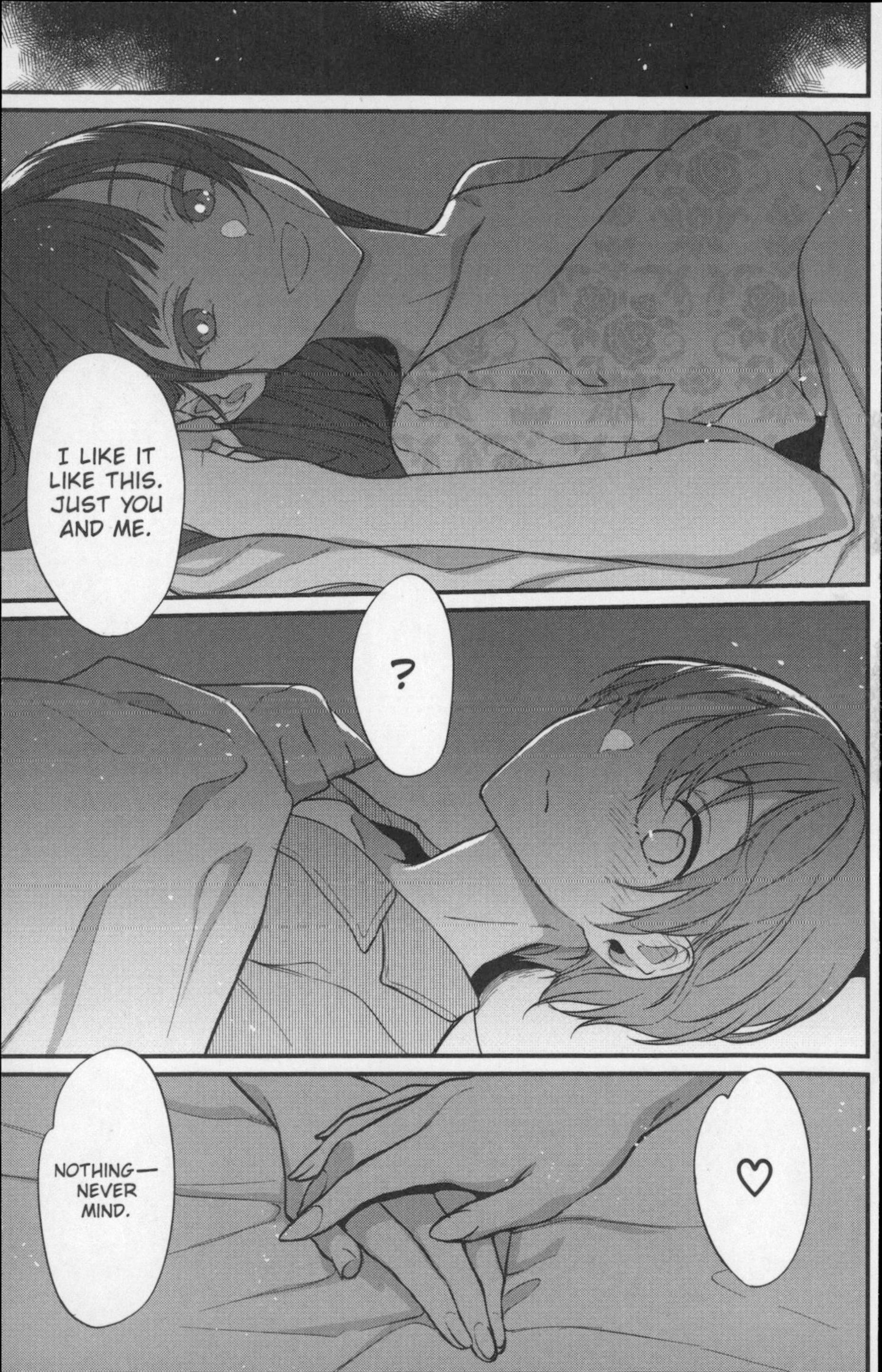
I LIKE IT LIKE THIS. JUST YOU AND ME.
?
♡
NOTHING— NEVER MIND.

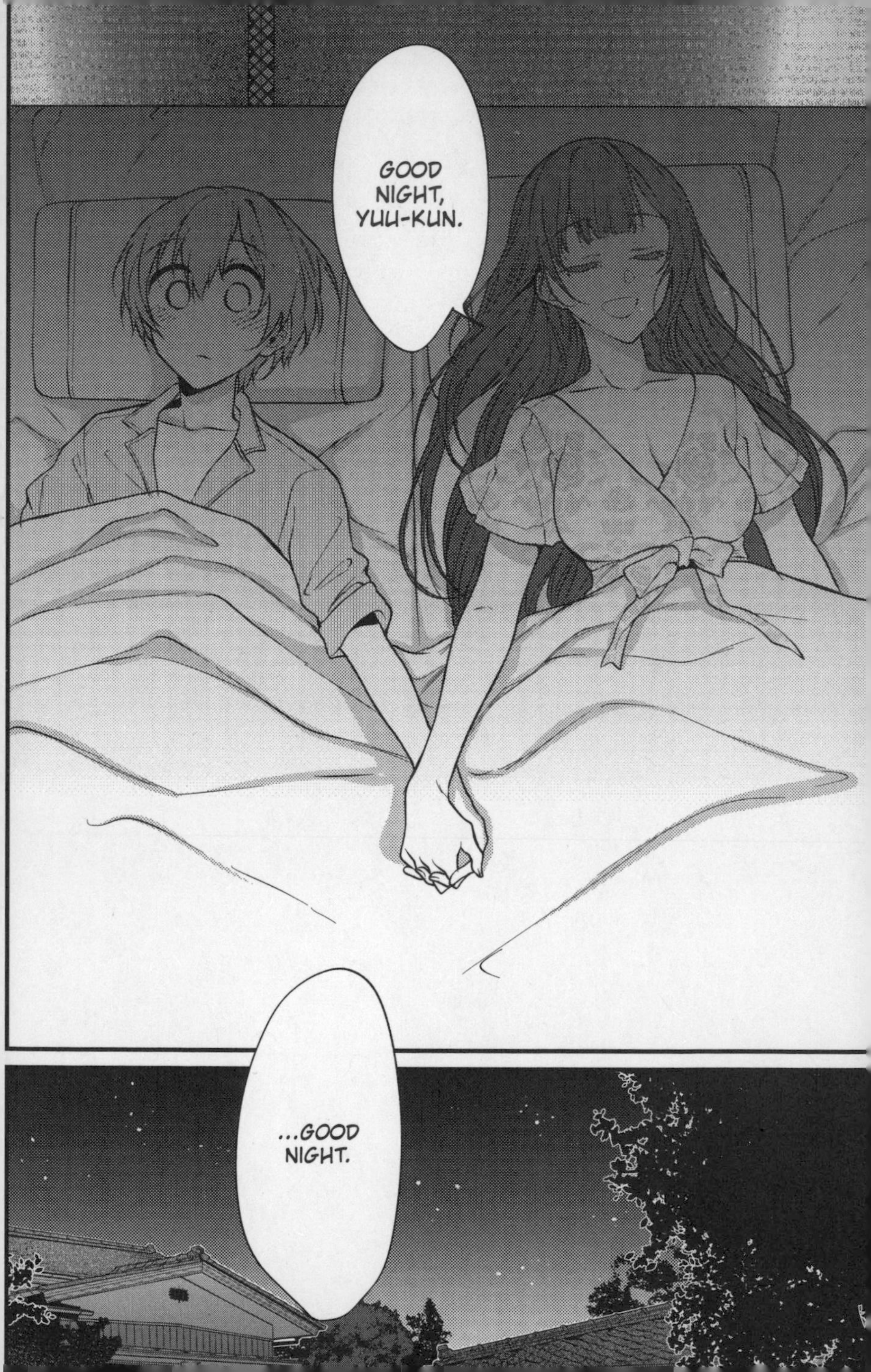
GOOD NIGHT, YUU-KUN.
...GOOD NIGHT.

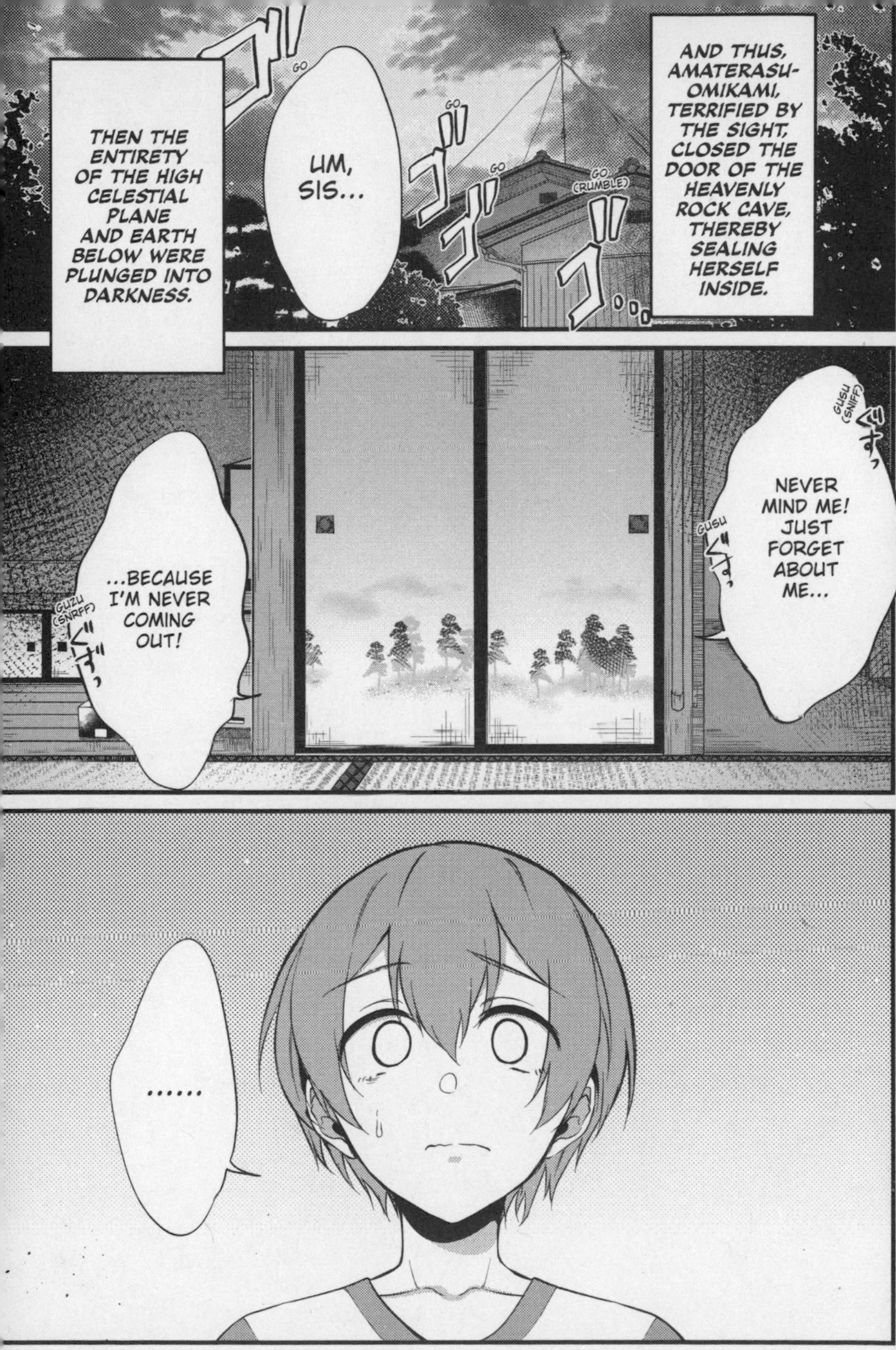
AND THUS, AMATERASU-OMIKAMI, TERRIFIED BY THE SIGHT, CLOSED THE DOOR OF THE HEAVENLY ROCK CAVE, THEREBY SEALING HERSELF INSIDE.
GO (RUMBLE)
GO
GO
GO
UM, SIS...
THEN THE ENTIRETY OF THE HIGH CELESTIAL PLANE AND EARTH BELOW WERE PLUNGED INTO DARKNESS.
GUSU (SNIFF)
GUSU
NEVER MIND ME! JUST FORGET ABOUT ME...
GUZU (SNRFF)
...BECAUSE I'M NEVER COMING OUT!
......

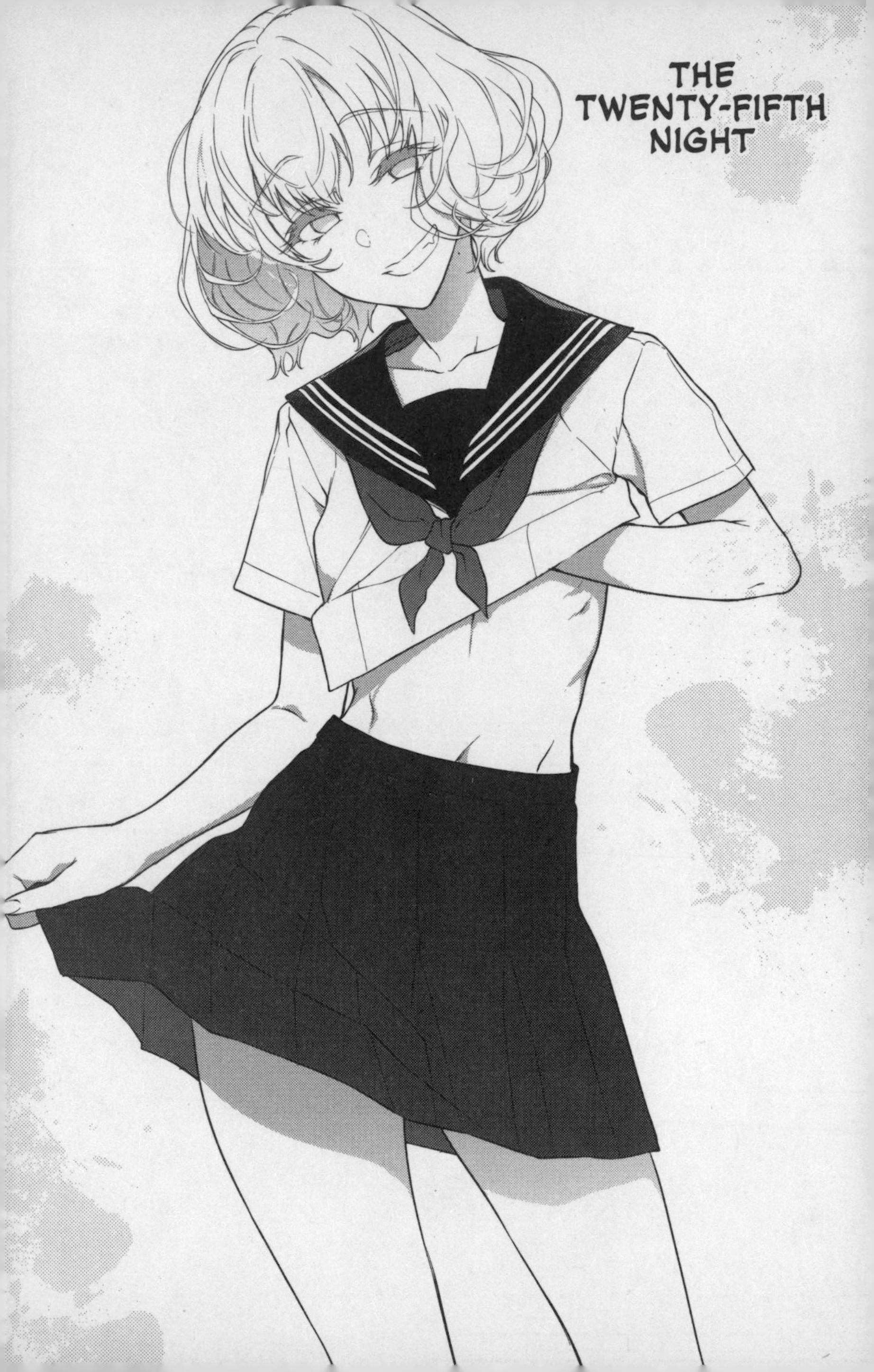
THE
TWENTY-FIFTH
NIGHT

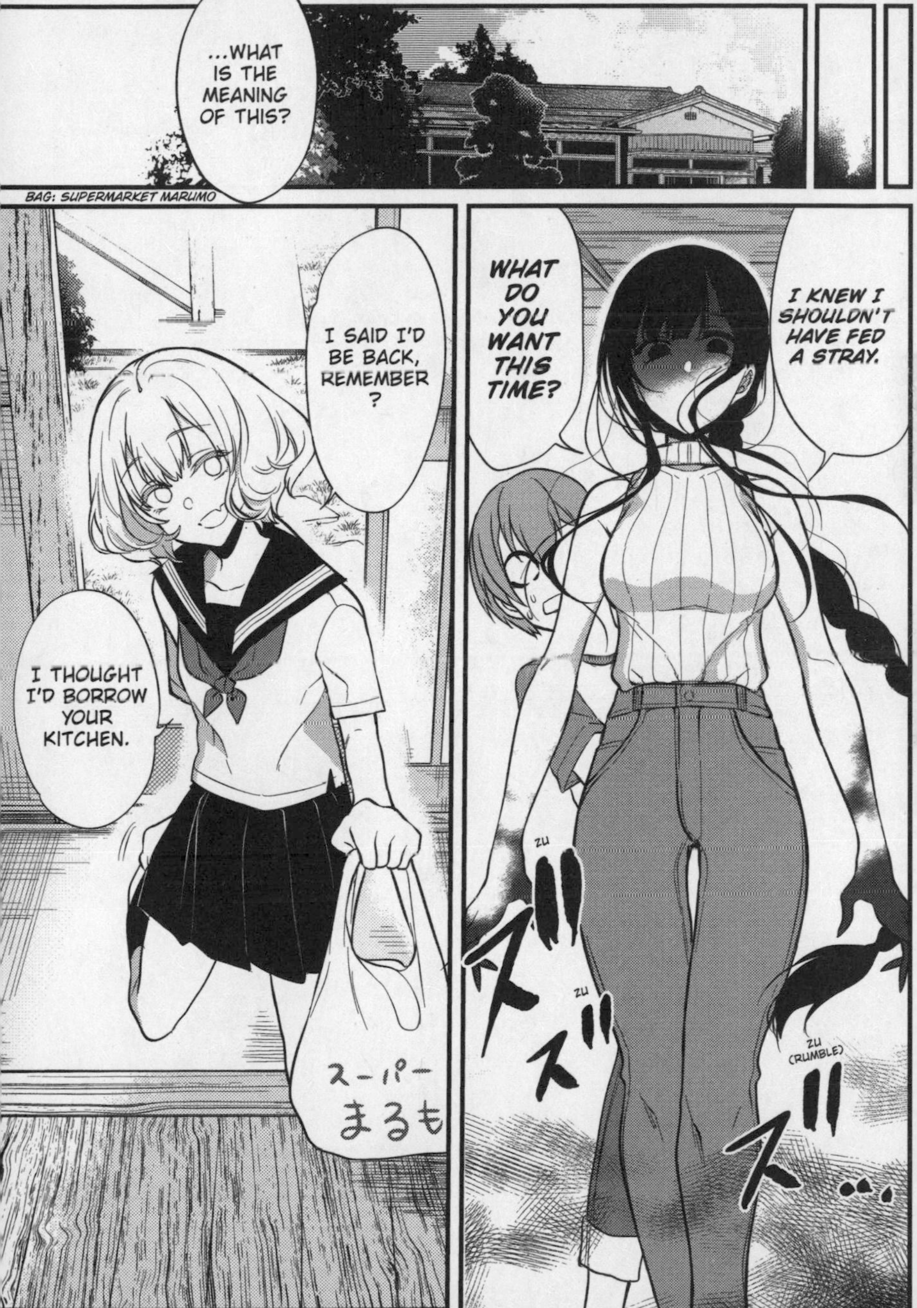
...WHAT IS THE MEANING OF THIS?
I KNEW I SHOULDN'T HAVE FED A STRAY.
WHAT DO YOU WANT THIS TIME?
ZU
ZU
ZU (RUMBLE)
I SAID I'D BE BACK, REMEMBER?
I THOUGHT I'D BORROW YOUR KITCHEN.
スーパー まるも
BAG: SUPERMARKET MARUMO

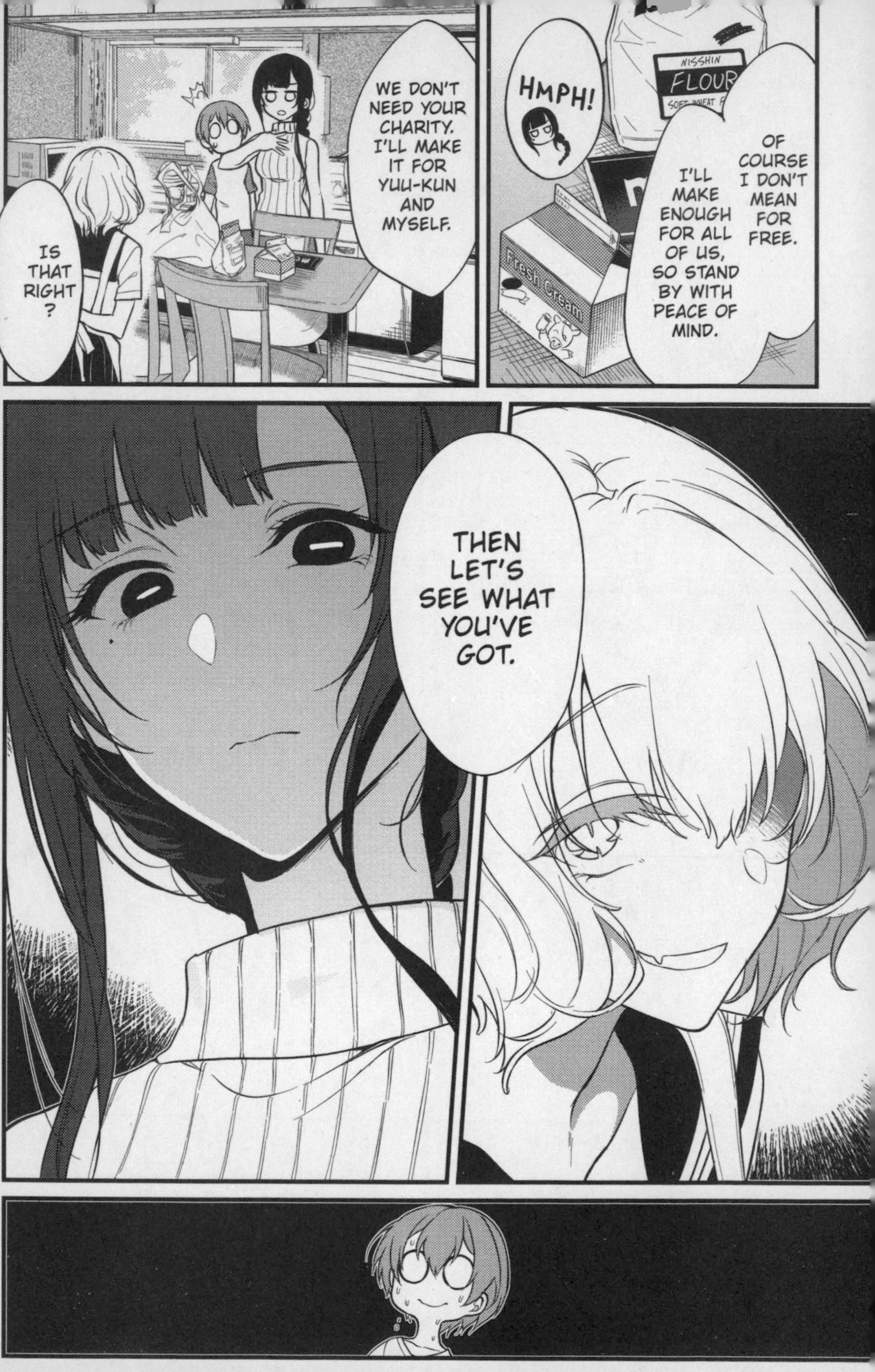
HMPH!
NISSHIN
FLOUR
Fresh Cream
OF COURSE I DON'T MEAN FOR FREE.
I'LL MAKE ENOUGH FOR ALL OF US, SO STAND BY WITH PEACE OF MIND.
WE DON'T NEED YOUR CHARITY. I'LL MAKE IT FOR YUU-KUN AND MYSELF.
IS THAT RIGHT?
THEN LET'S SEE WHAT YOU'VE GOT.

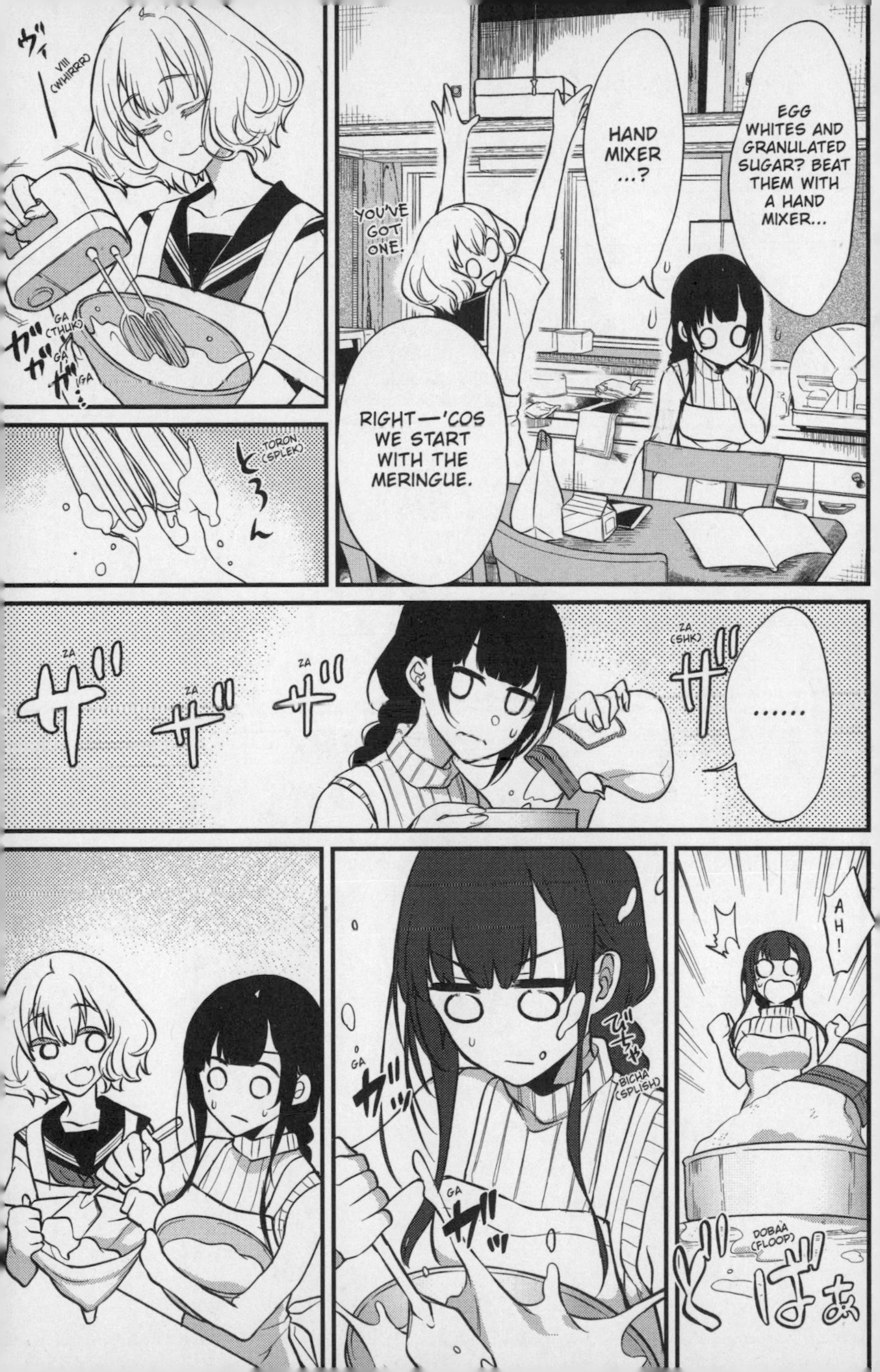
EGG WHITES AND GRANULATED SUGAR? BEAT THEM WITH A HAND MIXER...
HAND MIXER ...?
YOU'VE GOT ONE.
RIGHT—'COS WE START WITH THE MERINGUE.
VIII (WHIRRR)
GA (THUK)
GA
IGA
TORON (SPLEK)
ZA (SHK)
......
ZA
ZA
ZA
AH!
DOBAA (FLOOP)
BICHA (SPLISH)
GA
GA

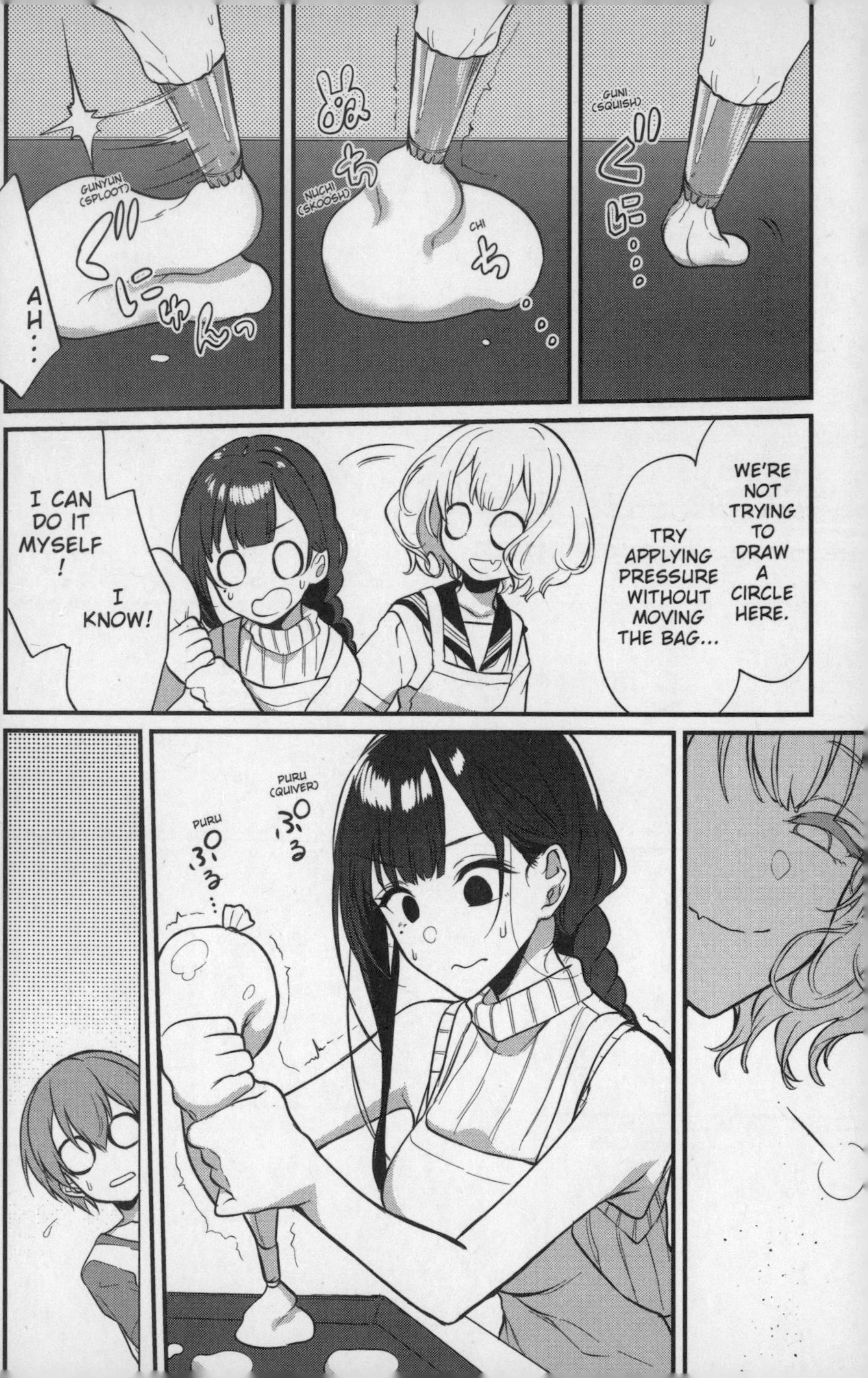

GUNI (SQUISH)
ぐぐに…
NUCHI (SKOOSH)
ぬち
CHI
ち…
GUNYUN (SPLOOT)
ぐにゅんっ
AH…
WE'RE NOT TRYING TO DRAW A CIRCLE HERE.
TRY APPLYING PRESSURE WITHOUT MOVING THE BAG…
I KNOW!
I CAN DO IT MYSELF!
PURU (QUIVER)
ぷる
PURU
ぷる…

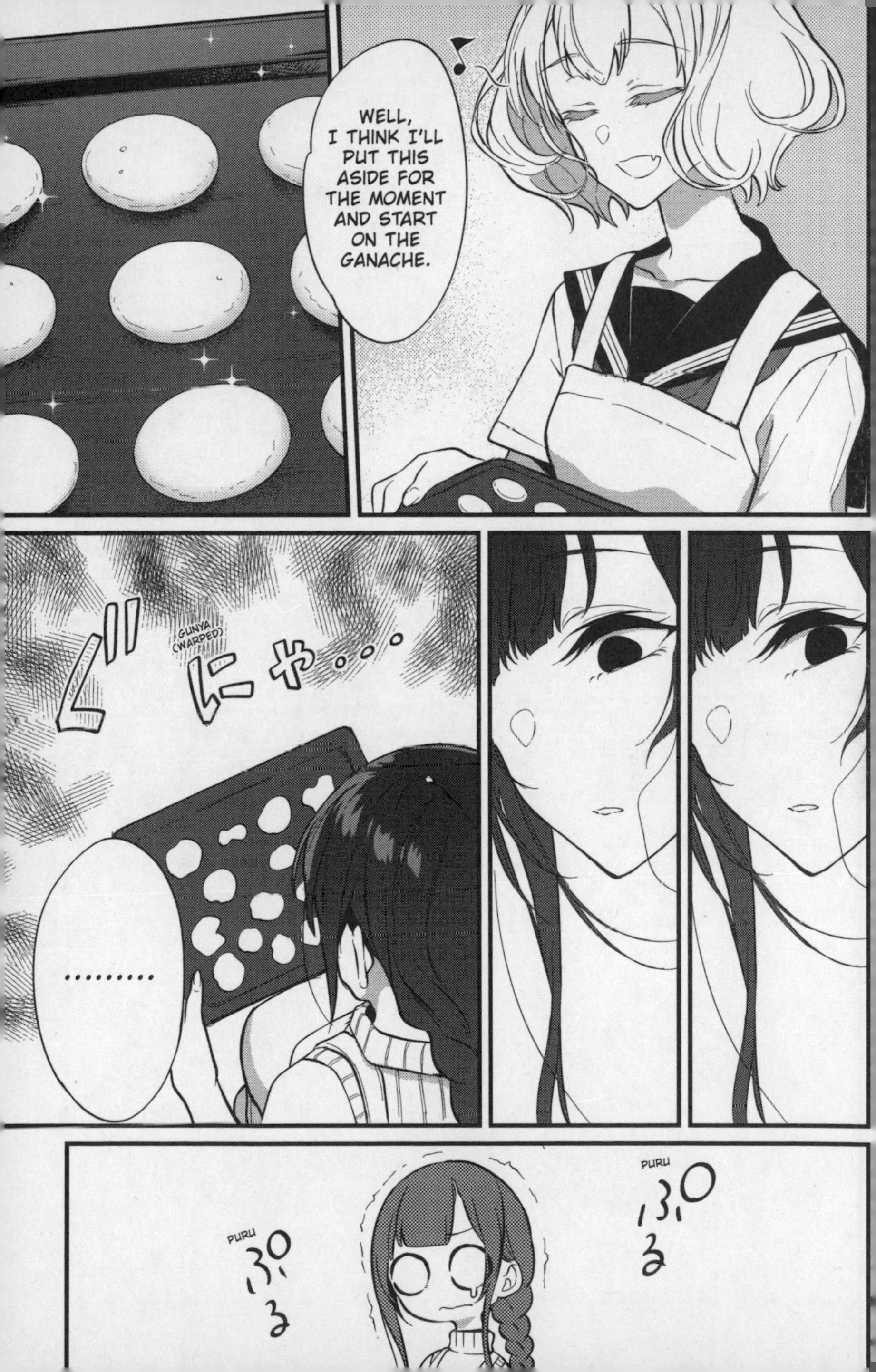
WELL, I THINK I'LL PUT THIS ASIDE FOR THE MOMENT AND START ON THE GANACHE.
ぐにゃ。。。
GUNYA (WARPED)
………
ぷるぷる
PURU
ぷるぷる
PURU

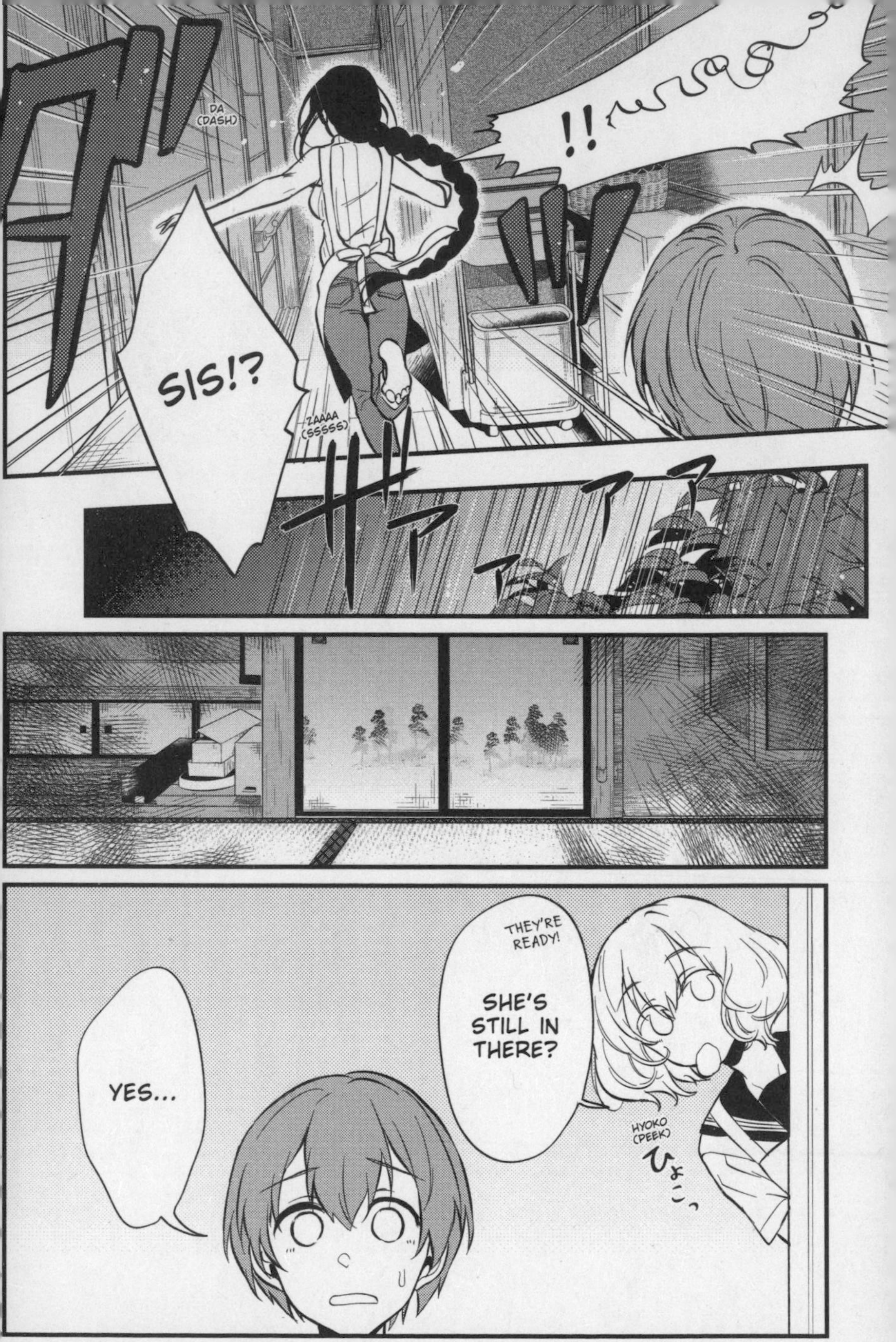
!!
DA (DASH)
SIS!?
ZAAAA (SSSSS)
HYOKO (PEEK)
THEY'RE READY!
SHE'S STILL IN THERE?
YES...

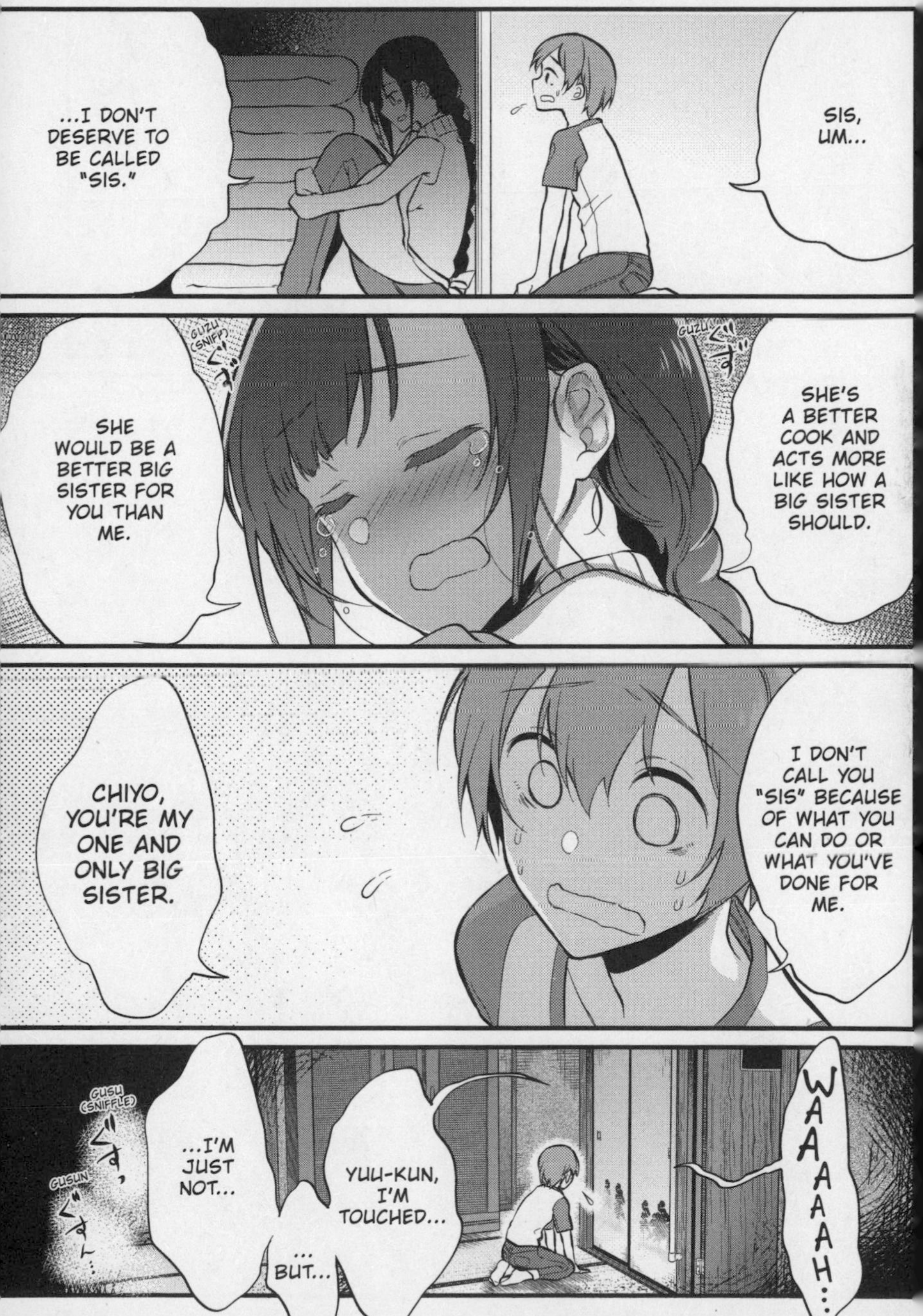
SIS, UM...
...I DON'T DESERVE TO BE CALLED "SIS."
GUZU
SHE'S A BETTER COOK AND ACTS MORE LIKE HOW A BIG SISTER SHOULD.
GUZU (SNIFF)
SHE WOULD BE A BETTER BIG SISTER FOR YOU THAN ME.
I DON'T CALL YOU "SIS" BECAUSE OF WHAT YOU CAN DO OR WHAT YOU'VE DONE FOR ME.
CHIYO, YOU'RE MY ONE AND ONLY BIG SISTER.
WAAAAAH...
YUU-KUN, I'M TOUCHED...
... BUT...
...I'M JUST NOT...
GUSU (SNIFFLE)
GUSUN

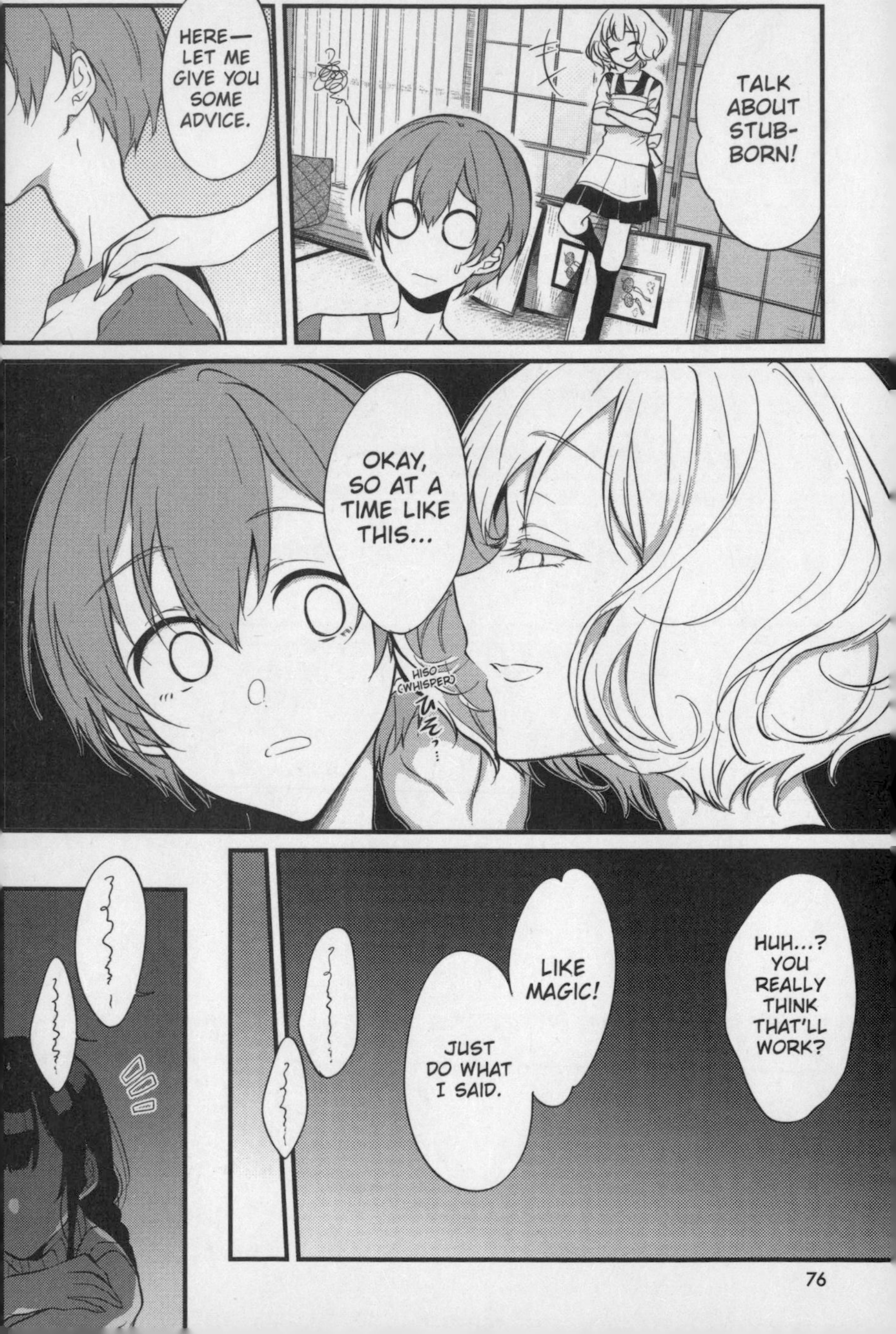
TALK ABOUT STUB-BORN!
HERE— LET ME GIVE YOU SOME ADVICE.
OKAY, SO AT A TIME LIKE THIS...
HISO (WHISPER)
HUH...? YOU REALLY THINK THAT'LL WORK?
LIKE MAGIC!
JUST DO WHAT I SAID.

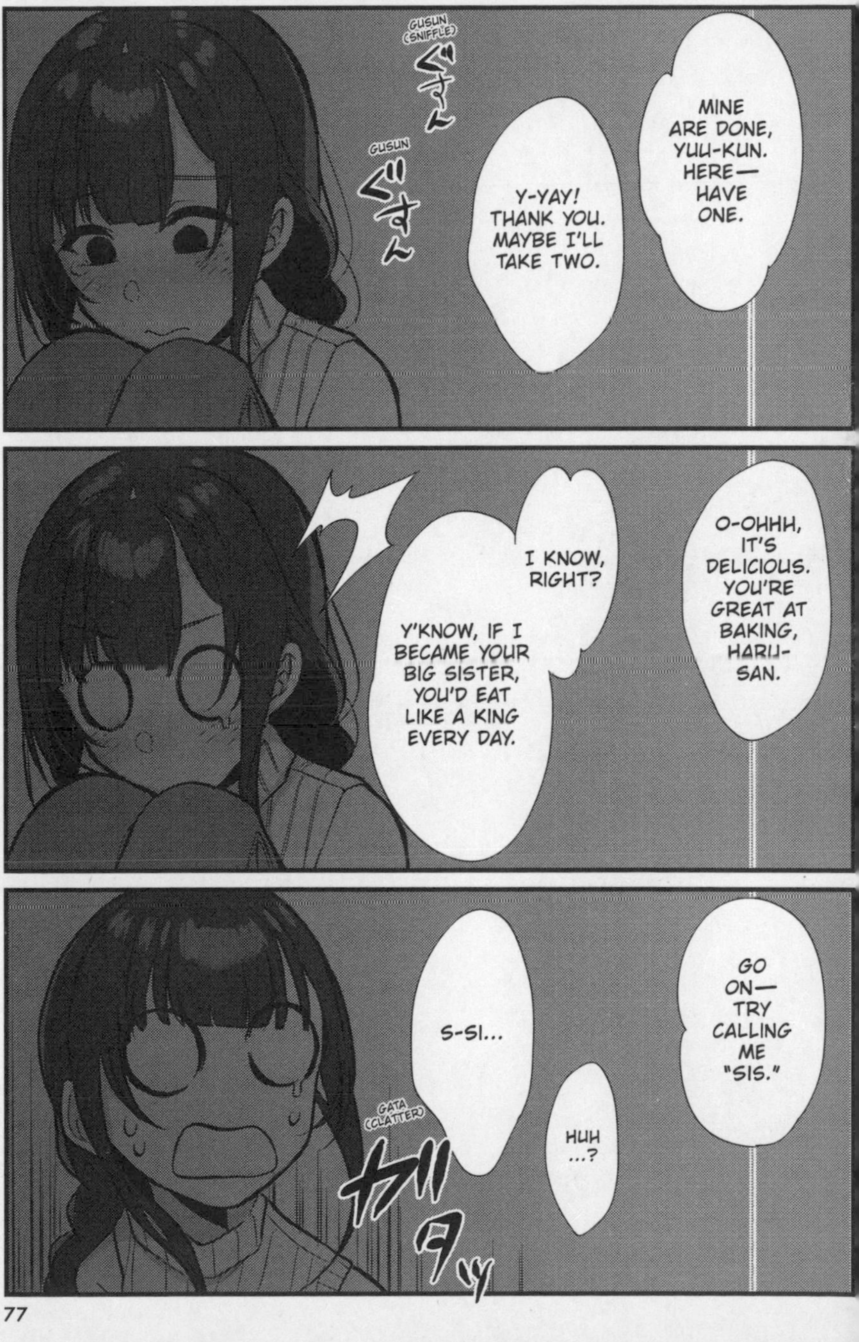
MINE ARE DONE, YUU-KUN. HERE—HAVE ONE.
Y-YAY! THANK YOU. MAYBE I'LL TAKE TWO.
GUSUN (SNIFFLE)
ぐすん
GUSUN
ぐすん
O-OHHH, IT'S DELICIOUS. YOU'RE GREAT AT BAKING, HARU-SAN.
I KNOW, RIGHT?
Y'KNOW, IF I BECAME YOUR BIG SISTER, YOU'D EAT LIKE A KING EVERY DAY.
GO ON—TRY CALLING ME "SIS."
HUH ...?
S-SI...
GATA (CLATTER)
ガタッ

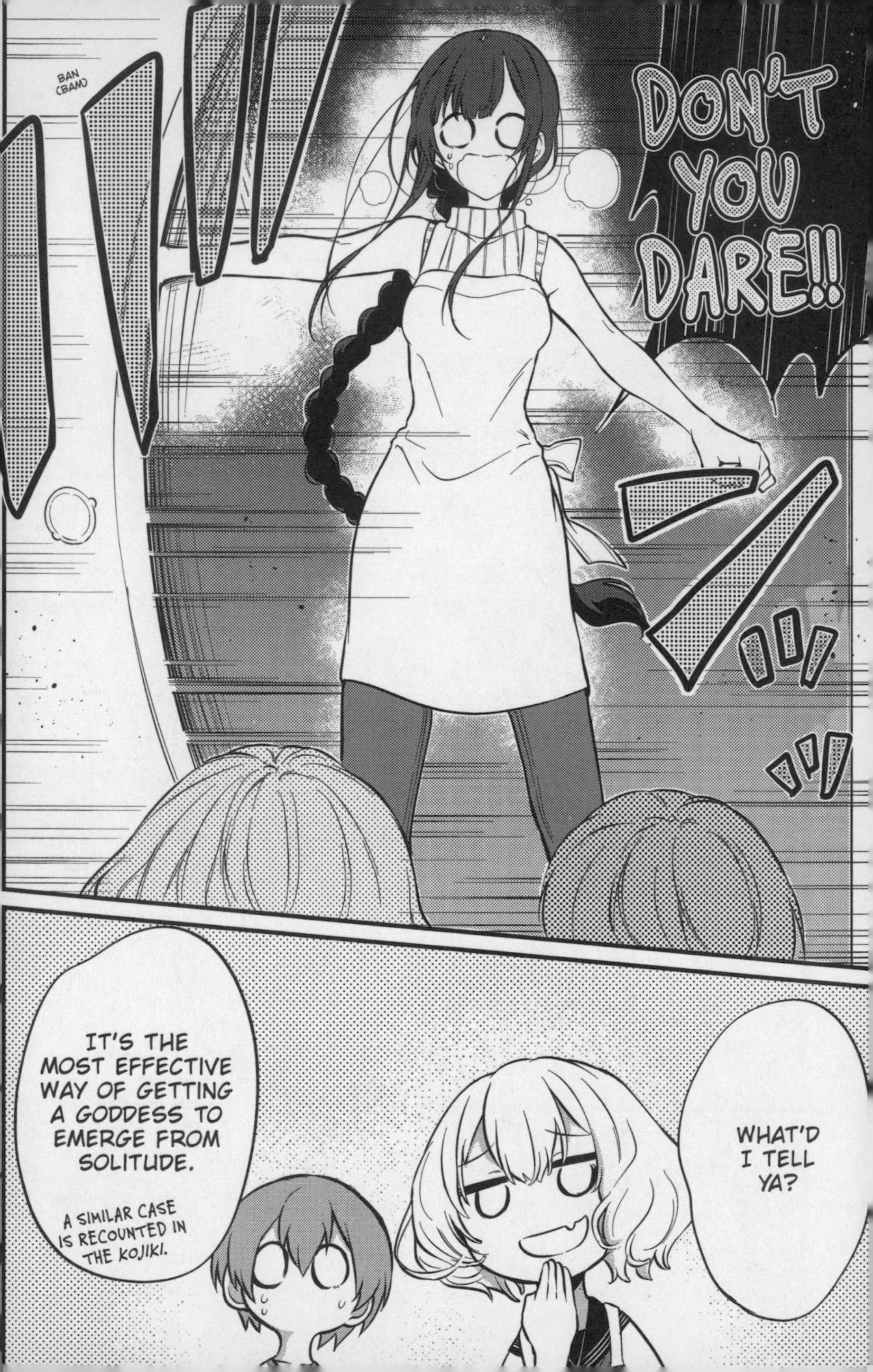
DON'T YOU DARE!!
BAN (BAM)
WHAT'D I TELL YA?
IT'S THE MOST EFFECTIVE WAY OF GETTING A GODDESS TO EMERGE FROM SOLITUDE.
A SIMILAR CASE IS RECOUNTED IN THE KOJIKI.

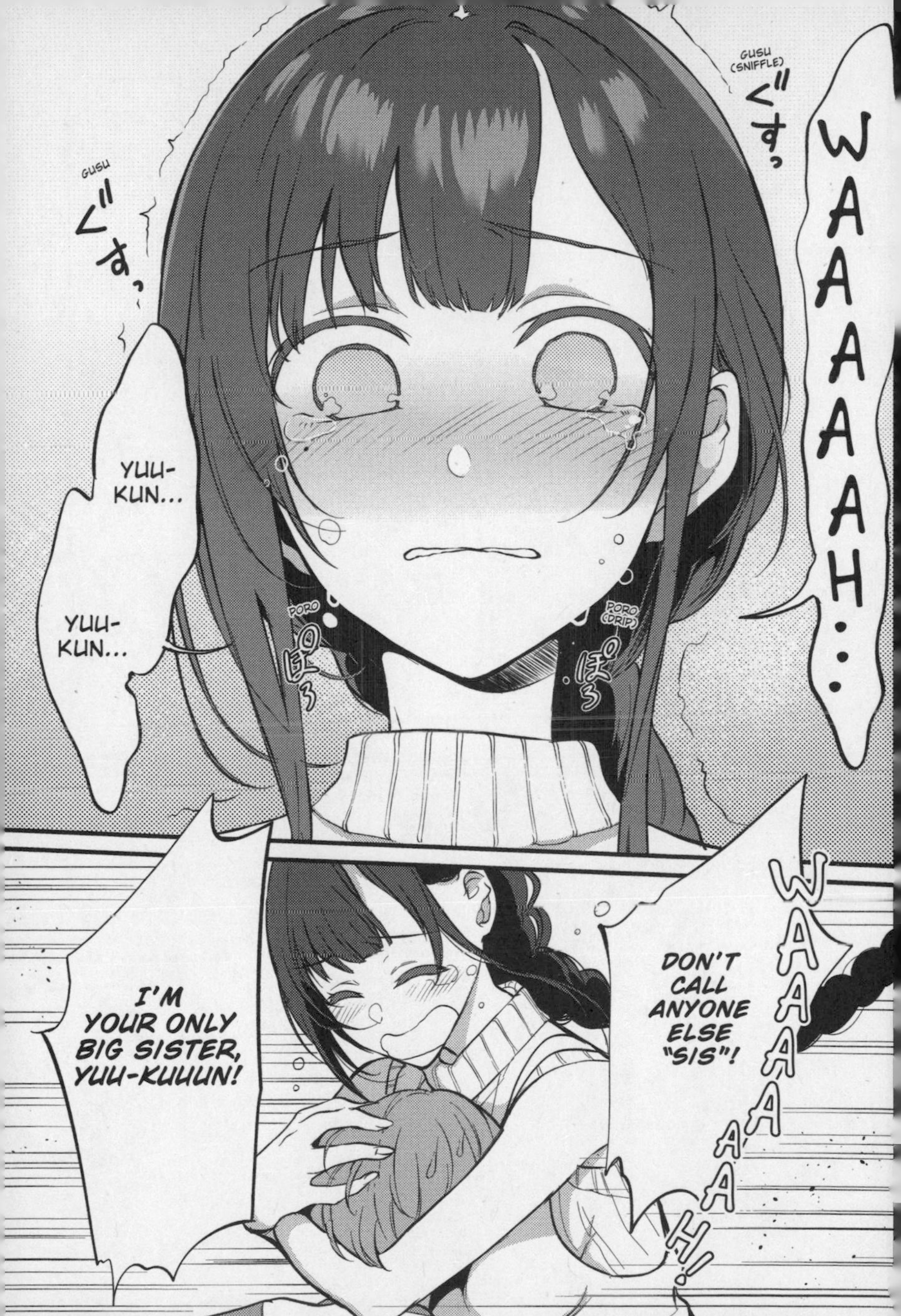
WAAAAAH...
GUSU (SNIFFLE)
ぐすっ
PORO (DRIP)
ぽろ
PORO
ぽろ
GUSU
ぐすっ
YUU-KUN...
YUU-KUN...
WAAAAAAH!
DON'T CALL ANYONE ELSE "SIS"!
I'M YOUR ONLY BIG SISTER, YUU-KUUUN!

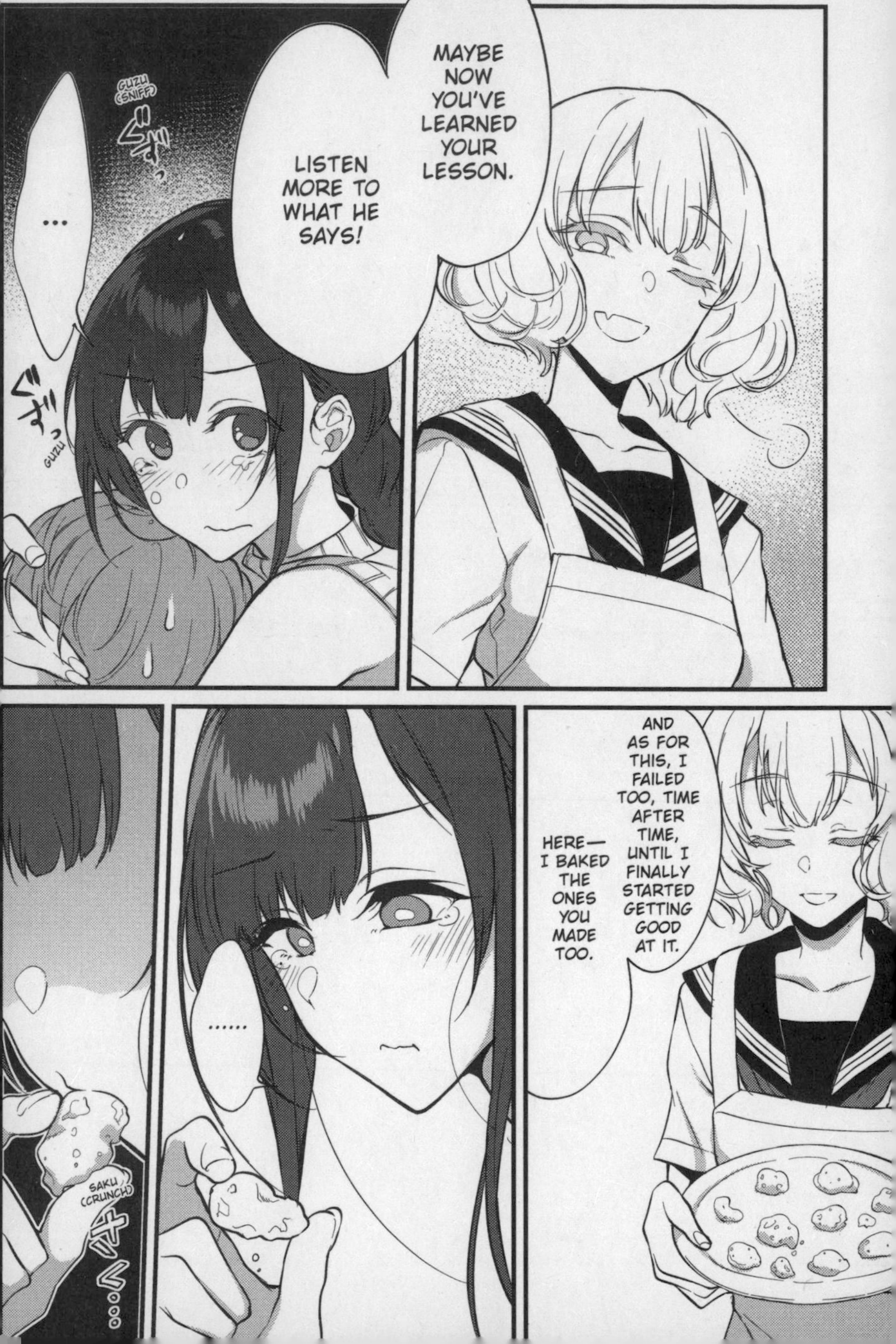
MAYBE NOW YOU'VE LEARNED YOUR LESSON.
LISTEN MORE TO WHAT HE SAYS!
GUZU (SNIFF)
ぐずっ
...
ぐずっ
GUZU
AND AS FOR THIS, I FAILED TOO, TIME AFTER TIME, UNTIL I FINALLY STARTED GETTING GOOD AT IT.
HERE— I BAKED THE ONES YOU MADE TOO.
......
SAKU (CRUNCH)
さく…

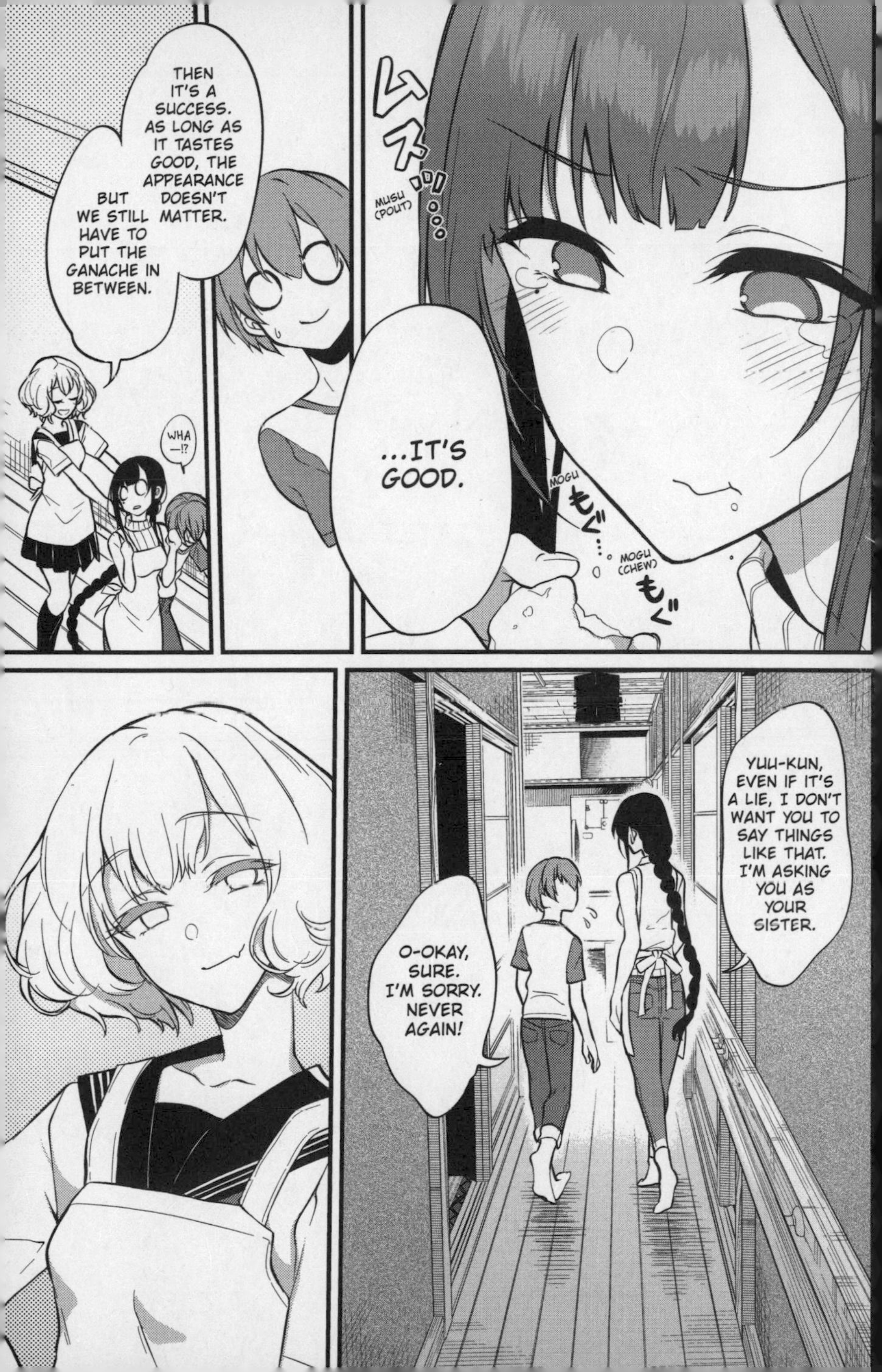
ムス
MUSU (POUT)
...IT'S GOOD.
MOGU もぐ...
MOGU (CHEW) もぐ
THEN IT'S A SUCCESS. AS LONG AS IT TASTES GOOD, THE APPEARANCE DOESN'T MATTER.
BUT WE STILL HAVE TO PUT THE GANACHE IN BETWEEN.
WHA—!?
YUU-KUN, EVEN IF IT'S A LIE, I DON'T WANT YOU TO SAY THINGS LIKE THAT. I'M ASKING YOU AS YOUR SISTER.
O-OKAY, SURE. I'M SORRY. NEVER AGAIN!

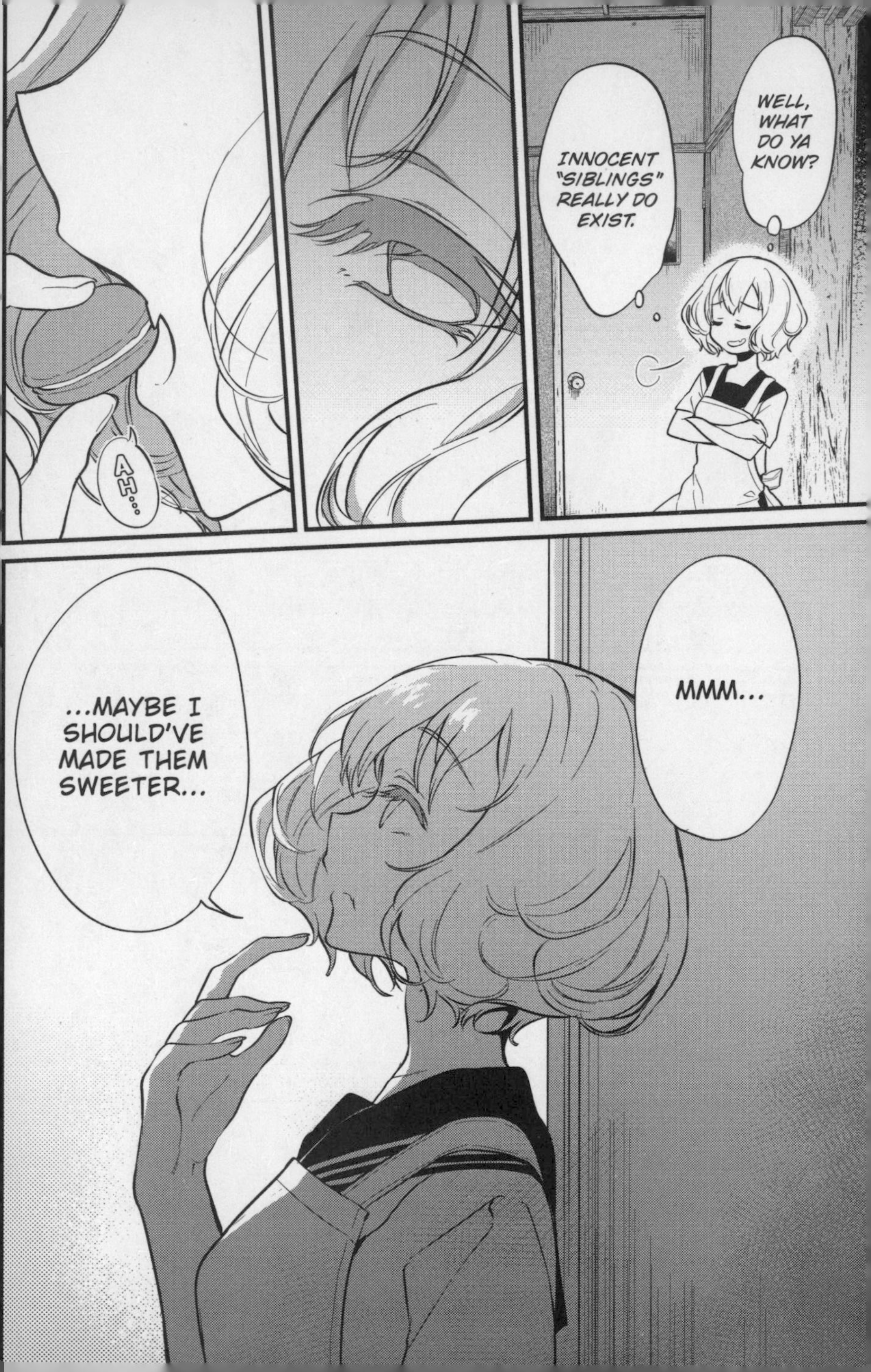
WELL, WHAT DO YA KNOW?
INNOCENT "SIBLINGS" REALLY DO EXIST.
AH...
MMM...
...MAYBE I SHOULD'VE MADE THEM SWEETER...

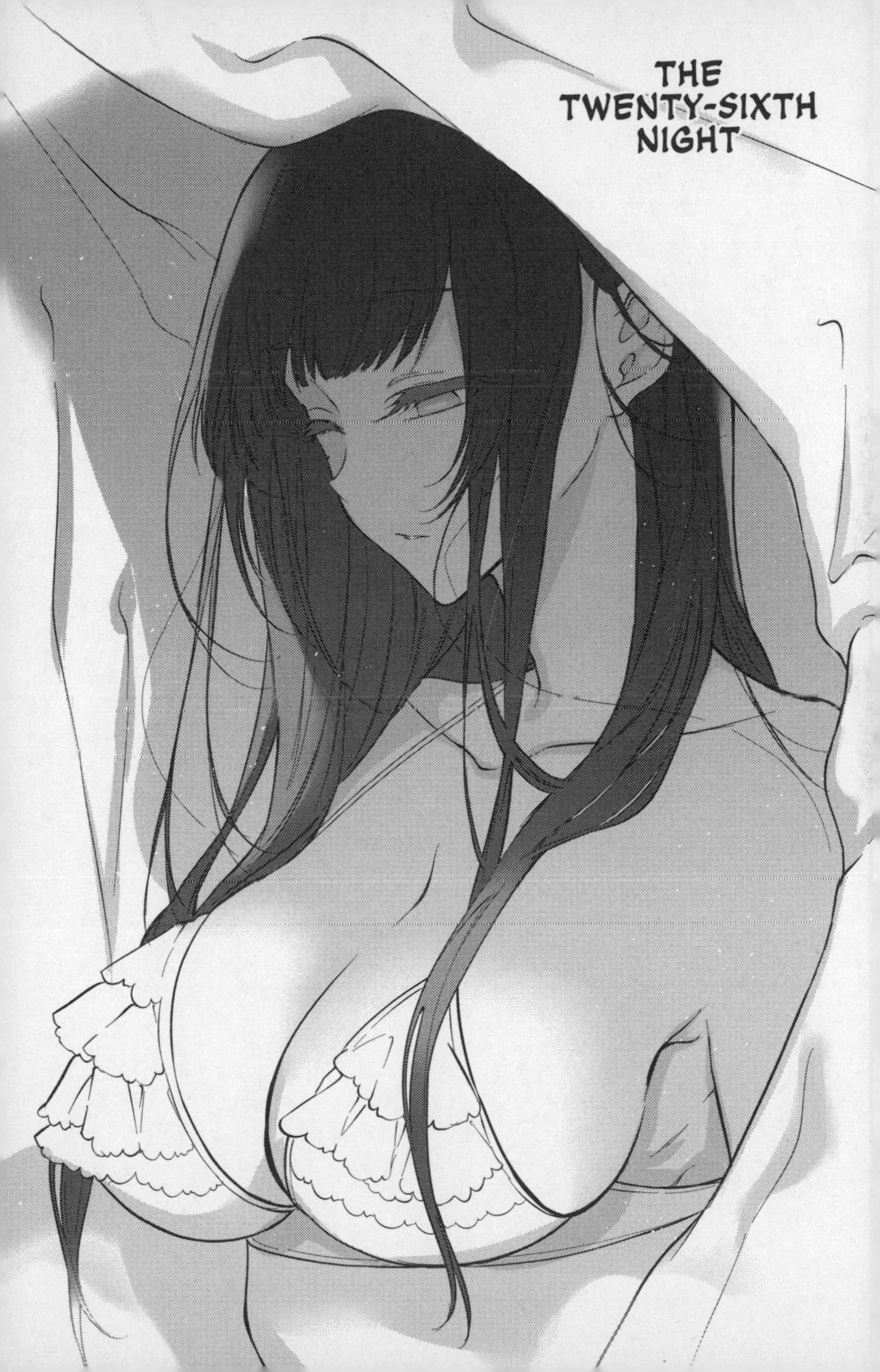
THE
TWENTY-SIXTH
NIGHT

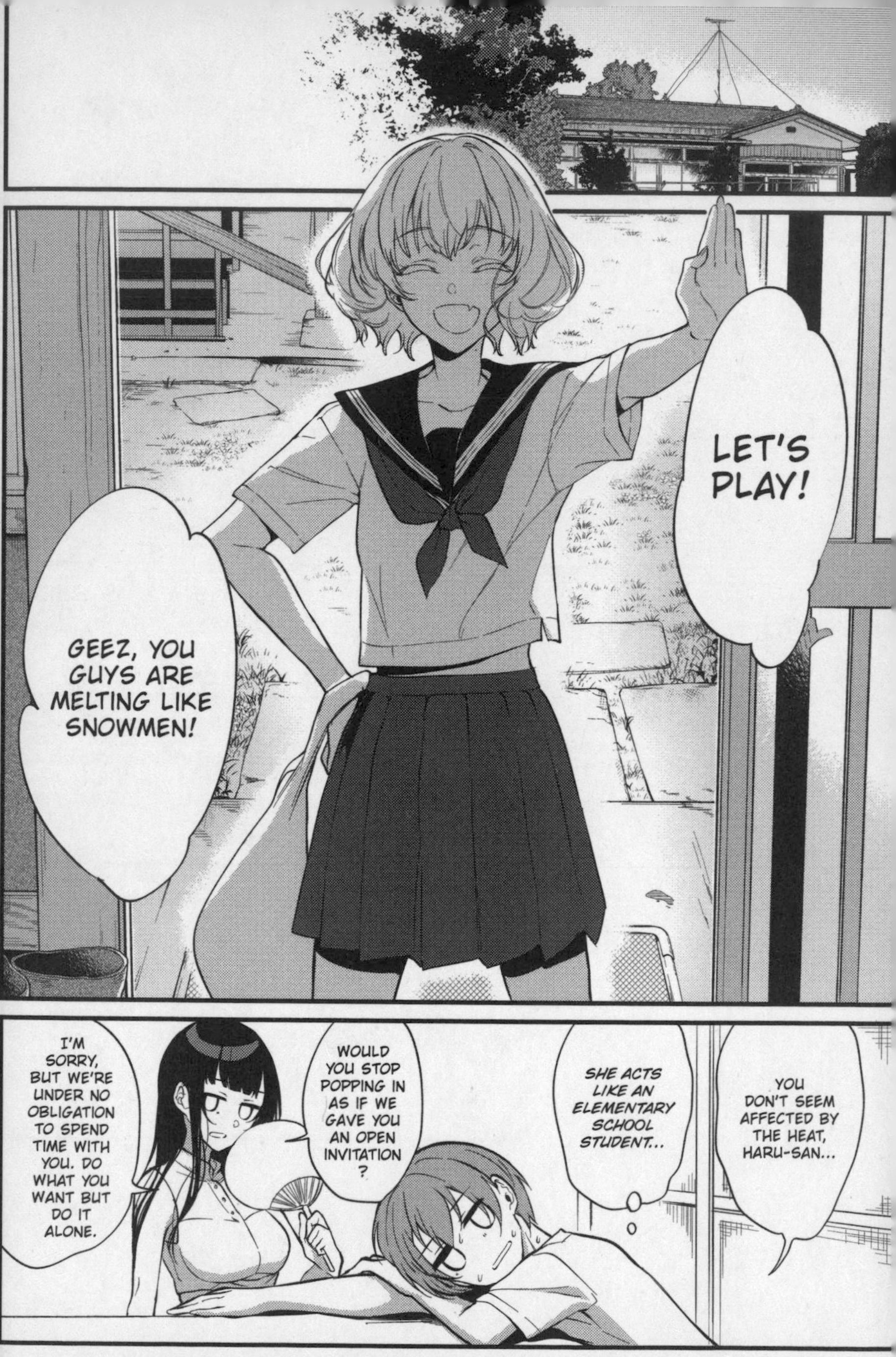
LET'S PLAY!
GEEZ, YOU GUYS ARE MELTING LIKE SNOWMEN!
YOU DON'T SEEM AFFECTED BY THE HEAT, HARU-SAN...
SHE ACTS LIKE AN ELEMENTARY SCHOOL STUDENT...
WOULD YOU STOP POPPING IN AS IF WE GAVE YOU AN OPEN INVITATION?
I'M SORRY, BUT WE'RE UNDER NO OBLIGATION TO SPEND TIME WITH YOU. DO WHAT YOU WANT BUT DO IT ALONE.

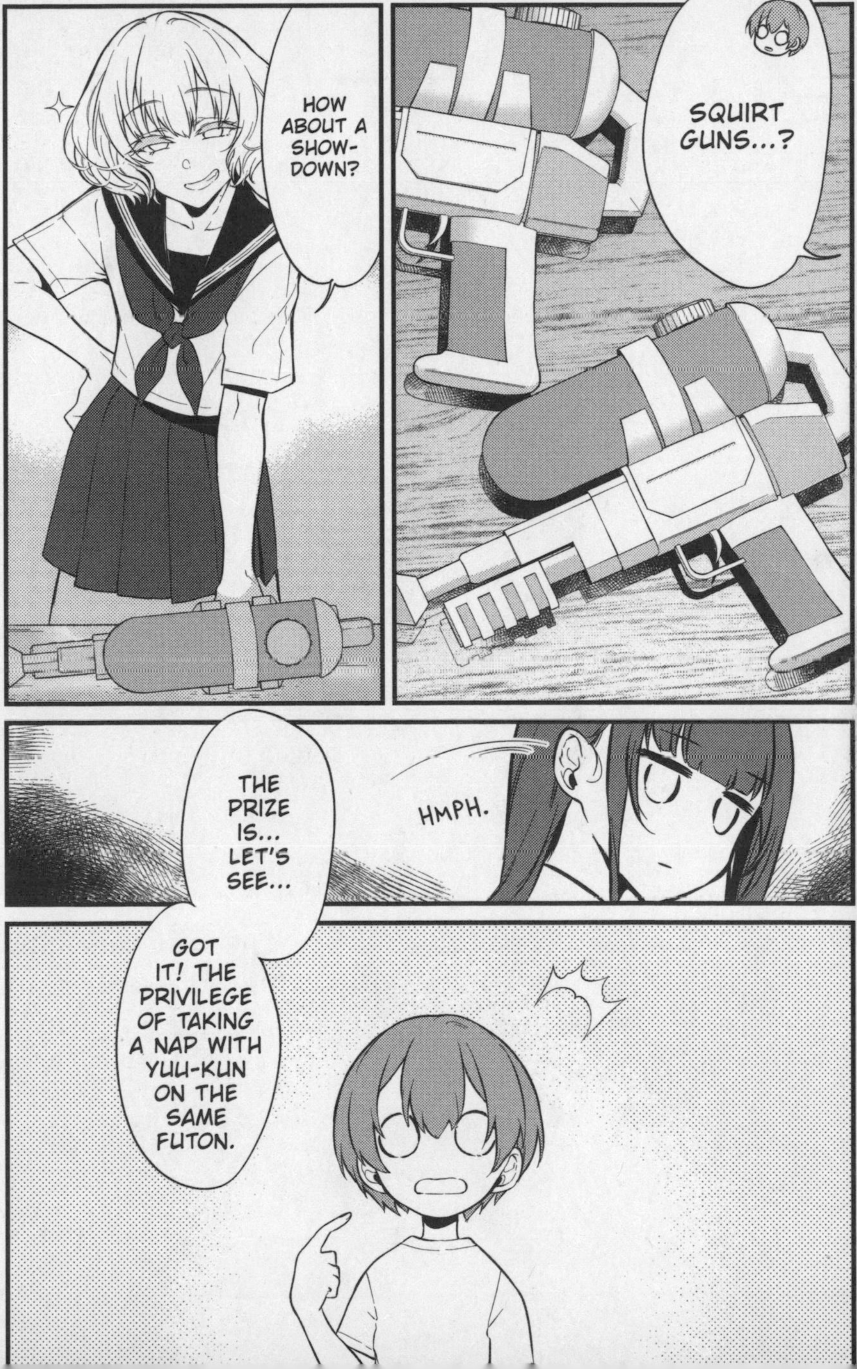
SQUIRT GUNS...?
HOW ABOUT A SHOW-DOWN?
HMPH.
THE PRIZE IS... LET'S SEE...
GOT IT! THE PRIVILEGE OF TAKING A NAP WITH YUU-KUN ON THE SAME FUTON.

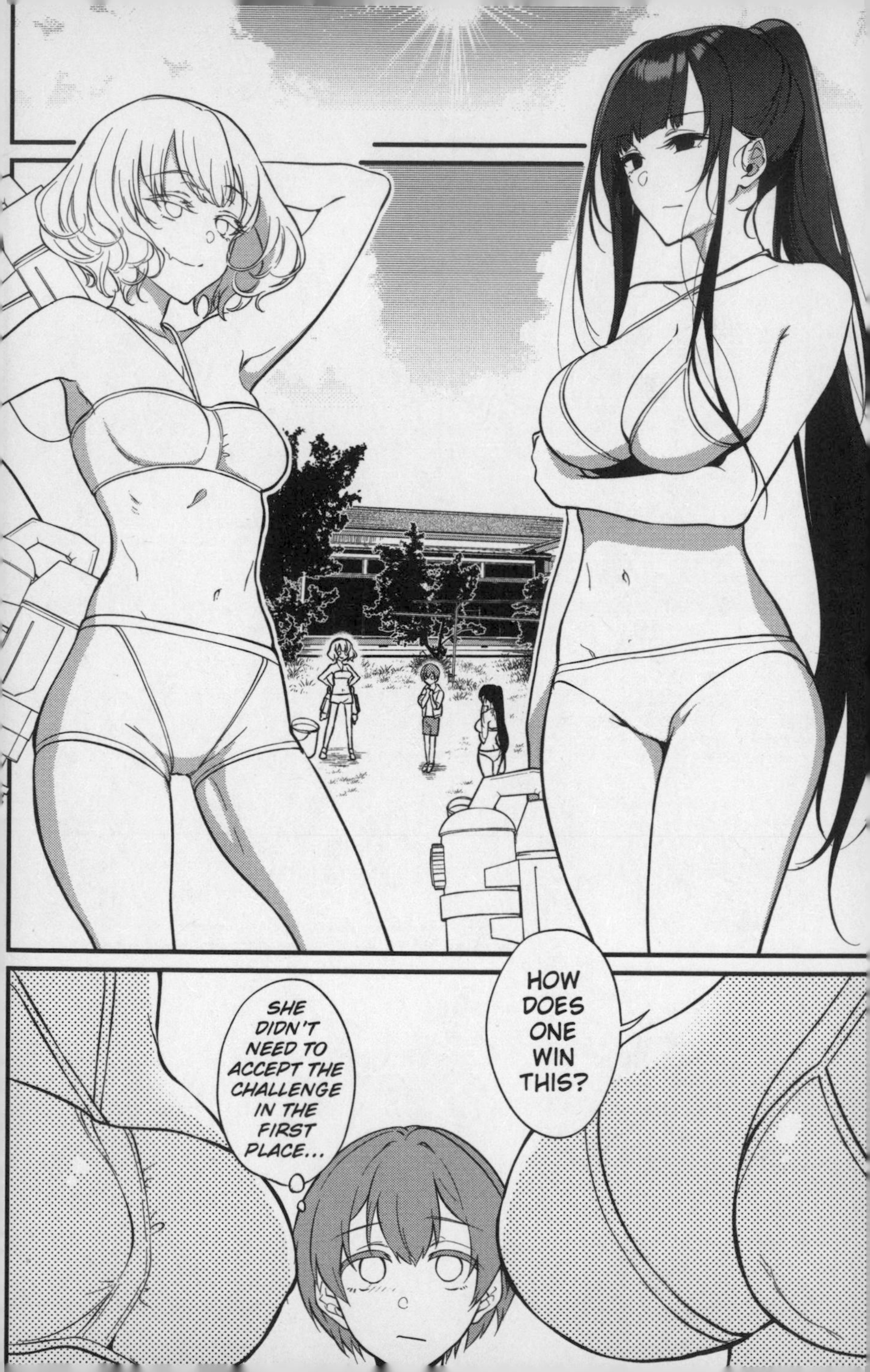
HOW DOES ONE WIN THIS?
SHE DIDN'T NEED TO ACCEPT THE CHALLENGE IN THE FIRST PLACE...

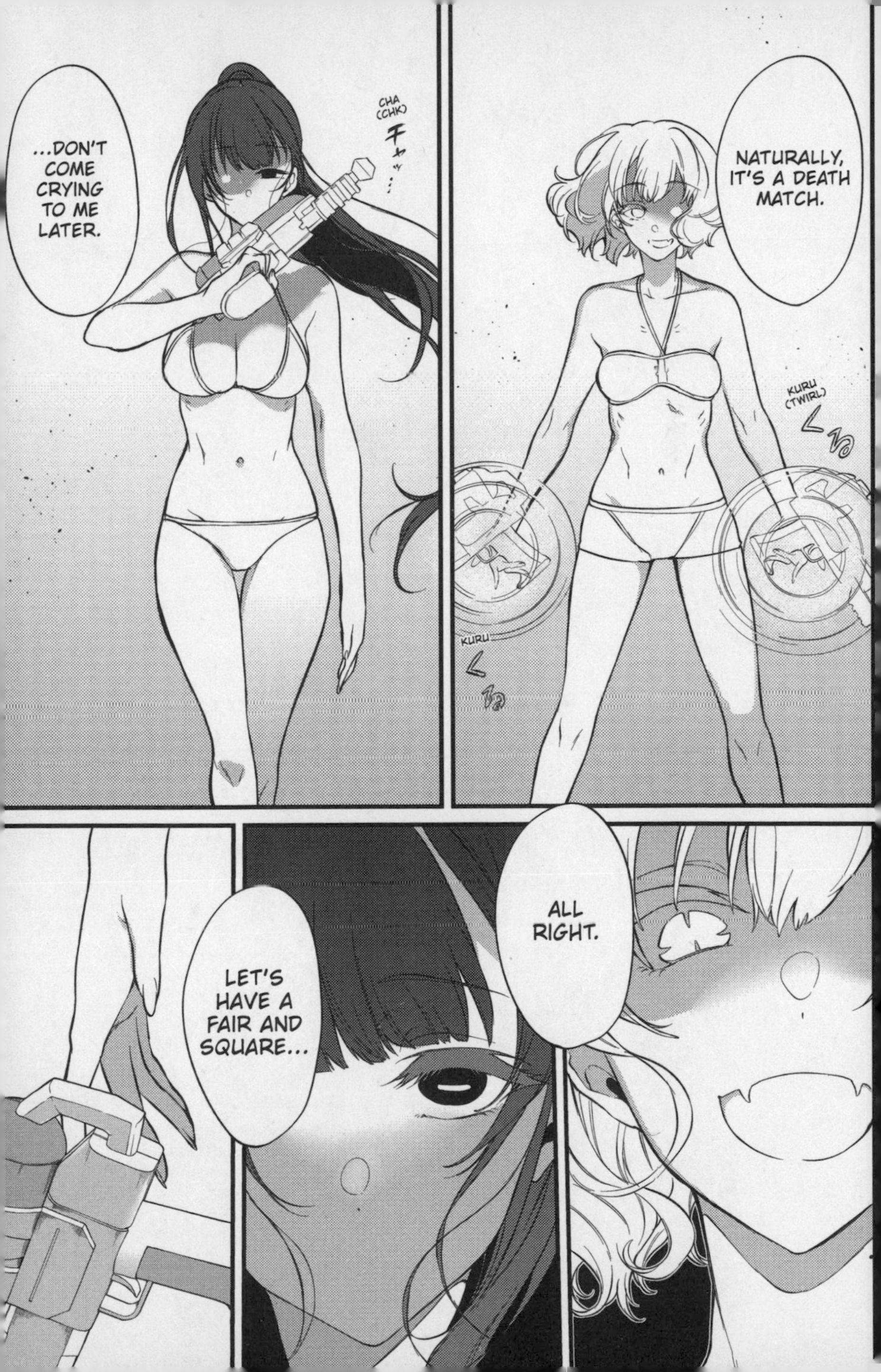
NATURALLY, IT'S A DEATH MATCH.
KURU (TWIRL)
くる
KURU
くる
...DON'T COME CRYING TO ME LATER.
CHA (CHK)
チャッ…
ALL RIGHT.
LET'S HAVE A FAIR AND SQUARE...

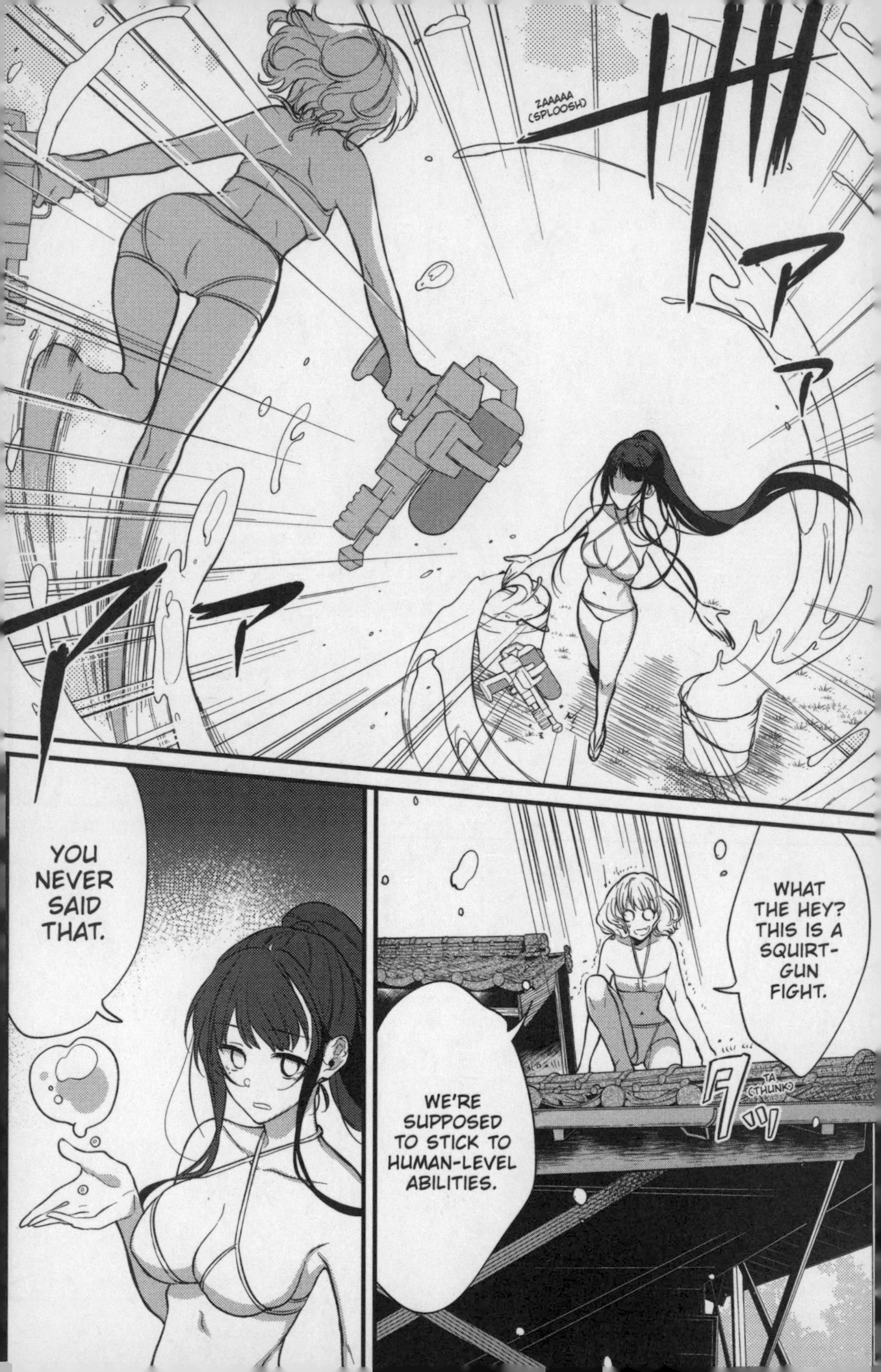
ZAAAAA (SPLOOSH)
WHAT THE HEY? THIS IS A SQUIRT-GUN FIGHT.
TA (THUNK)
WE'RE SUPPOSED TO STICK TO HUMAN-LEVEL ABILITIES.
YOU NEVER SAID THAT.

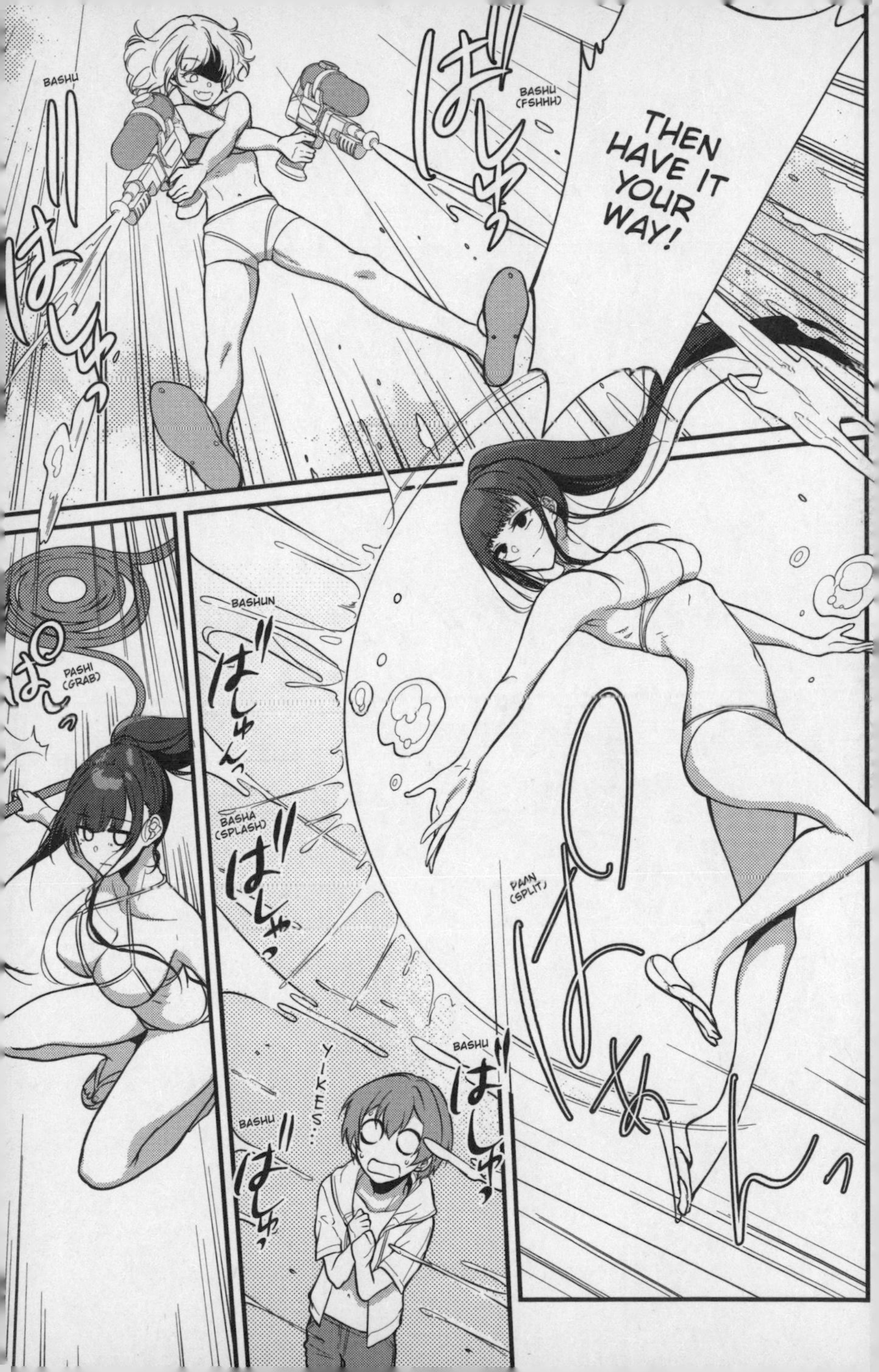
THEN HAVE IT YOUR WAY!
DAAN (SPLIT)
BASHU (FSHHH)
BASHU
BASHUN
BASHA (SPLASH)
BASHU
YIKES...
BASHU
PASHI (GRAB)

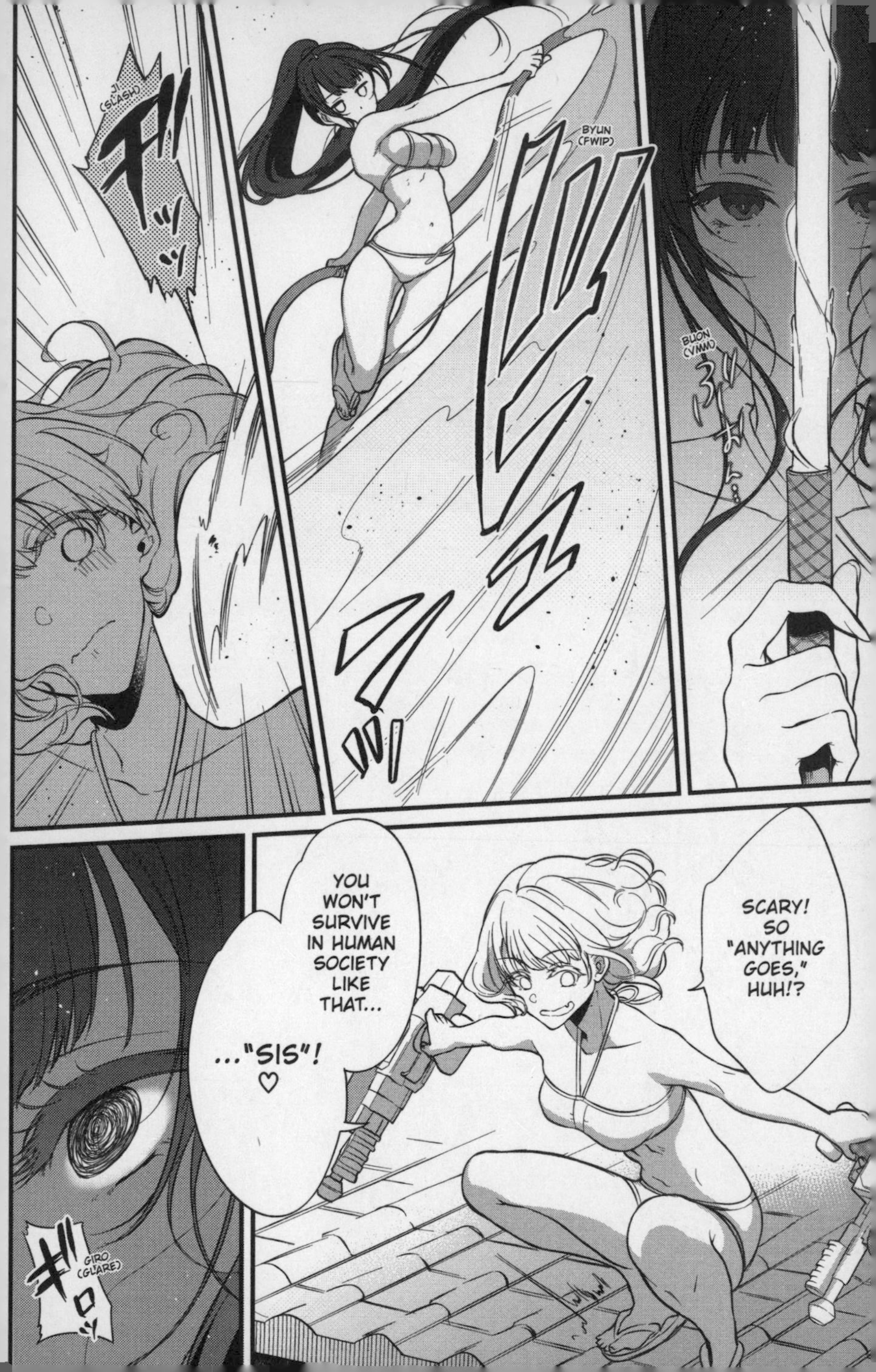
BUON (VMMM)
BYUN (FWIP)
JI (SLASH)
SCARY! SO "ANYTHING GOES," HUH!?
YOU WON'T SURVIVE IN HUMAN SOCIETY LIKE THAT...
..."SIS"! ♡
GIRO (GLARE)

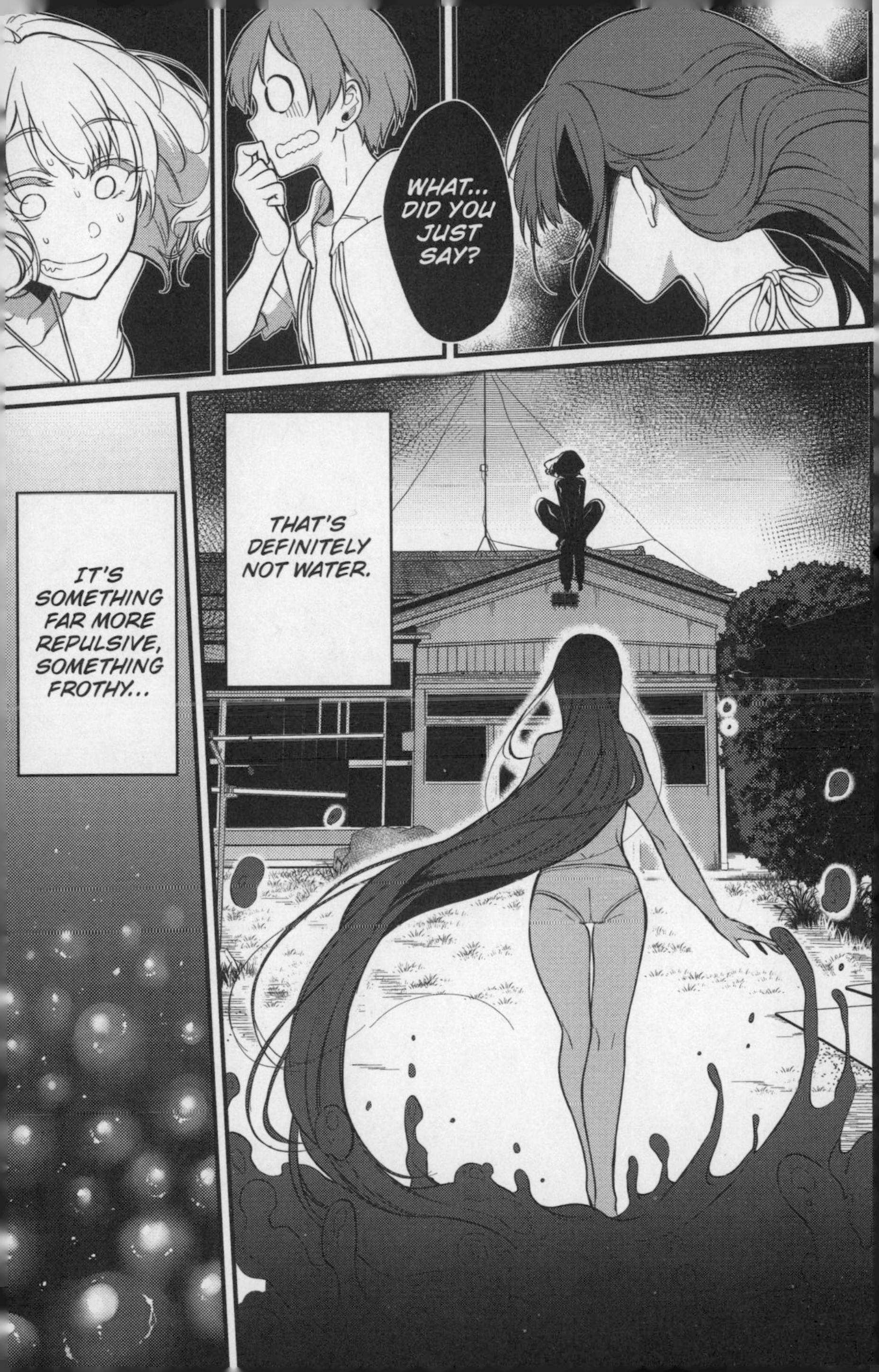
WHAT... DID YOU JUST SAY?
THAT'S DEFINITELY NOT WATER.
IT'S SOMETHING FAR MORE REPULSIVE, SOMETHING FROTHY...

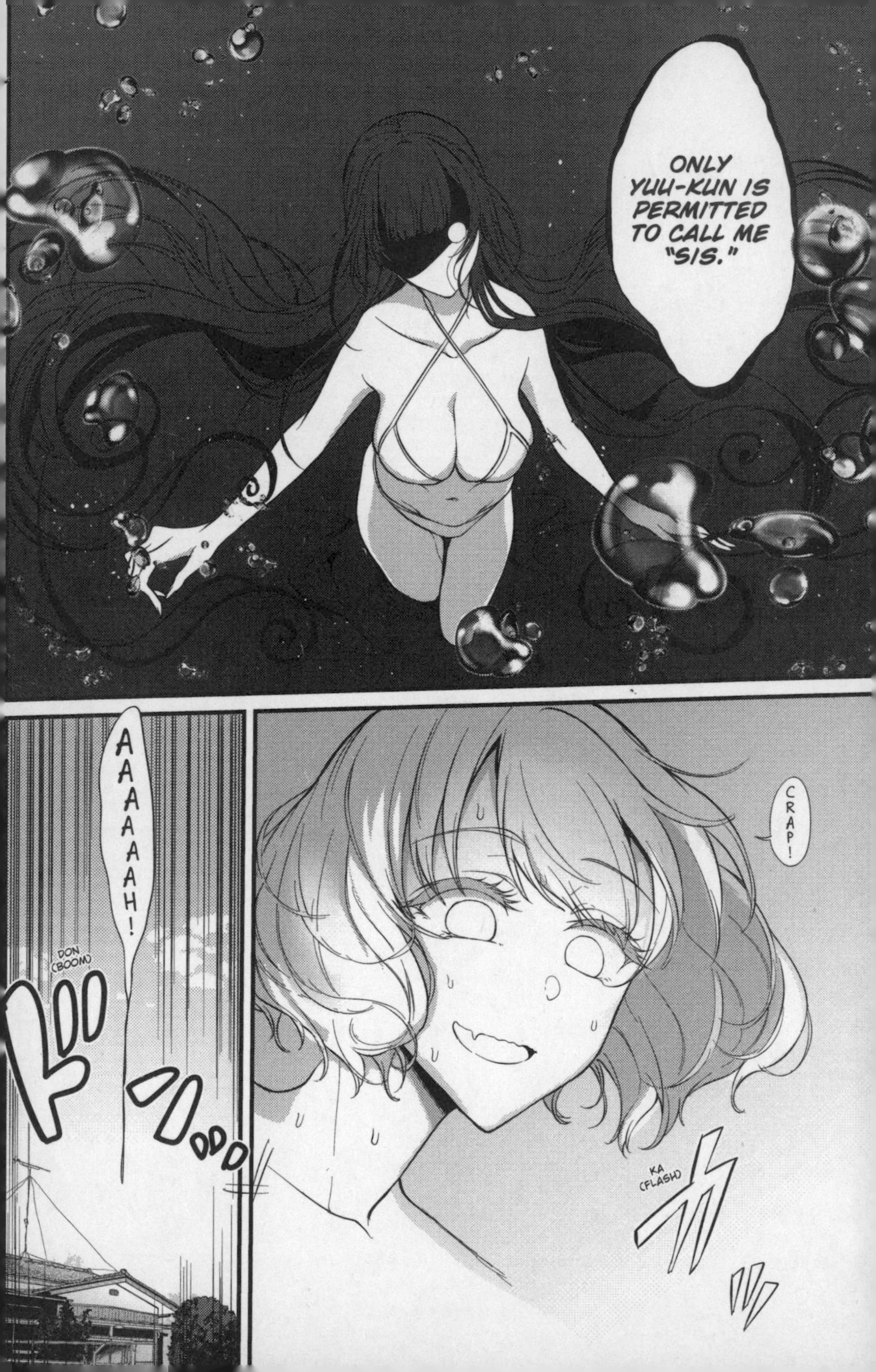
ONLY YUU-KUN IS PERMITTED TO CALL ME "SIS."
CRAP!
KA (FLASH)
AAAAAAAH!
DON (BOOM)

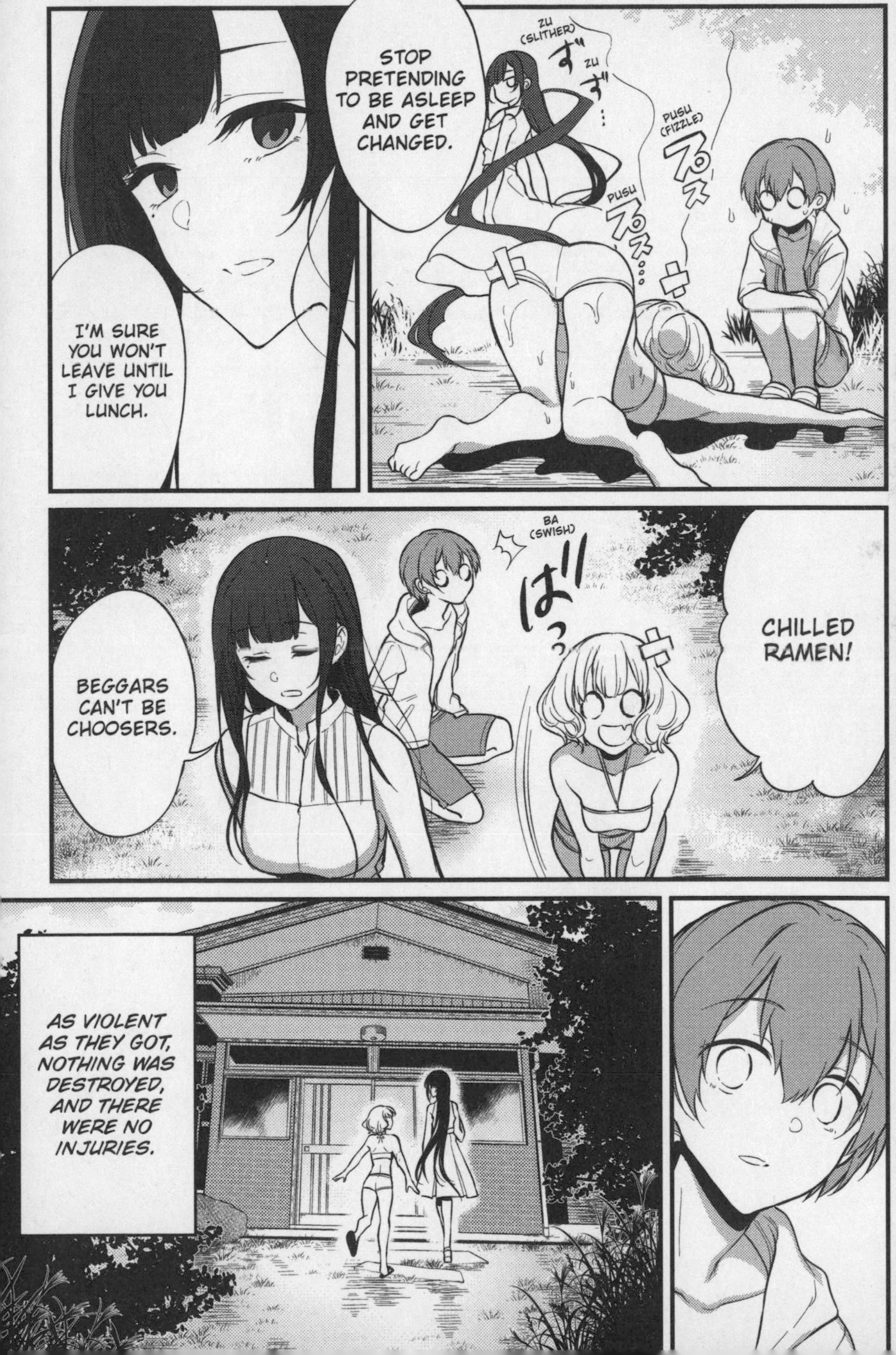
ZU (SLITHER)
ずず…
PUSU (FIZZLE)
プス
PUSU
プス…
STOP PRETENDING TO BE ASLEEP AND GET CHANGED.
I'M SURE YOU WON'T LEAVE UNTIL I GIVE YOU LUNCH.
CHILLED RAMEN!
BA (SWISH)
ばっ
BEGGARS CAN'T BE CHOOSERS.
AS VIOLENT AS THEY GOT, NOTHING WAS DESTROYED, AND THERE WERE NO INJURIES.

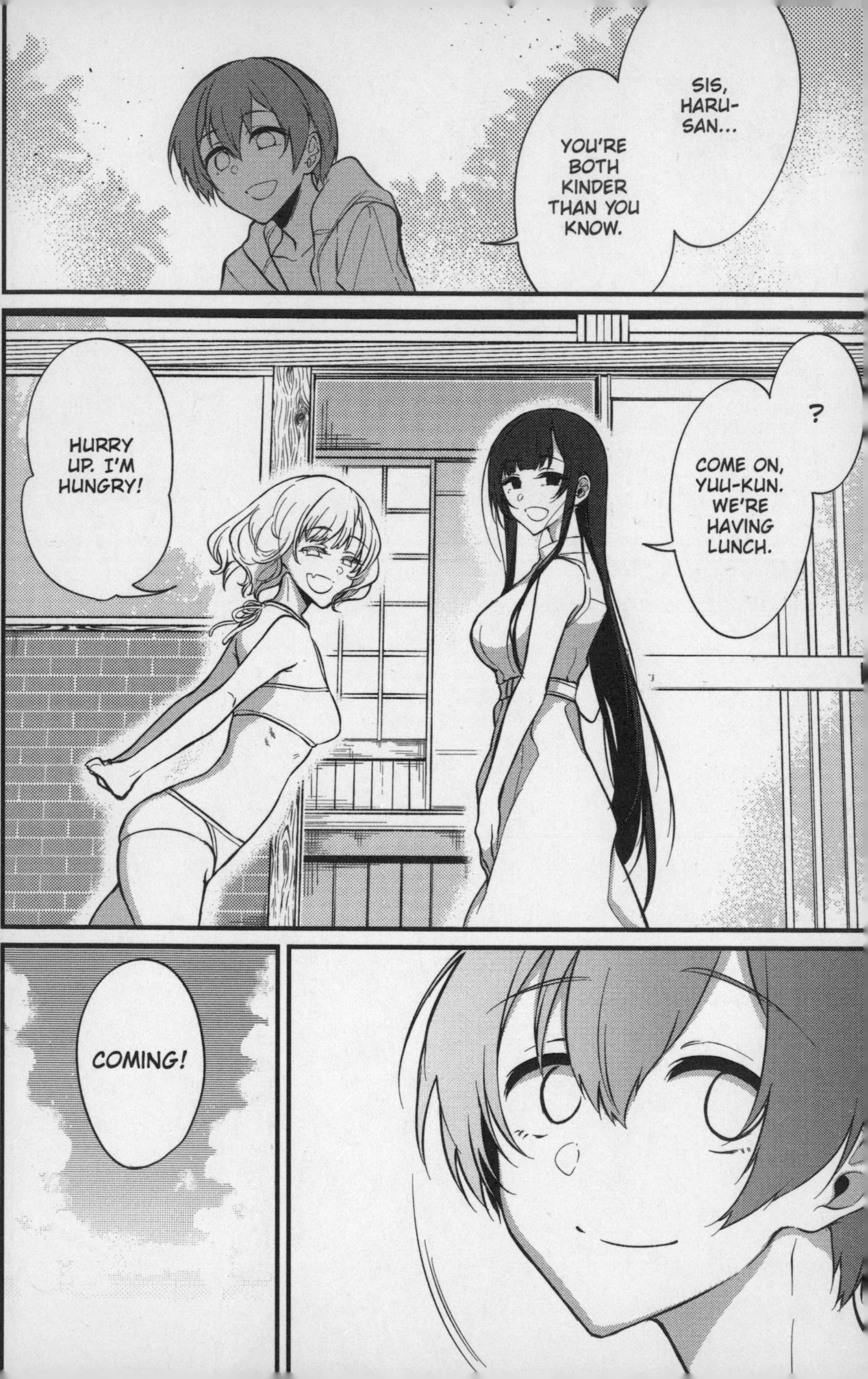
SIS, HARU-SAN...
YOU'RE BOTH KINDER THAN YOU KNOW.
?
COME ON, YUU-KUN. WE'RE HAVING LUNCH.
HURRY UP. I'M HUNGRY!
COMING!

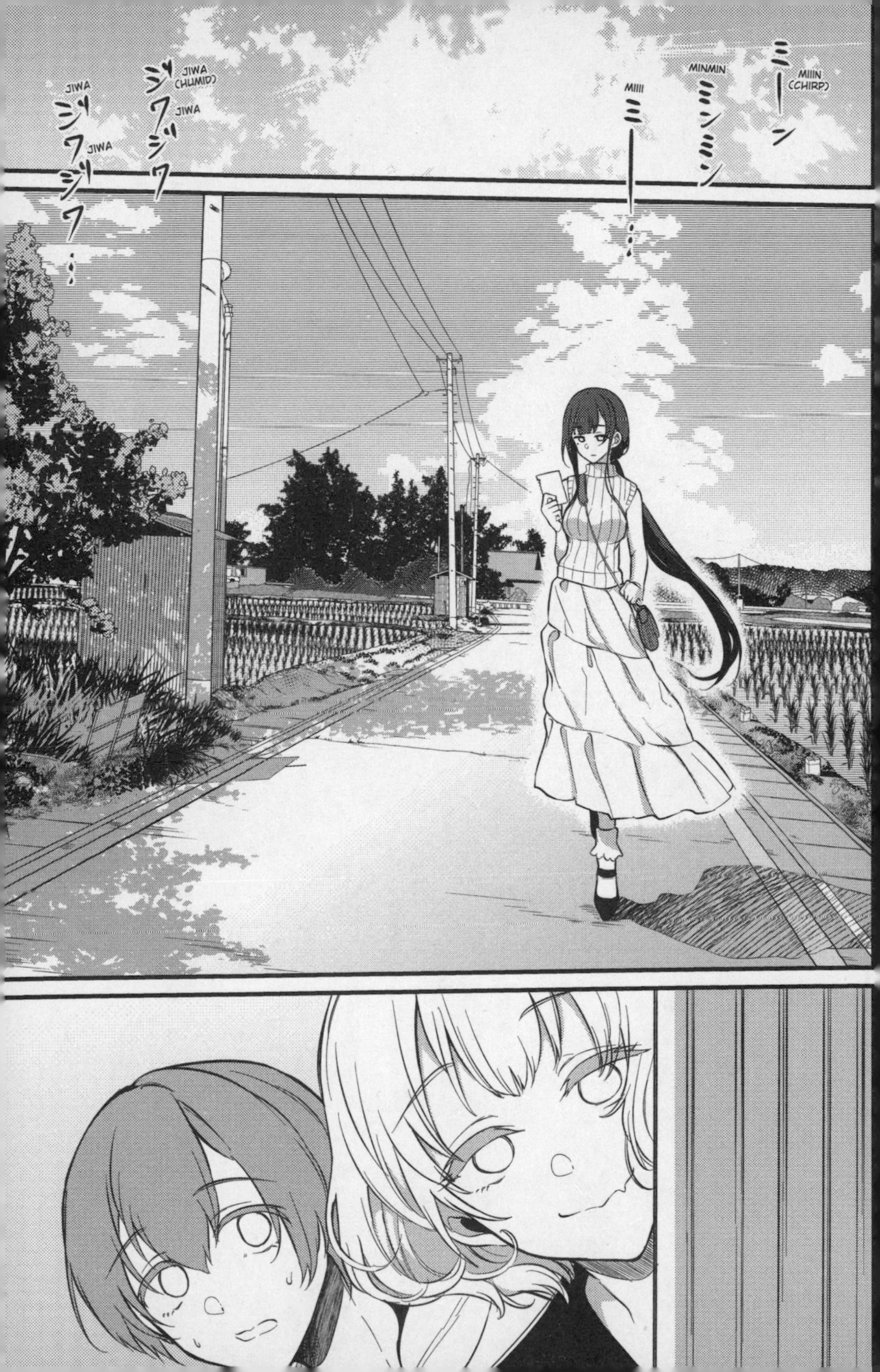
ミーン
MIIN (CHIRP)
ミンミン
MINMIN
ミーー…
MIIII
ジワジワ
JIWA (HUMID) JIWA
ジワジワ…
JIWA JIWA

THE TWENTY-SEVENTH NIGHT

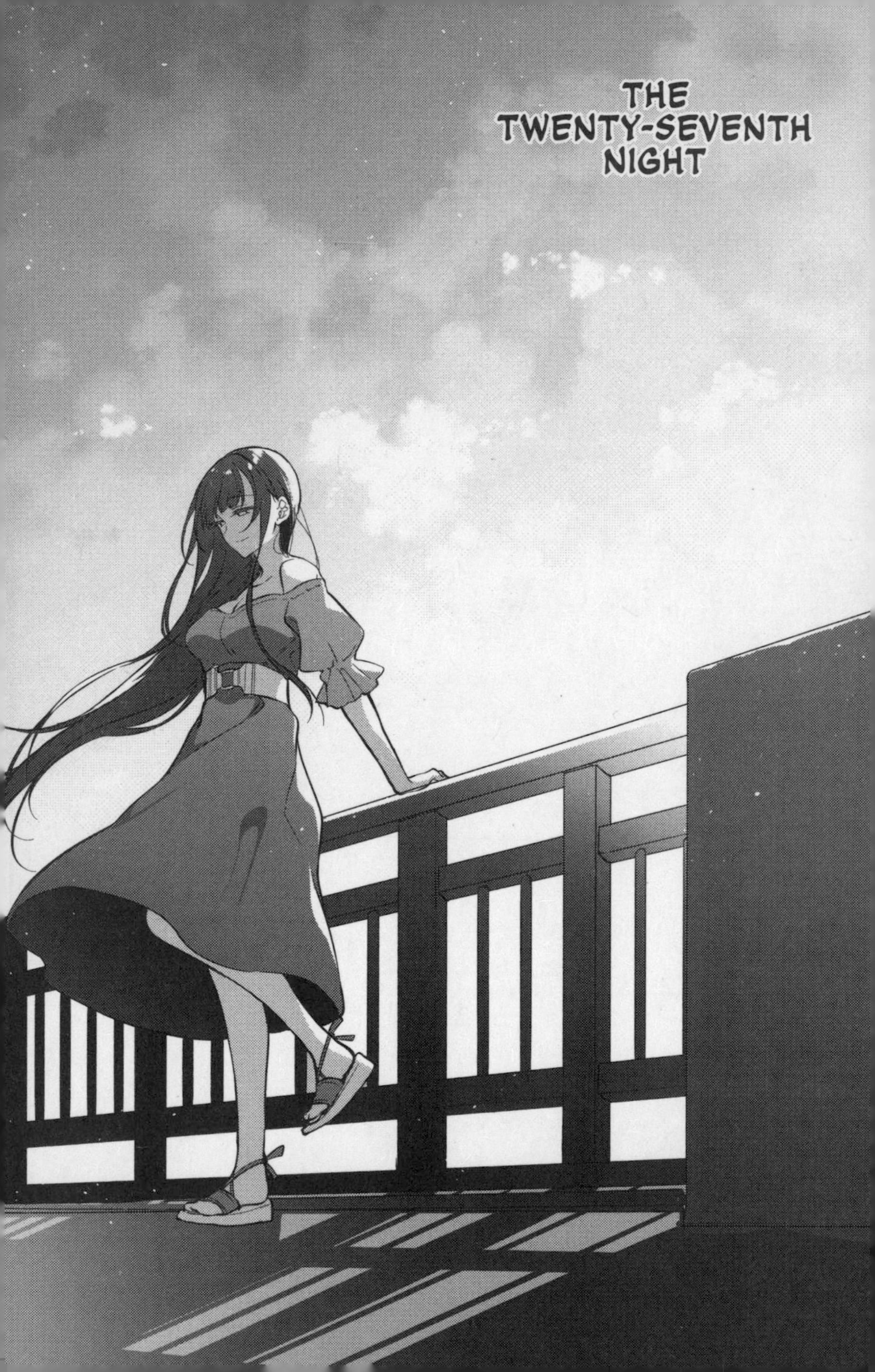

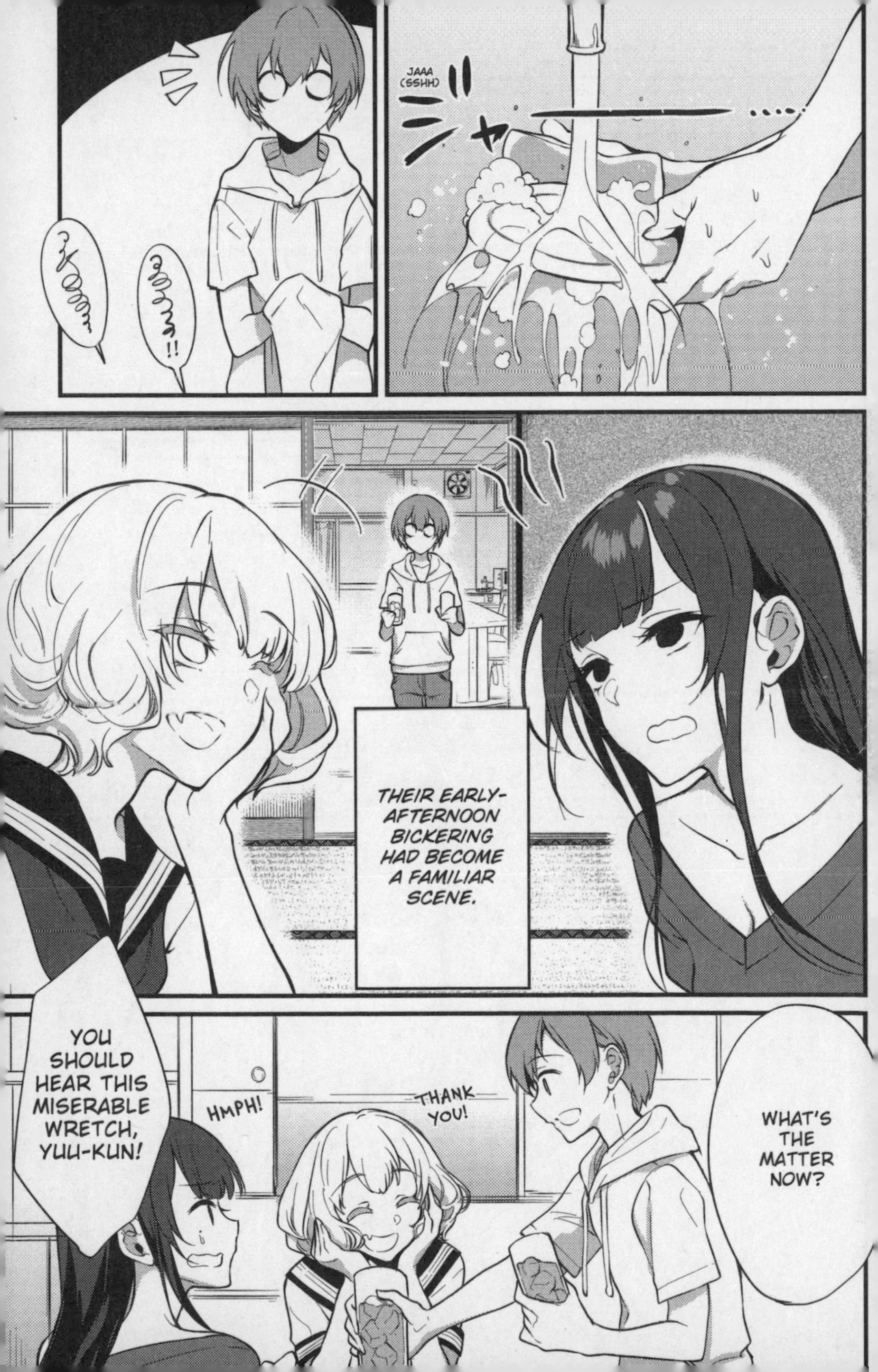
JAAA (SSHH)
......
THEIR EARLY-AFTERNOON BICKERING HAD BECOME A FAMILIAR SCENE.
WHAT'S THE MATTER NOW?
THANK YOU!
HMPH!
YOU SHOULD HEAR THIS MISERABLE WRETCH, YUU-KUN!

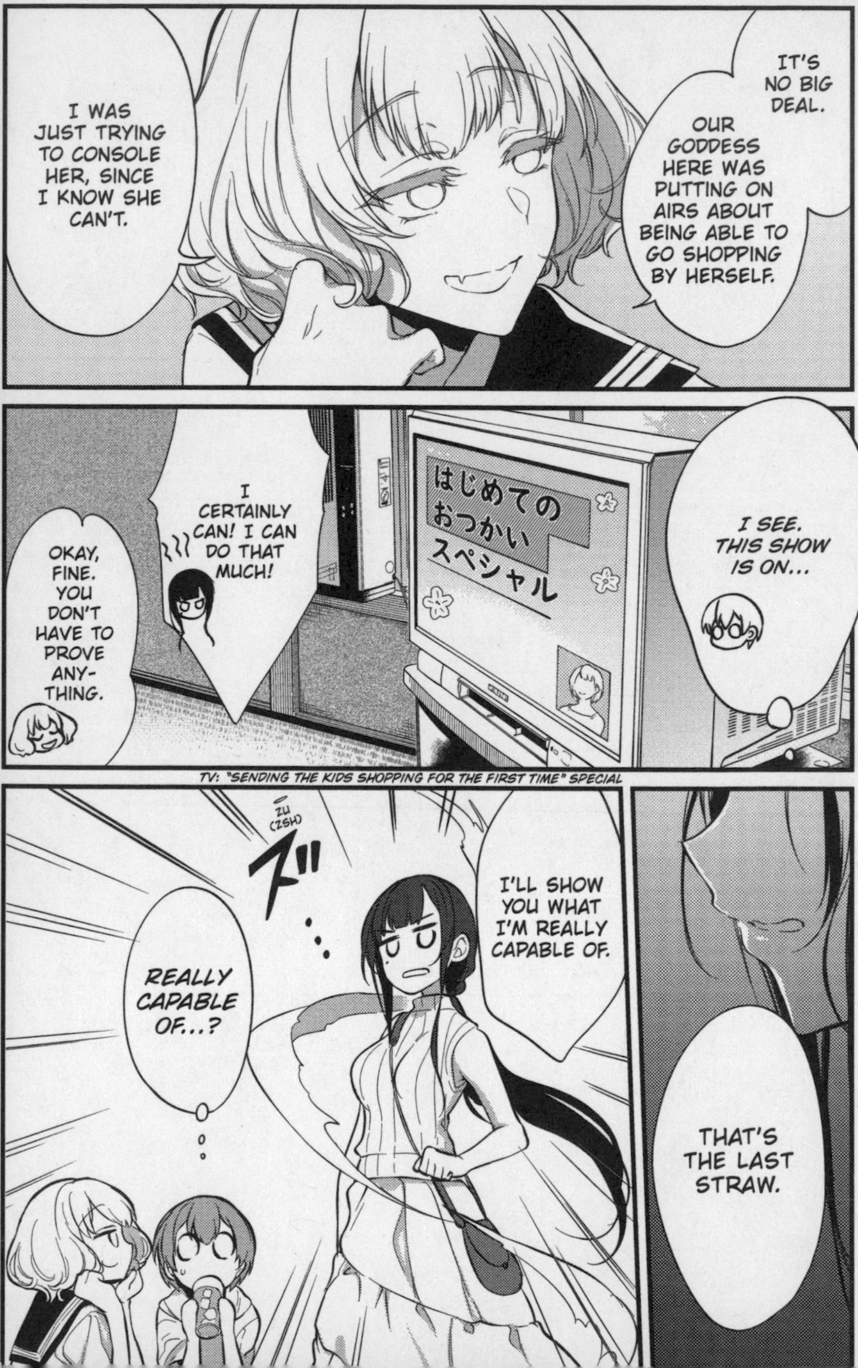
IT'S NO BIG DEAL.
OUR GODDESS HERE WAS PUTTING ON AIRS ABOUT BEING ABLE TO GO SHOPPING BY HERSELF.
I WAS JUST TRYING TO CONSOLE HER, SINCE I KNOW SHE CAN'T.
I SEE. THIS SHOW IS ON...
はじめてのおつかいスペシャル
I CERTAINLY CAN! I CAN DO THAT MUCH!
OKAY, FINE. YOU DON'T HAVE TO PROVE ANY-THING.
TV: "SENDING THE KIDS SHOPPING FOR THE FIRST TIME" SPECIAL
THAT'S THE LAST STRAW.
I'LL SHOW YOU WHAT I'M REALLY CAPABLE OF.
ZU (ZSH)
REALLY CAPABLE OF...?

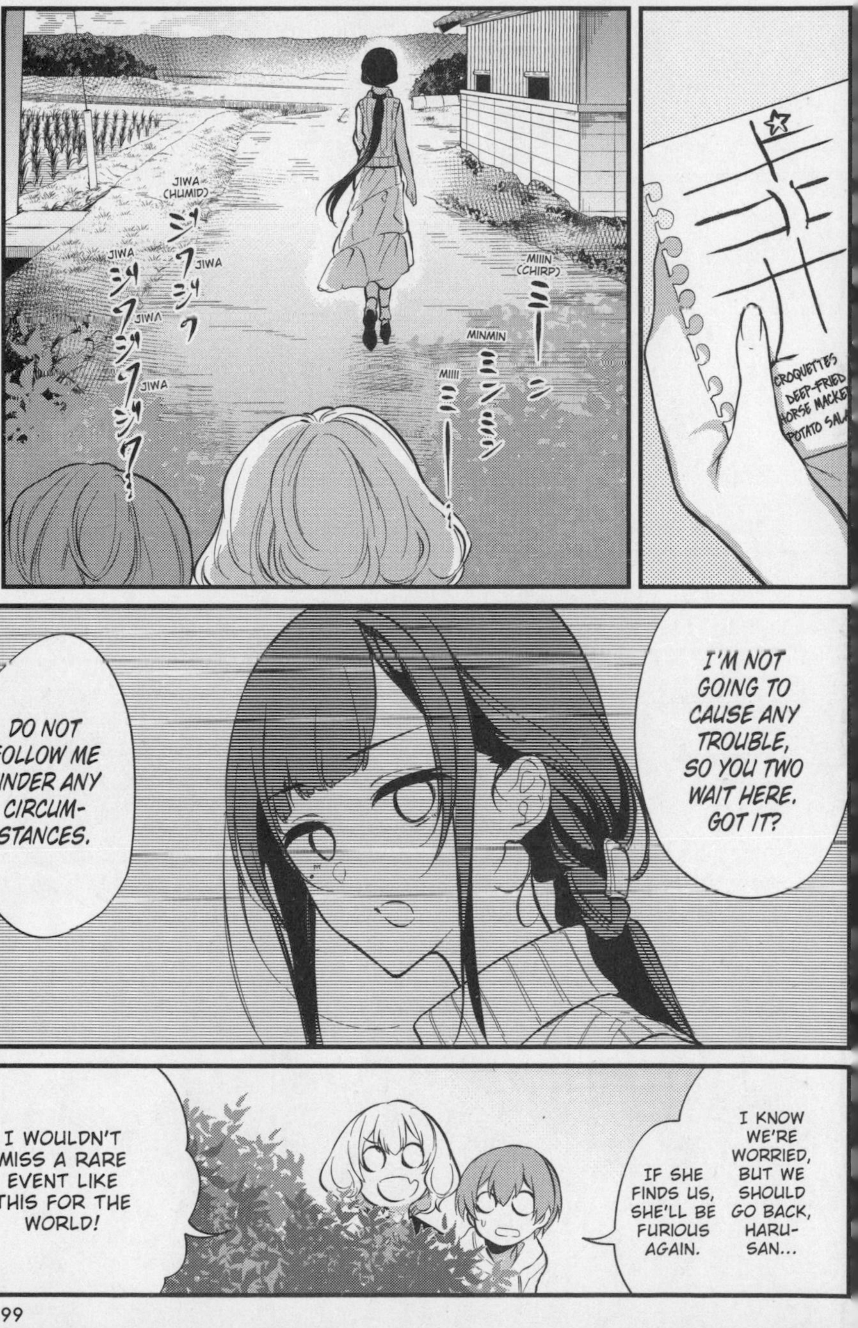
CROQUETTES
DEEP-FRIED
HORSE MACKE
POTATO SALA
MIIIN (CHIRP)
MINMIN
MIIII
JIWA (HUMID)
JIWA
JIWA
JIWA
JIWA
I'M NOT GOING TO CAUSE ANY TROUBLE, SO YOU TWO WAIT HERE. GOT IT?
DO NOT FOLLOW ME UNDER ANY CIRCUM-STANCES.
I KNOW WE'RE WORRIED, BUT WE SHOULD GO BACK, HARU-SAN...
IF SHE FINDS US, SHE'LL BE FURIOUS AGAIN.
I WOULDN'T MISS A RARE EVENT LIKE THIS FOR THE WORLD!

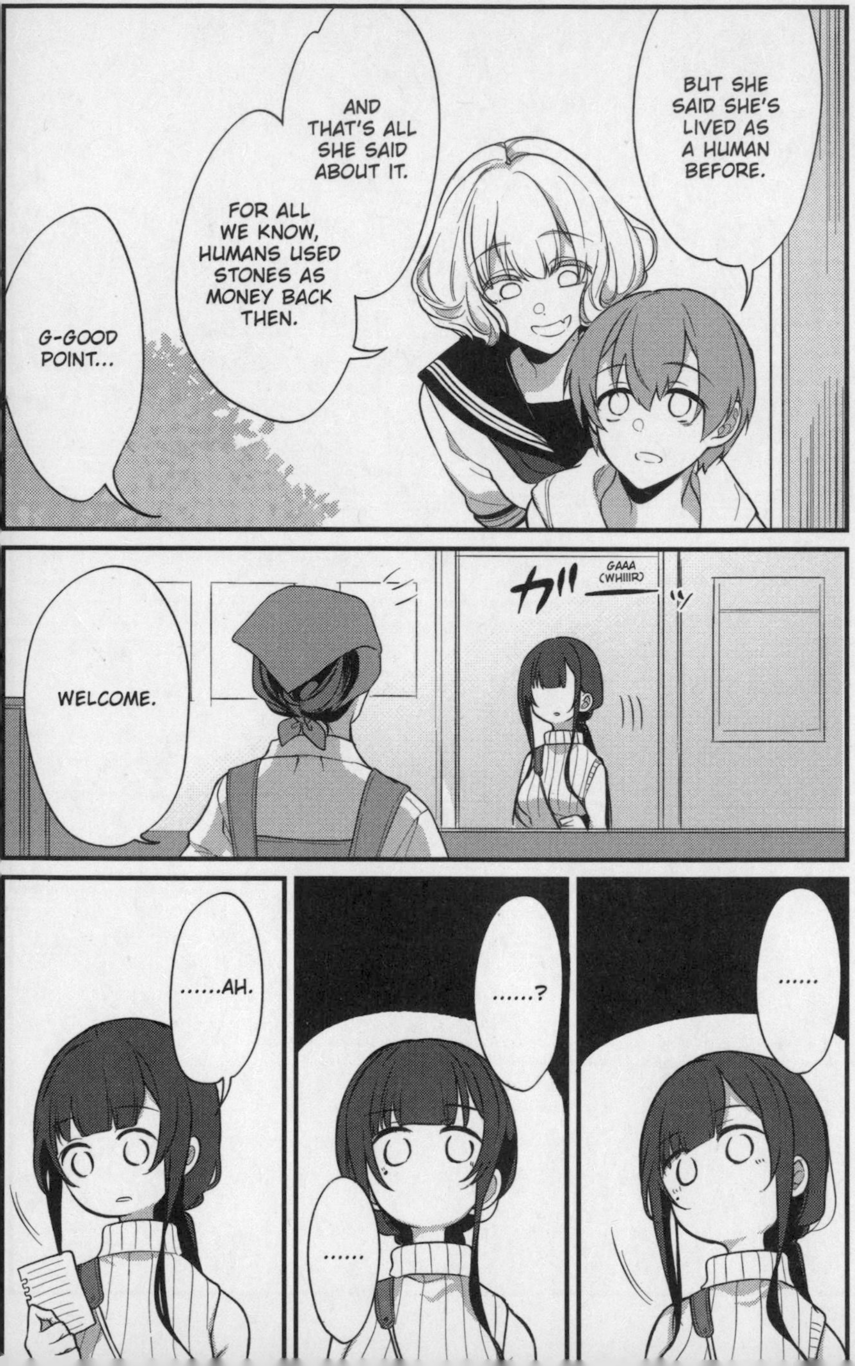
BUT SHE SAID SHE'S LIVED AS A HUMAN BEFORE.
AND THAT'S ALL SHE SAID ABOUT IT.
FOR ALL WE KNOW, HUMANS USED STONES AS MONEY BACK THEN.
G-GOOD POINT...
GAAA (WHIIIR)
WELCOME.
......
......?
......
......AH.

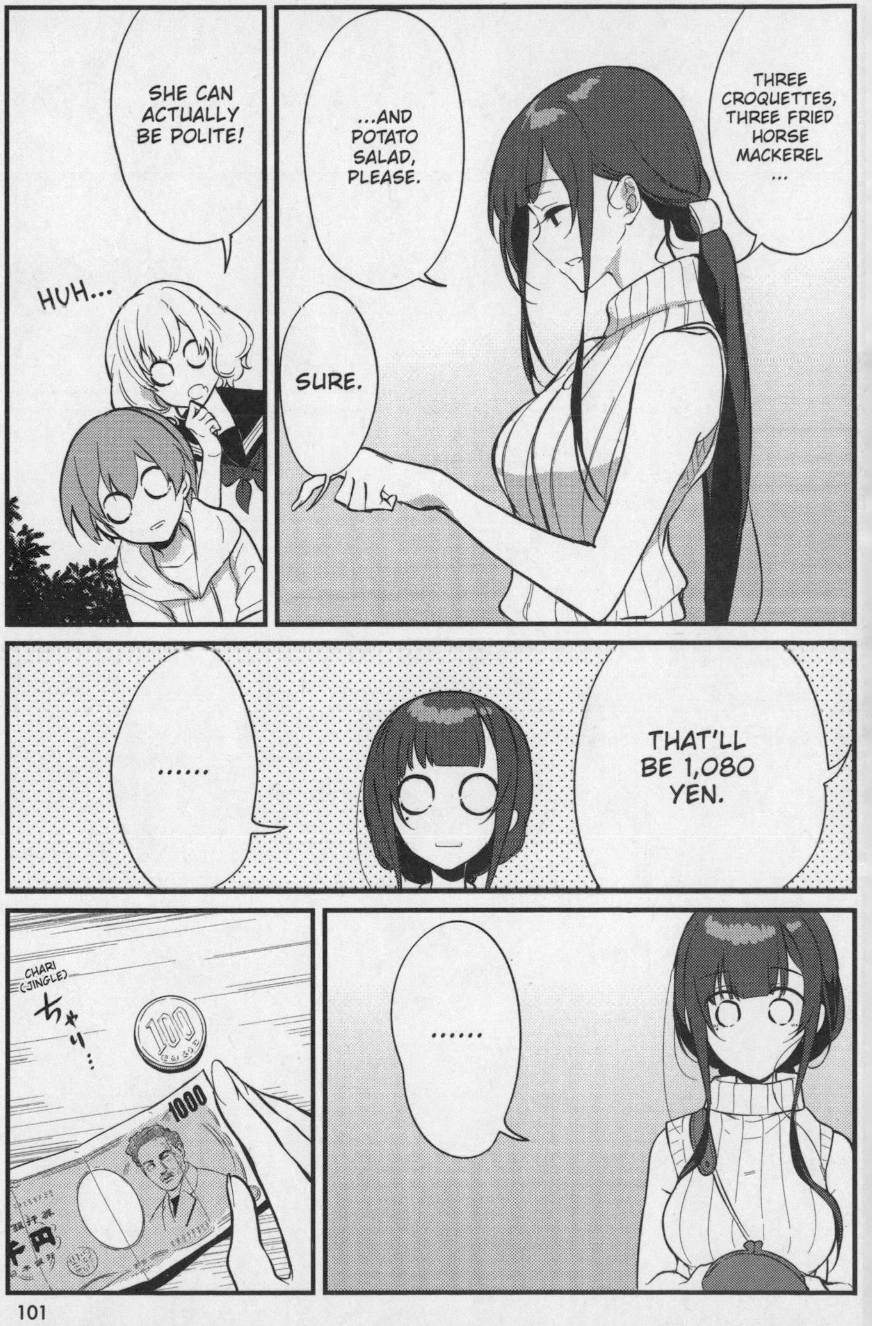
THREE CROQUETTES, THREE FRIED HORSE MACKEREL ...
...AND POTATO SALAD, PLEASE.
SURE.
SHE CAN ACTUALLY BE POLITE!
HUH...
THAT'LL BE 1,080 YEN.
......
......
CHARI (-JINGLE)
ちゃり…

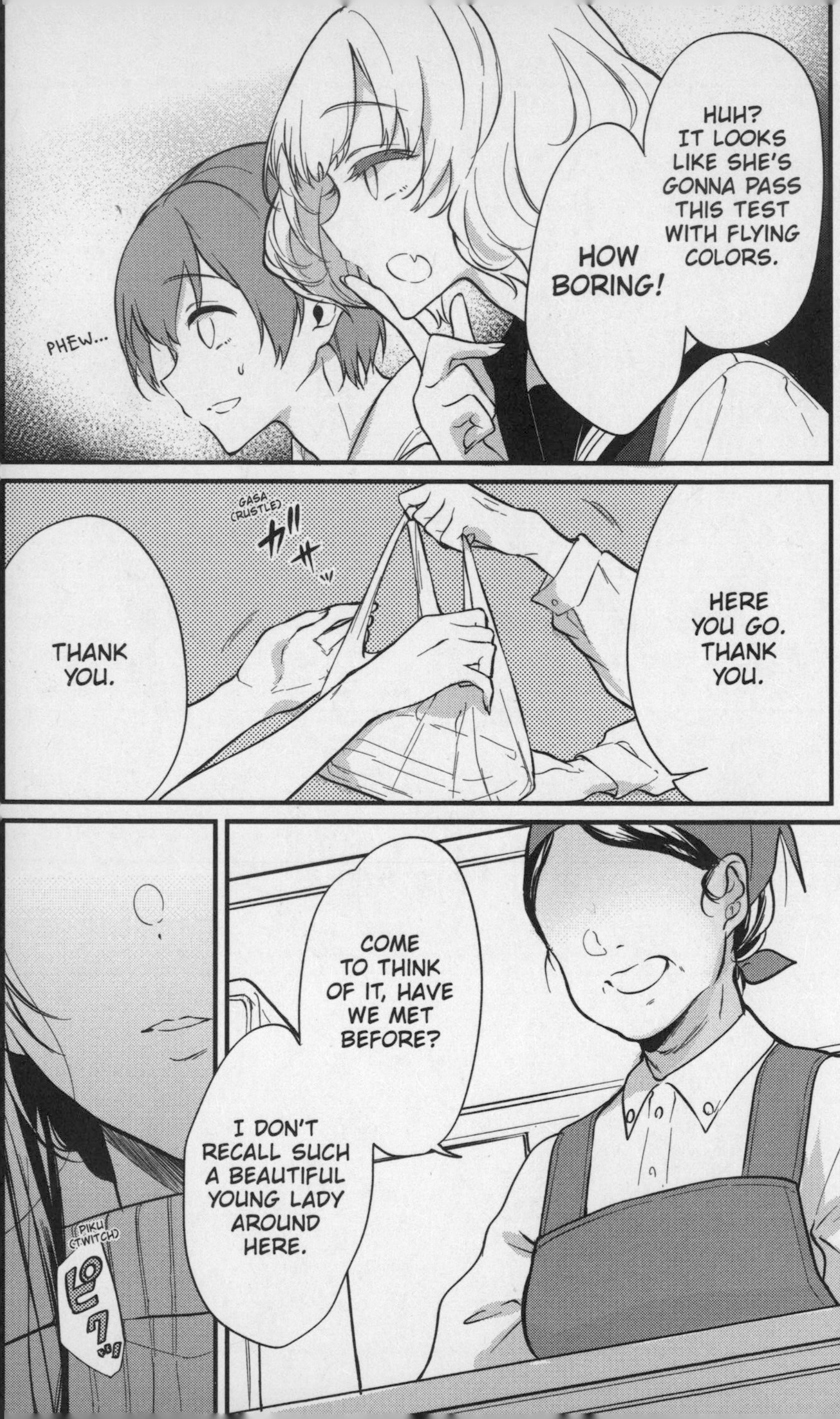
HUH? IT LOOKS LIKE SHE'S GONNA PASS THIS TEST WITH FLYING COLORS.
HOW BORING!
PHEW...
HERE YOU GO. THANK YOU.
GASA (RUSTLE)
THANK YOU.
COME TO THINK OF IT, HAVE WE MET BEFORE?
I DON'T RECALL SUCH A BEAUTIFUL YOUNG LADY AROUND HERE.
PIKU (TWITCH)

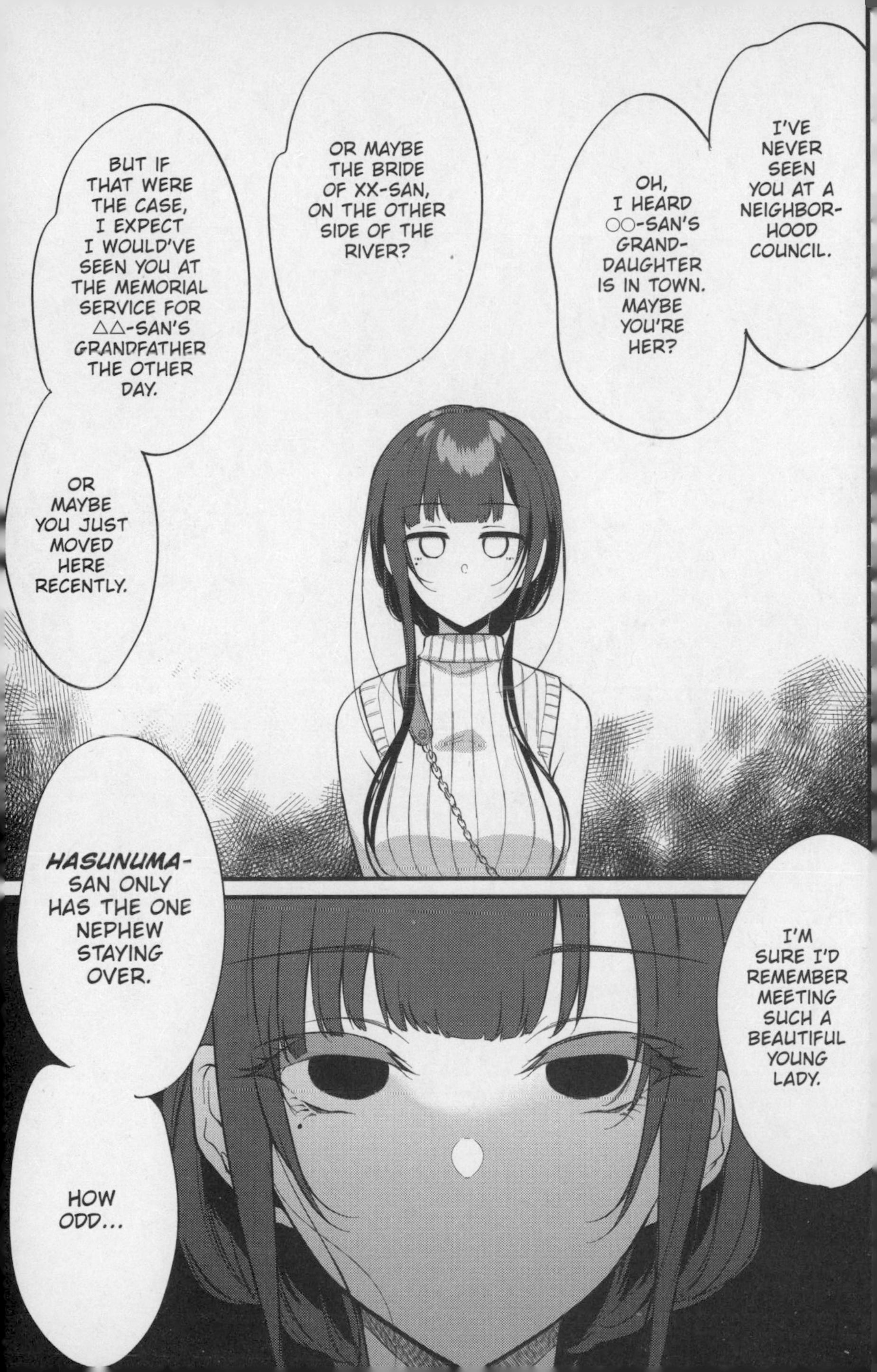
I'VE NEVER SEEN YOU AT A NEIGHBOR-HOOD COUNCIL.
OH, I HEARD ○○-SAN'S GRAND-DAUGHTER IS IN TOWN. MAYBE YOU'RE HER?
OR MAYBE THE BRIDE OF XX-SAN, ON THE OTHER SIDE OF THE RIVER?
BUT IF THAT WERE THE CASE, I EXPECT I WOULD'VE SEEN YOU AT THE MEMORIAL SERVICE FOR △△-SAN'S GRANDFATHER THE OTHER DAY.
OR MAYBE YOU JUST MOVED HERE RECENTLY.
HASUNUMA-SAN ONLY HAS THE ONE NEPHEW STAYING OVER.
I'M SURE I'D REMEMBER MEETING SUCH A BEAUTIFUL YOUNG LADY.
HOW ODD...

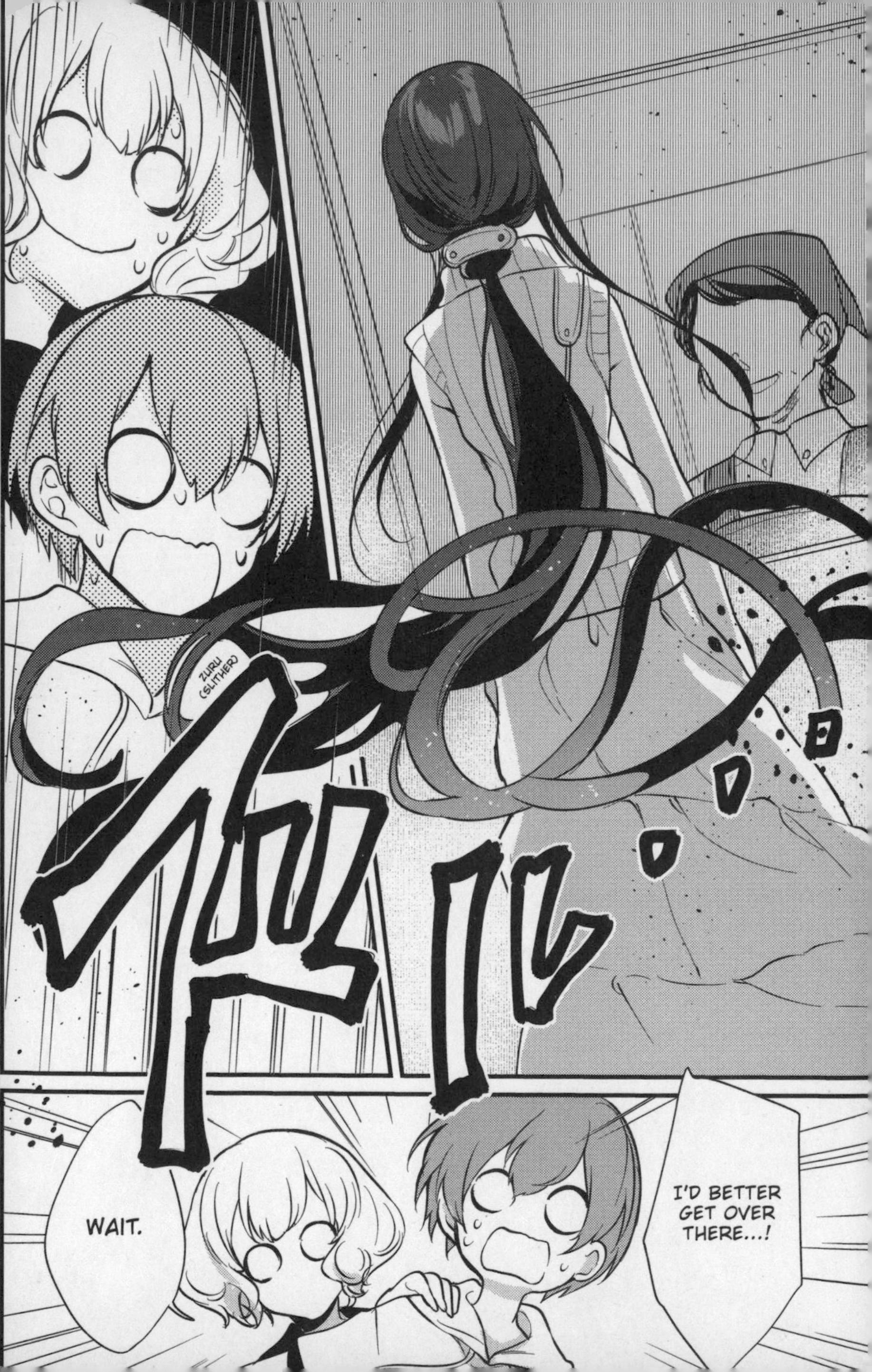
ZURU (SLITHER)
I'D BETTER GET OVER THERE...!
WAIT.

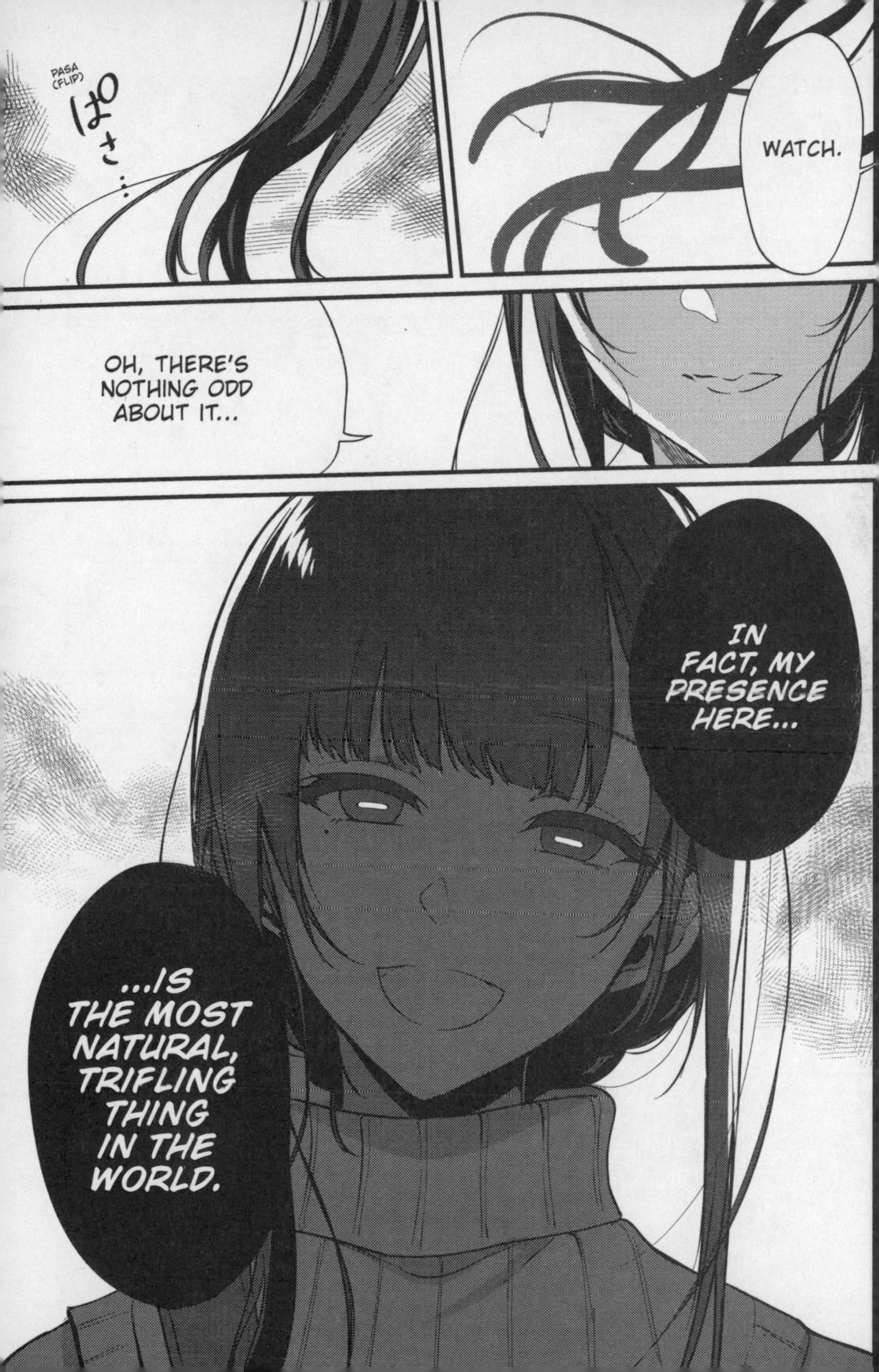
WATCH.
PASA (FLIP)
ぱさ…
OH, THERE'S NOTHING ODD ABOUT IT...
IN FACT, MY PRESENCE HERE...
...IS THE MOST NATURAL, TRIFLING THING IN THE WORLD.

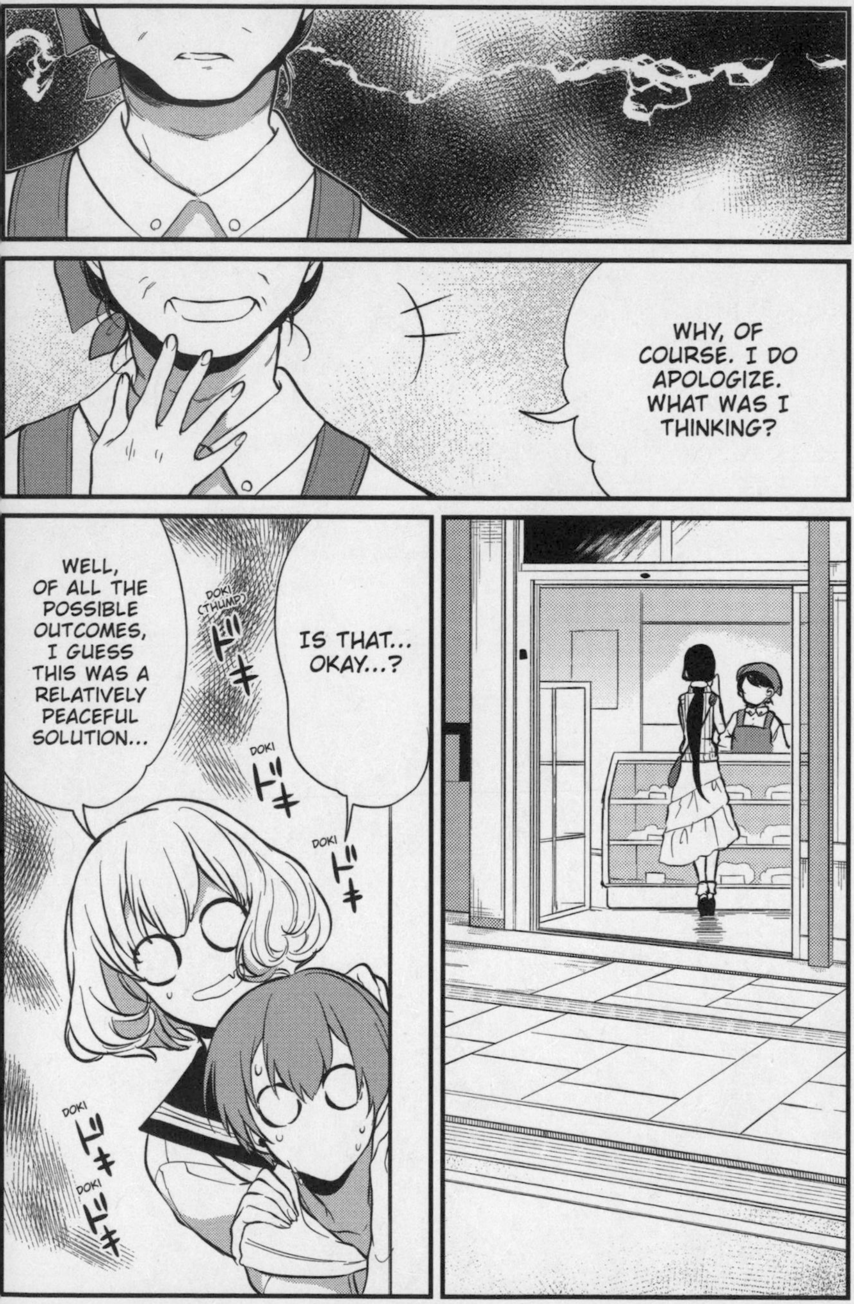
WHY, OF COURSE. I DO APOLOGIZE. WHAT WAS I THINKING?
IS THAT... OKAY...?
DOKI (THUMP) ドキ
WELL, OF ALL THE POSSIBLE OUTCOMES, I GUESS THIS WAS A RELATIVELY PEACEFUL SOLUTION...
DOKI ドキ
DOKI ドキ
DOKI ドキ
DOKI ドキ

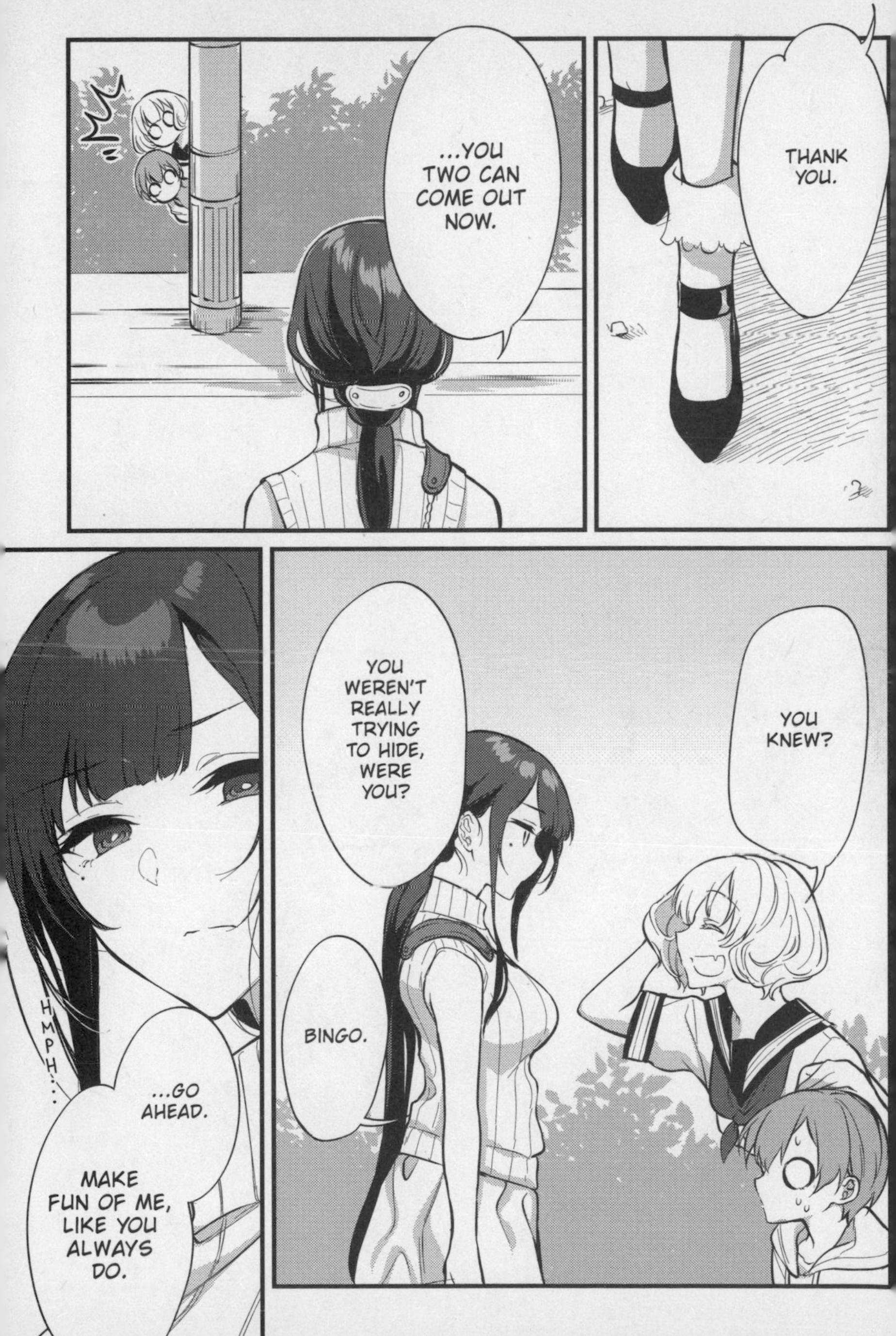
THANK YOU.
...YOU TWO CAN COME OUT NOW.
YOU KNEW?
YOU WEREN'T REALLY TRYING TO HIDE, WERE YOU?
BINGO.
HMPH...
...GO AHEAD.
MAKE FUN OF ME, LIKE YOU ALWAYS DO.

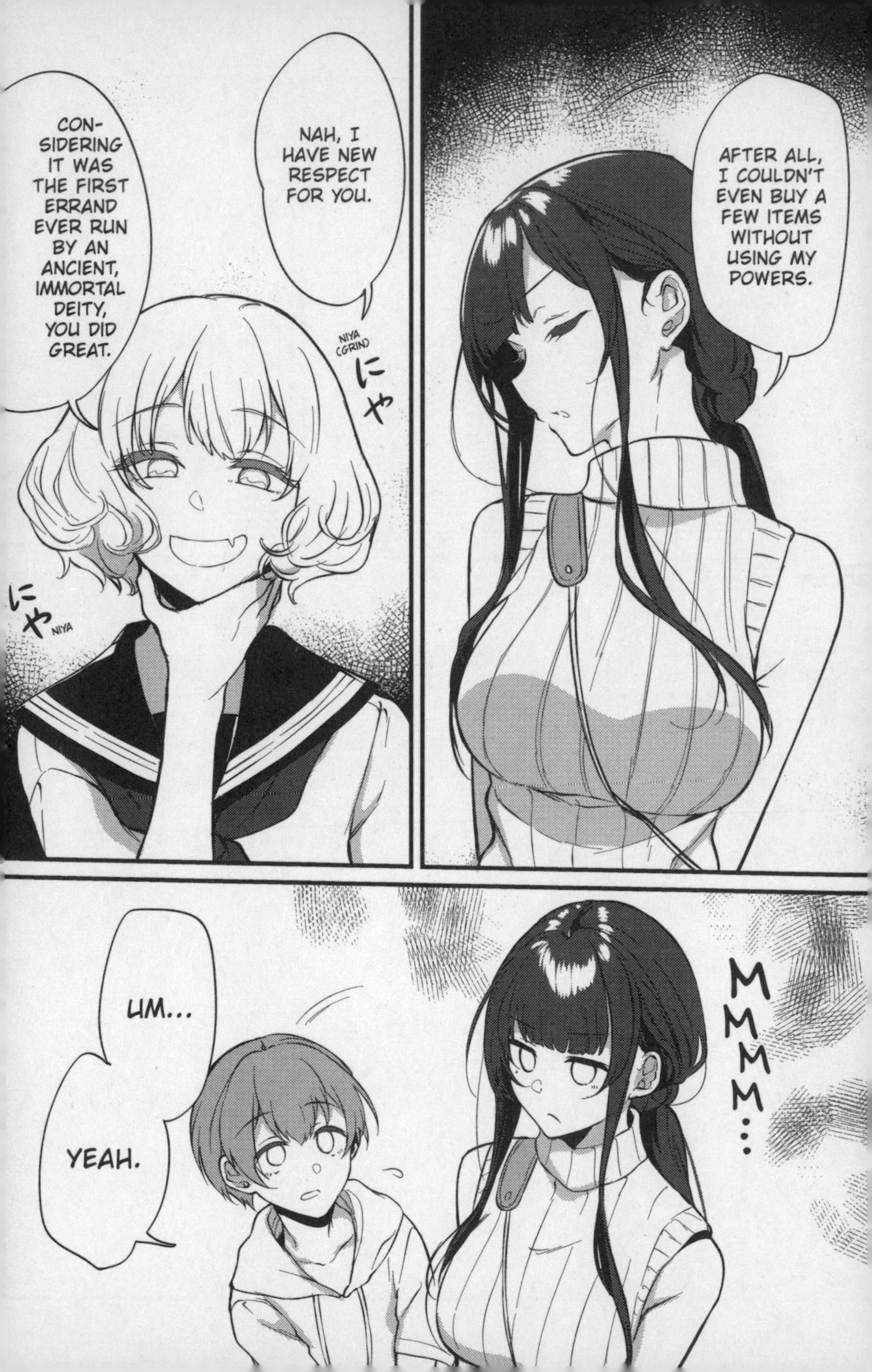
AFTER ALL, I COULDN'T EVEN BUY A FEW ITEMS WITHOUT USING MY POWERS.
NAH, I HAVE NEW RESPECT FOR YOU.
NIYA (GRIN)
にゃ
CON-SIDERING IT WAS THE FIRST ERRAND EVER RUN BY AN ANCIENT, IMMORTAL DEITY, YOU DID GREAT.
にゃ
NIYA
MMMM...
UM...
YEAH.

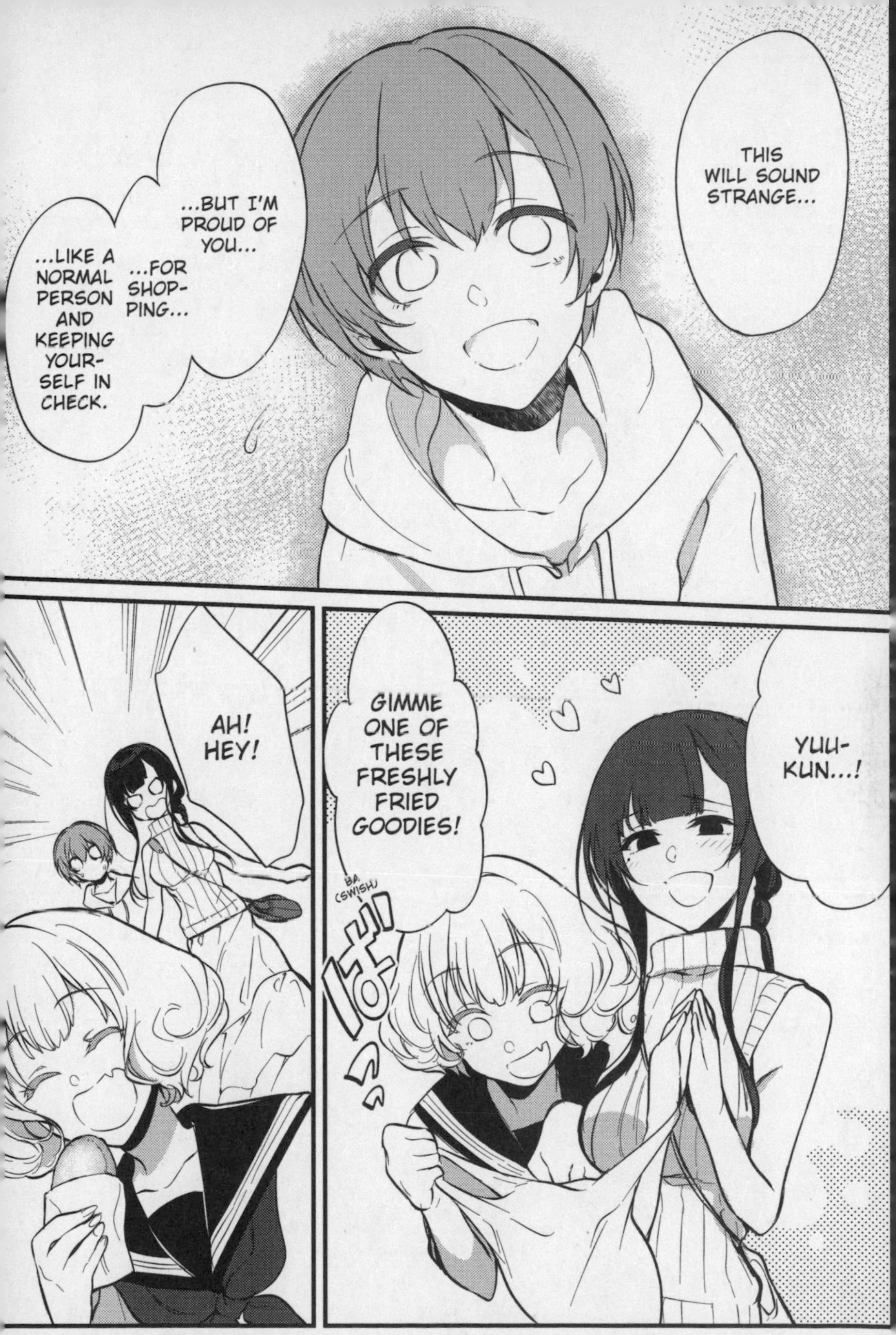
THIS WILL SOUND STRANGE...
...BUT I'M PROUD OF YOU...
...FOR SHOP-PING...
...LIKE A NORMAL PERSON AND KEEPING YOUR-SELF IN CHECK.
YUU-KUN...!
GIMME ONE OF THESE FRESHLY FRIED GOODIES!
BA (SWISH)
AH! HEY!

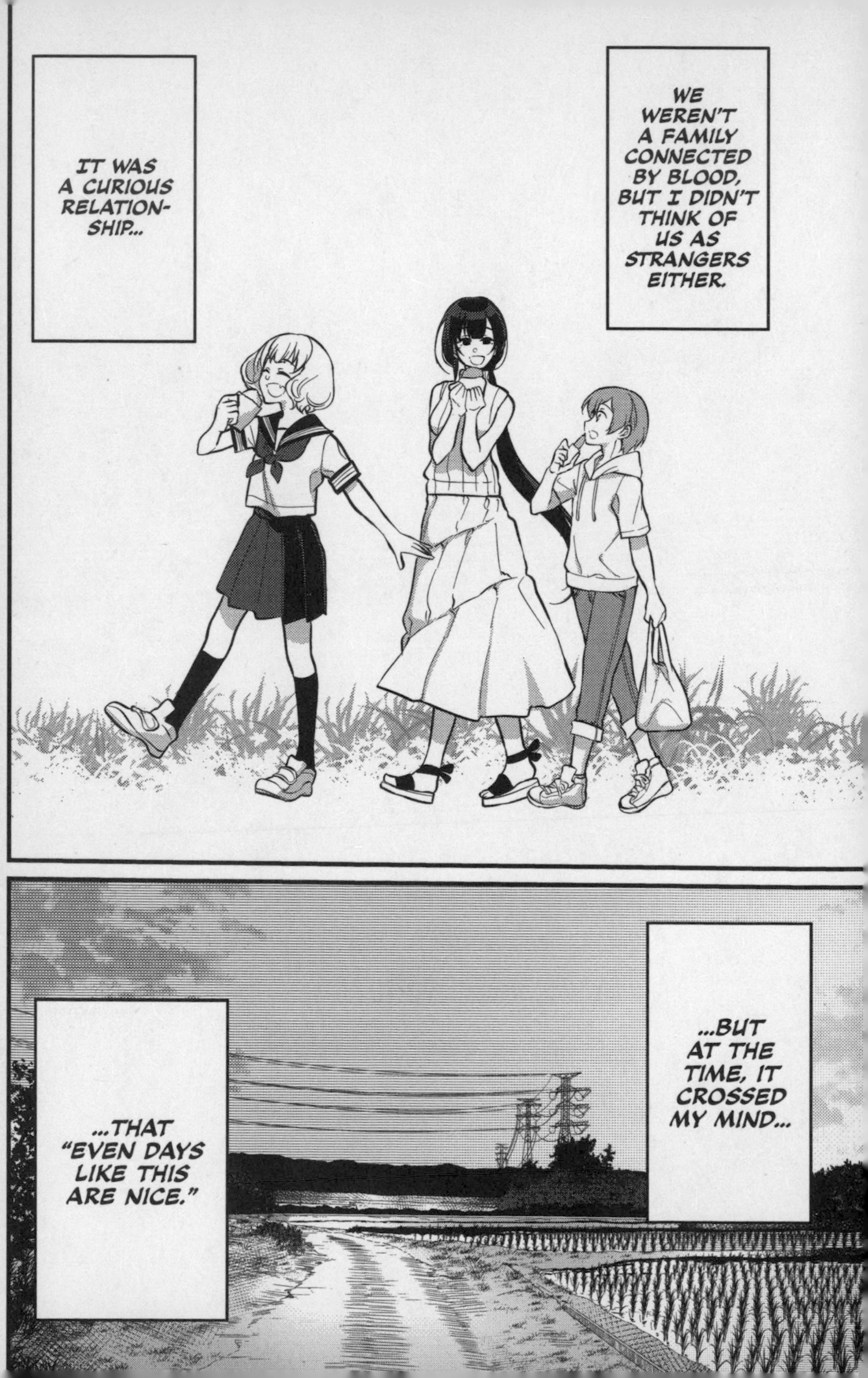
WE WEREN'T A FAMILY CONNECTED BY BLOOD, BUT I DIDN'T THINK OF US AS STRANGERS EITHER.
IT WAS A CURIOUS RELATION-SHIP...
...BUT AT THE TIME, IT CROSSED MY MIND...
...THAT "EVEN DAYS LIKE THIS ARE NICE."

THE TWENTY-EIGHTH NIGHT

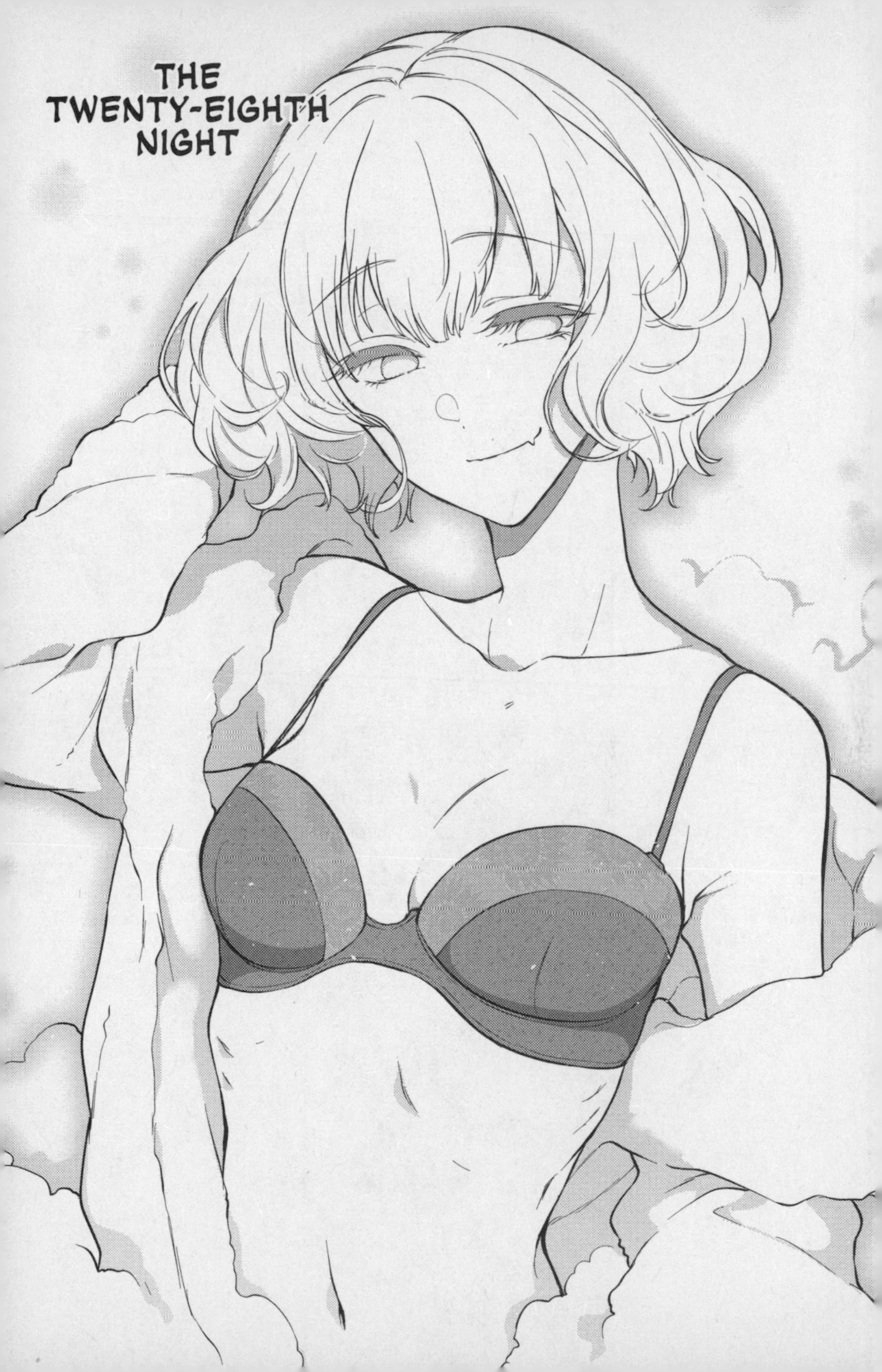

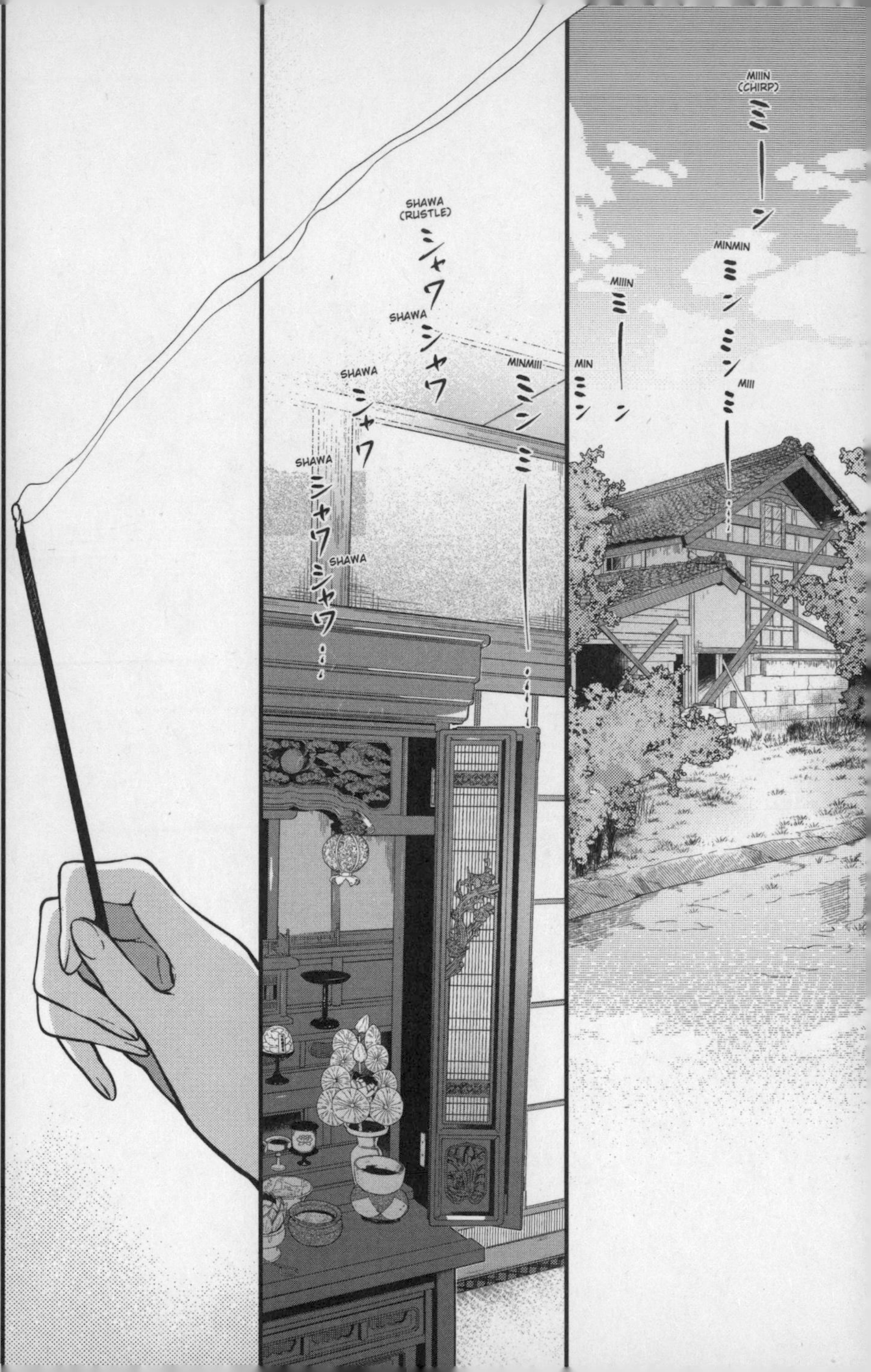
MIIIN (CHIRP)
ミーン
MINMIN
ミンミンミー
MIII
MIIIN
ミーーン
MIN
ミン
MINMIII
ミンミー…
SHAWA (RUSTLE)
シャワ
SHAWA
シャワ
SHAWA
シャワ
SHAWA
シャワ
SHAWA
シャワ…

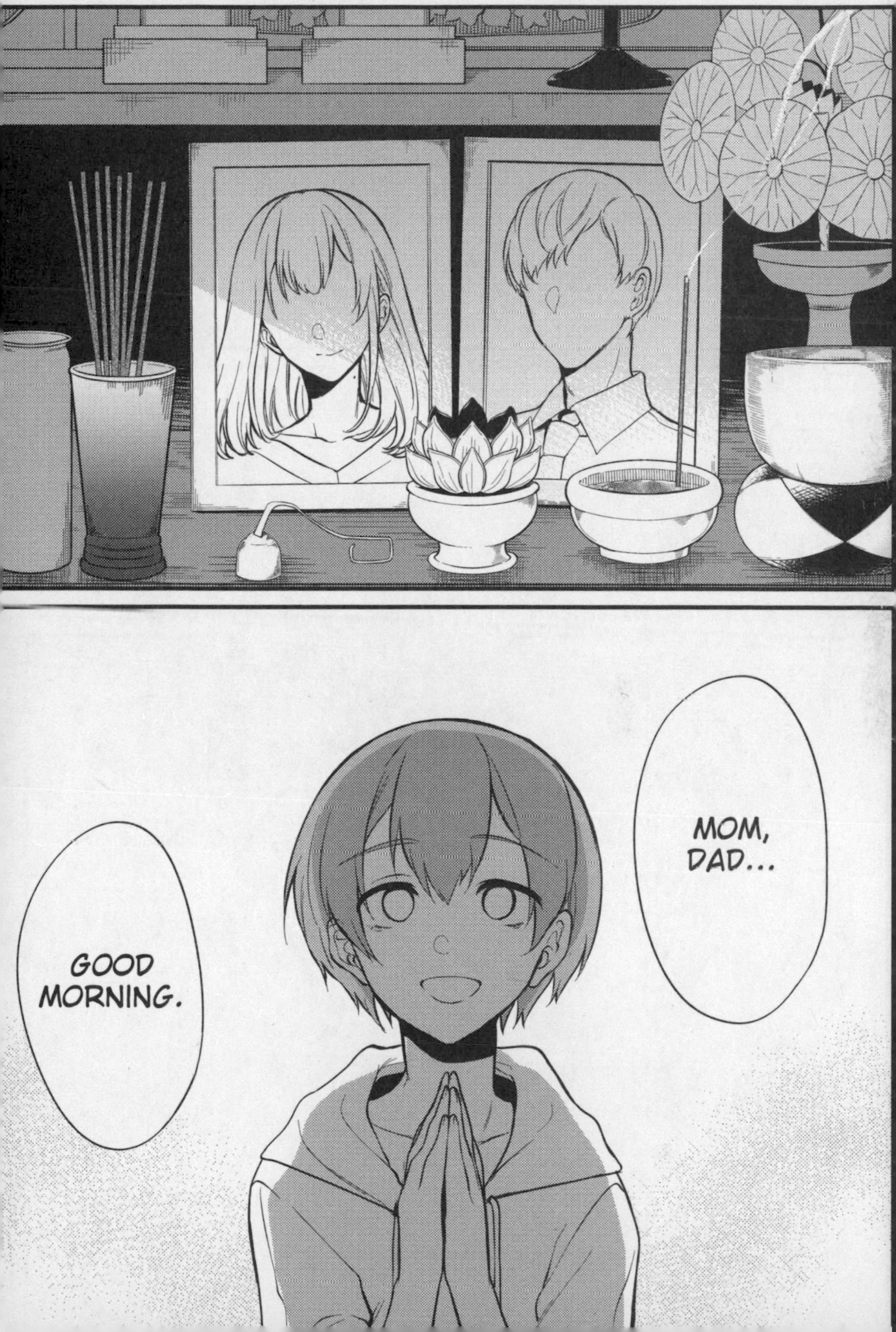
MOM, DAD...
GOOD MORNING.

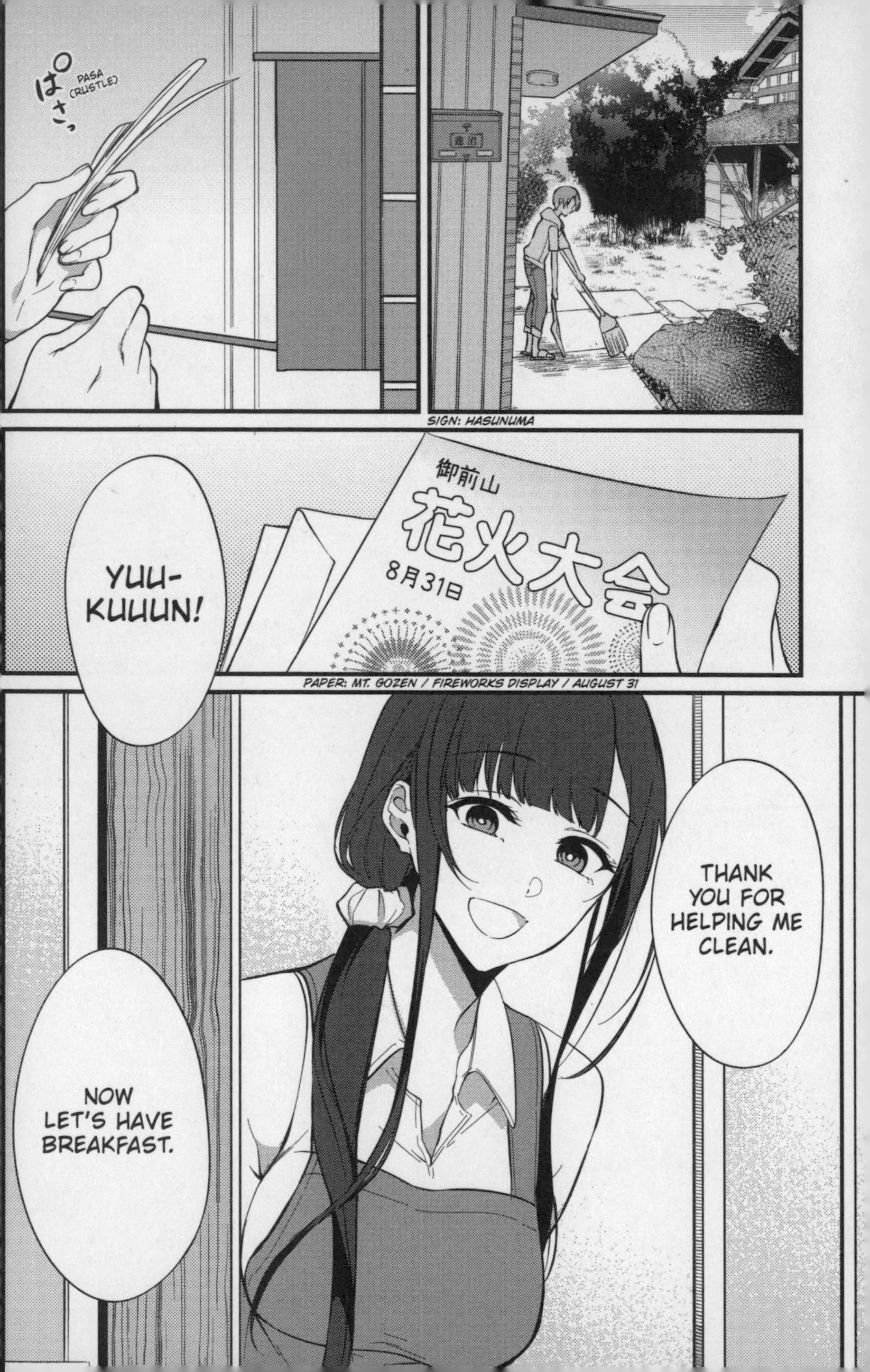
SIGN: HASUNUMA
ぱさっ
PASA (RUSTLE)
御前山
花火大会
8月31日
PAPER: MT. GOZEN / FIREWORKS DISPLAY / AUGUST 31
YUU-KUUUN!
THANK YOU FOR HELPING ME CLEAN.
NOW LET'S HAVE BREAKFAST.

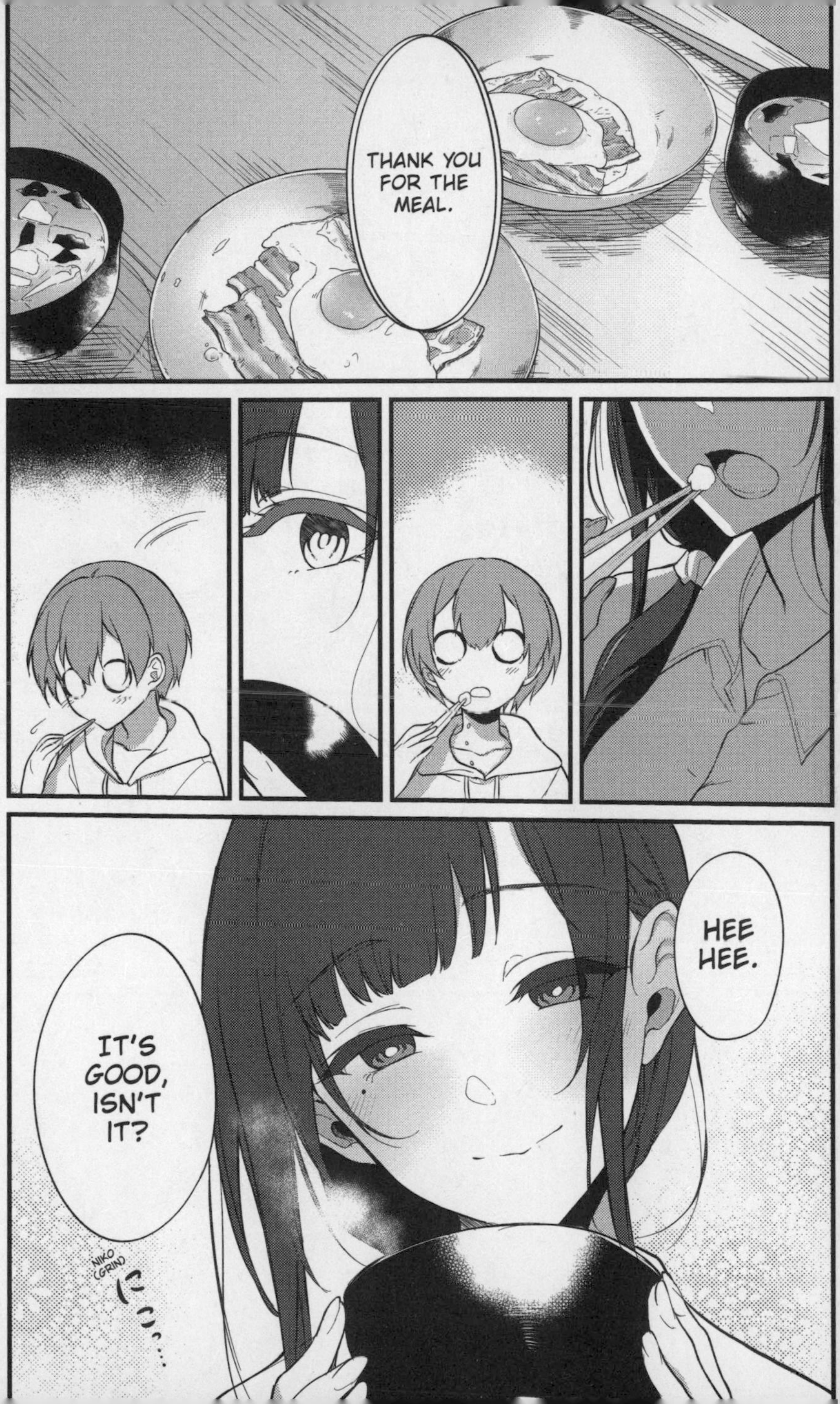
THANK YOU FOR THE MEAL.
HEE HEE.
IT'S GOOD, ISN'T IT?
NIKO (GRIN)

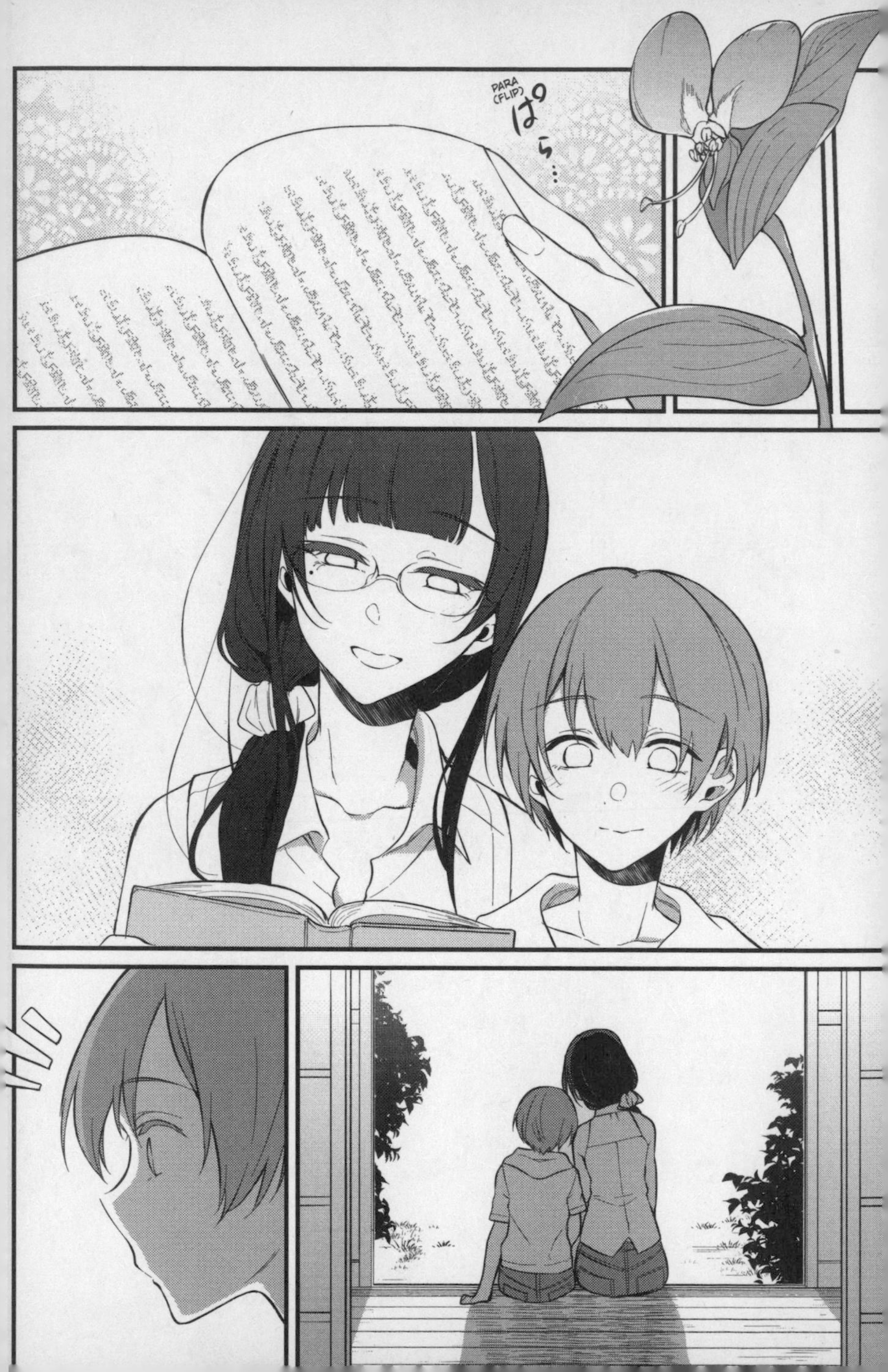
PARA (FLIP)
ぱら…

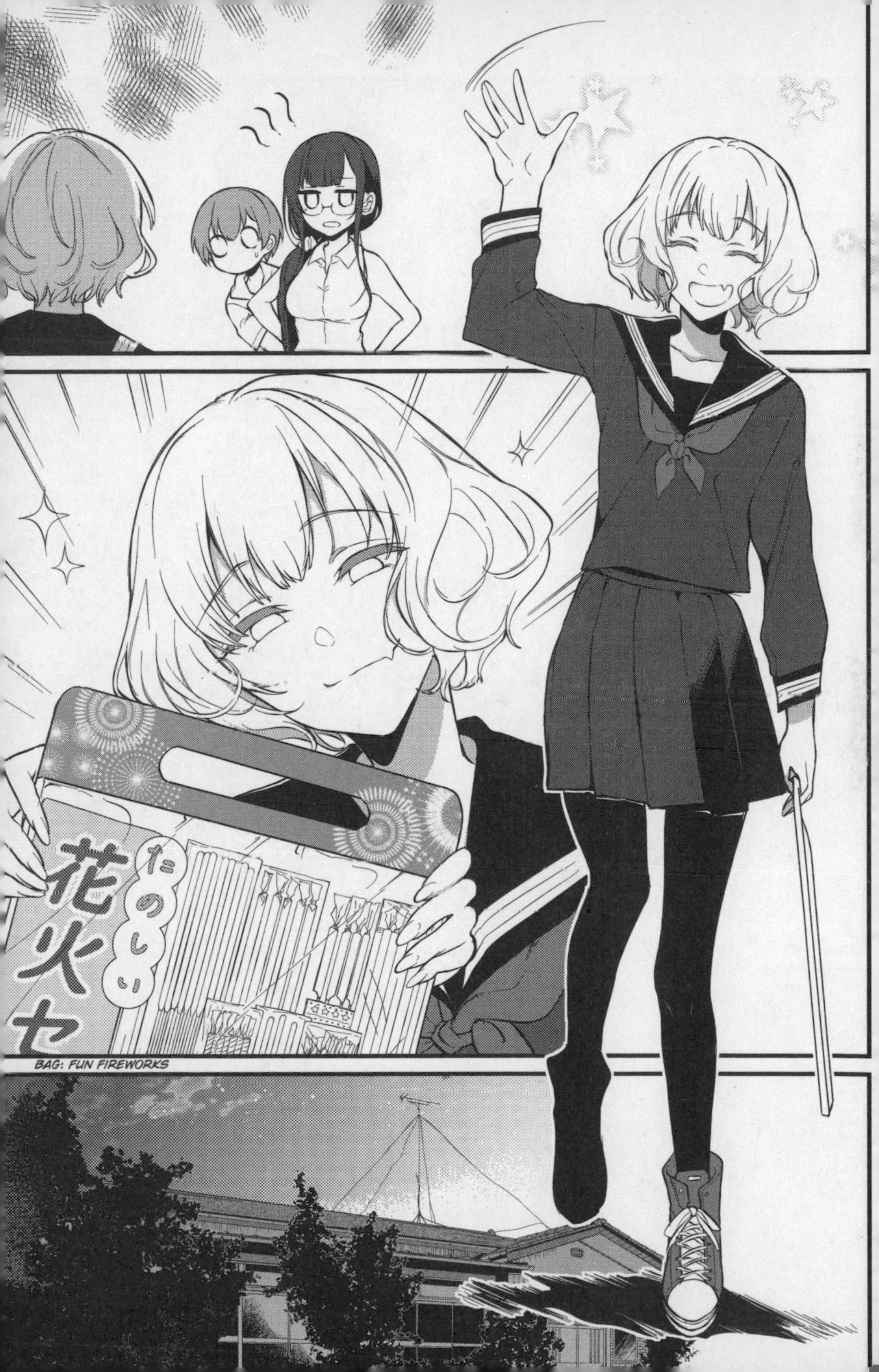
たのしい花火セ
BAG: FUN FIREWORKS

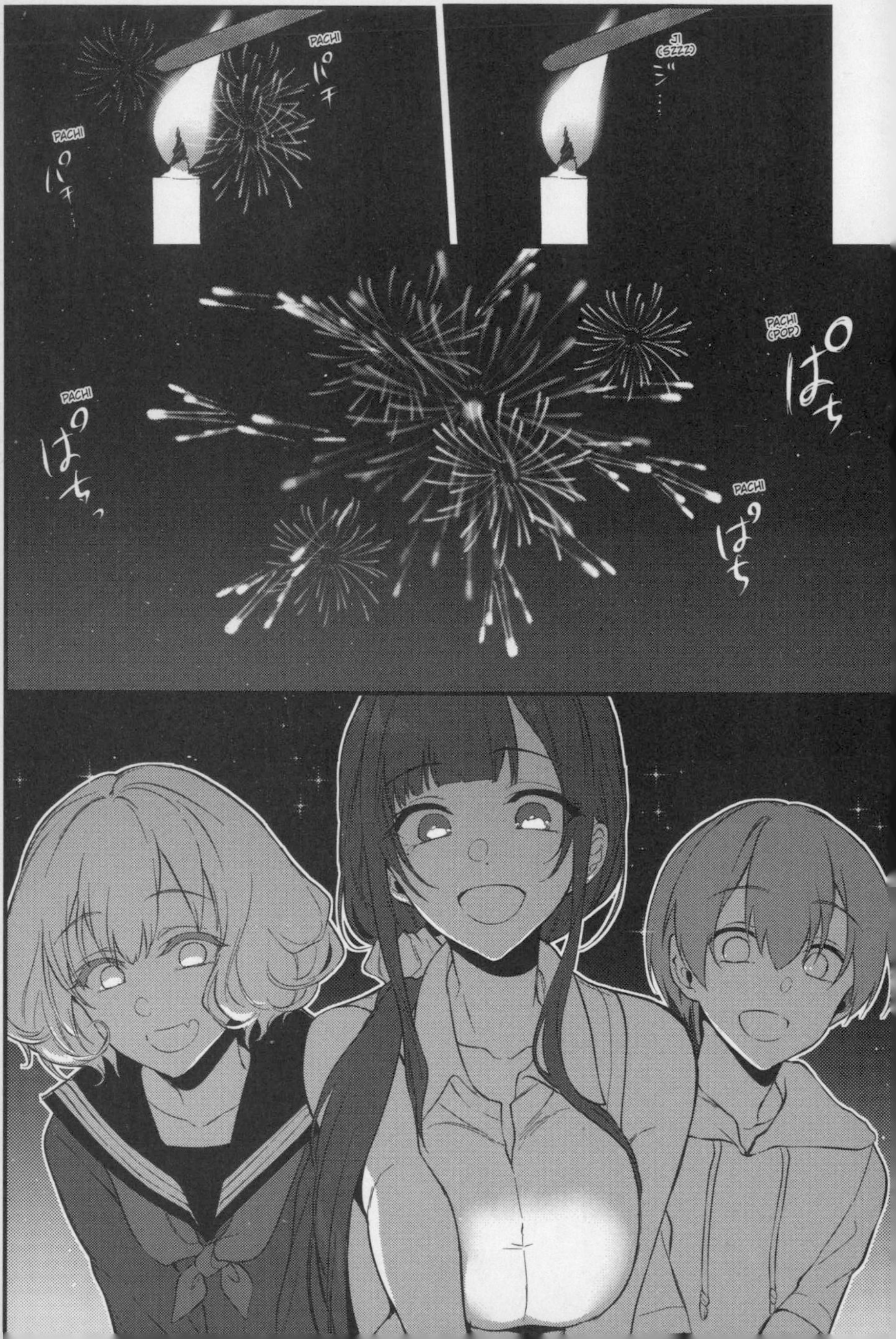
JI (SZZZ)
ジ…
PACHI
パチ
PACHI
パチ…
PACHI (POP)
ぱち
PACHI
ぱち
PACHI
ぱちっ

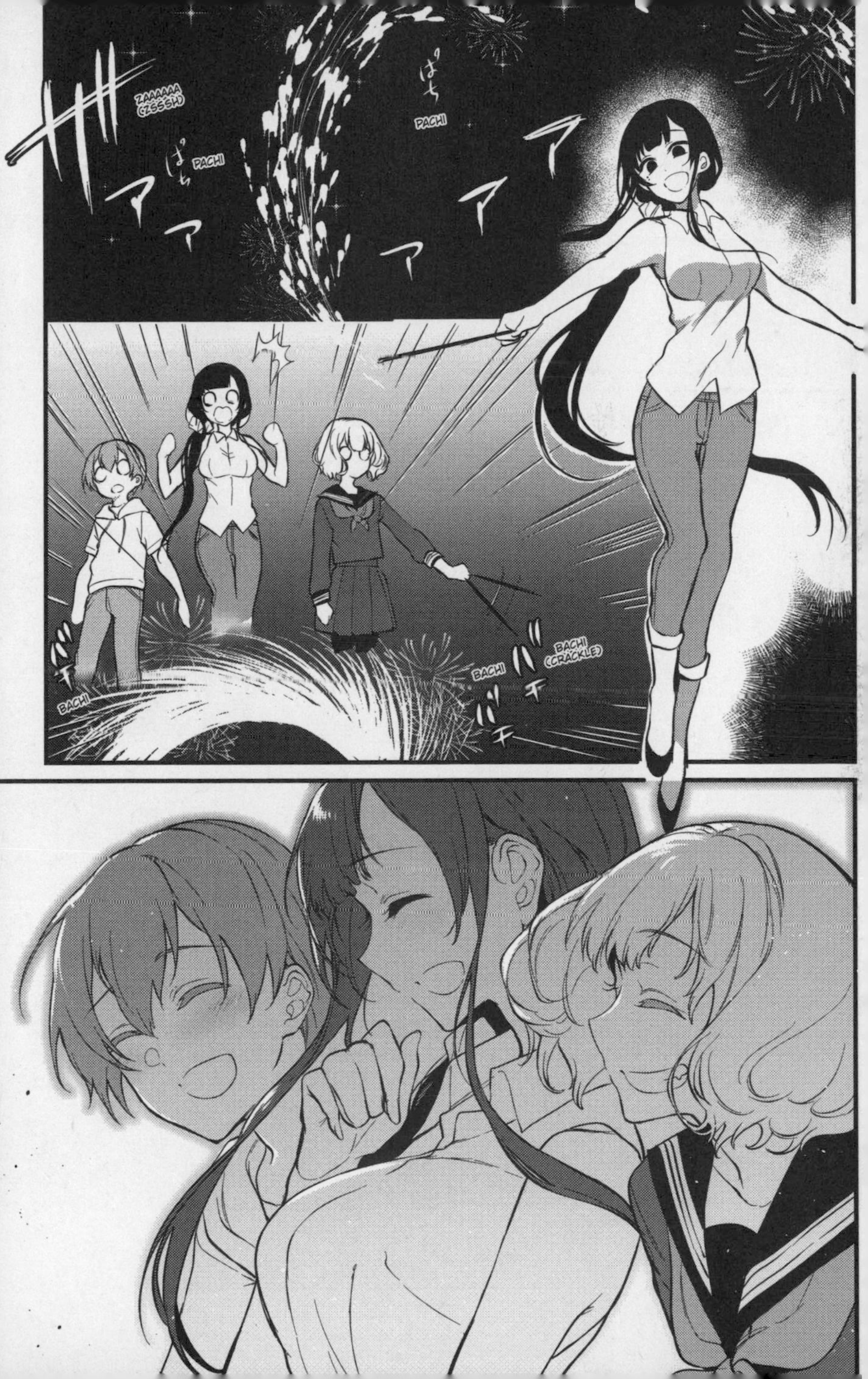
ぱち
PACHI
ZAAAAAA (ZSSSH)
ぱち
PACHI
BACHI (CRACKLE)
BACHI
BACHI

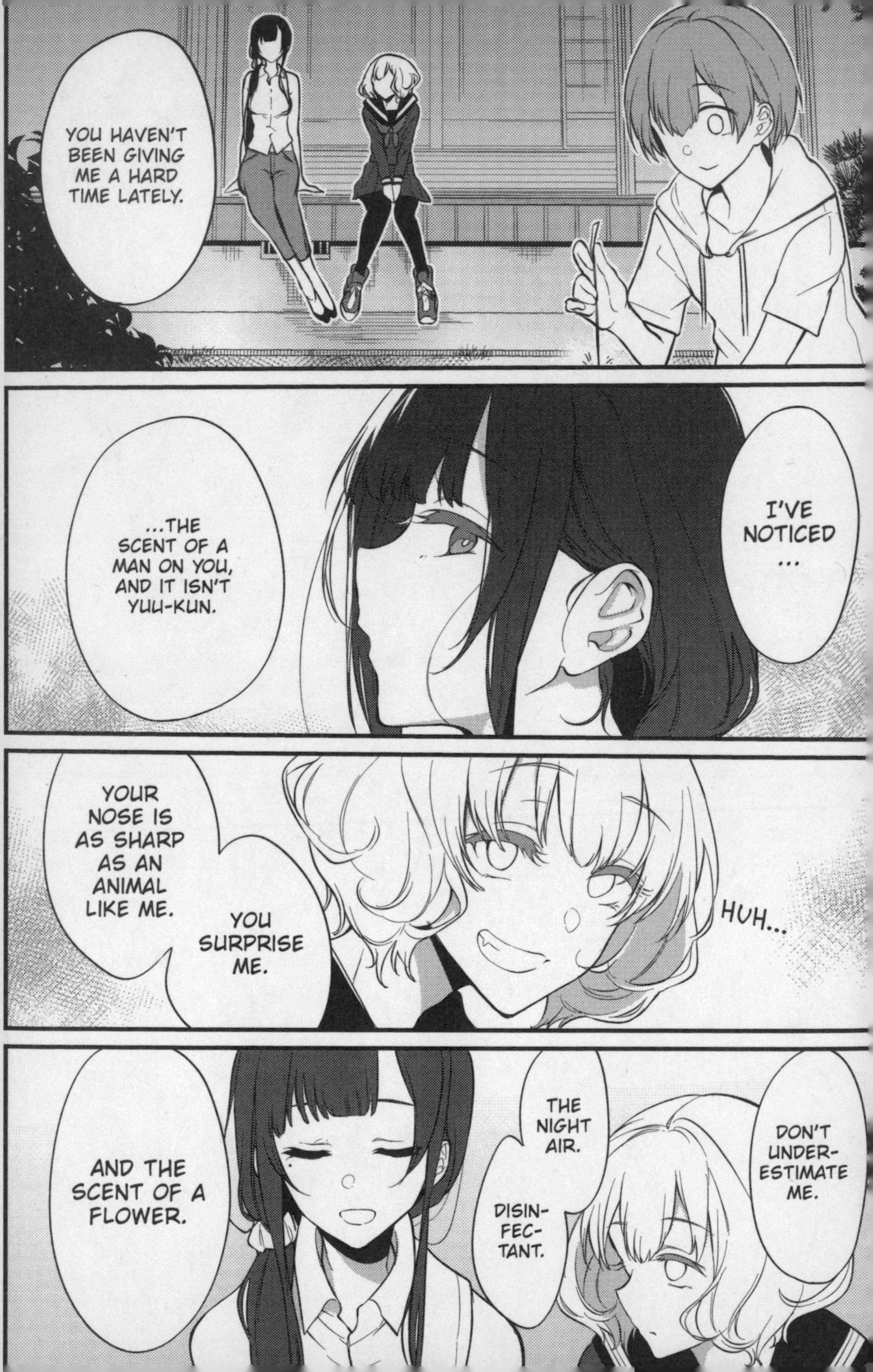
YOU HAVEN'T BEEN GIVING ME A HARD TIME LATELY.
I'VE NOTICED ...
...THE SCENT OF A MAN ON YOU, AND IT ISN'T YUU-KUN.
HUH...
YOU SURPRISE ME.
YOUR NOSE IS AS SHARP AS AN ANIMAL LIKE ME.
DON'T UNDER-ESTIMATE ME.
THE NIGHT AIR.
DISIN-FEC-TANT.
AND THE SCENT OF A FLOWER.

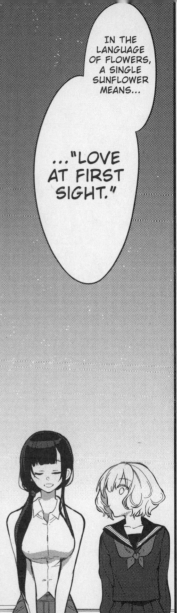

IN THE LANGUAGE OF FLOWERS, A SINGLE SUNFLOWER MEANS...

..."LOVE AT FIRST SIGHT."

WELL, WELL, WELL.

YOU SEE RIGHT THROUGH ME, HUH?

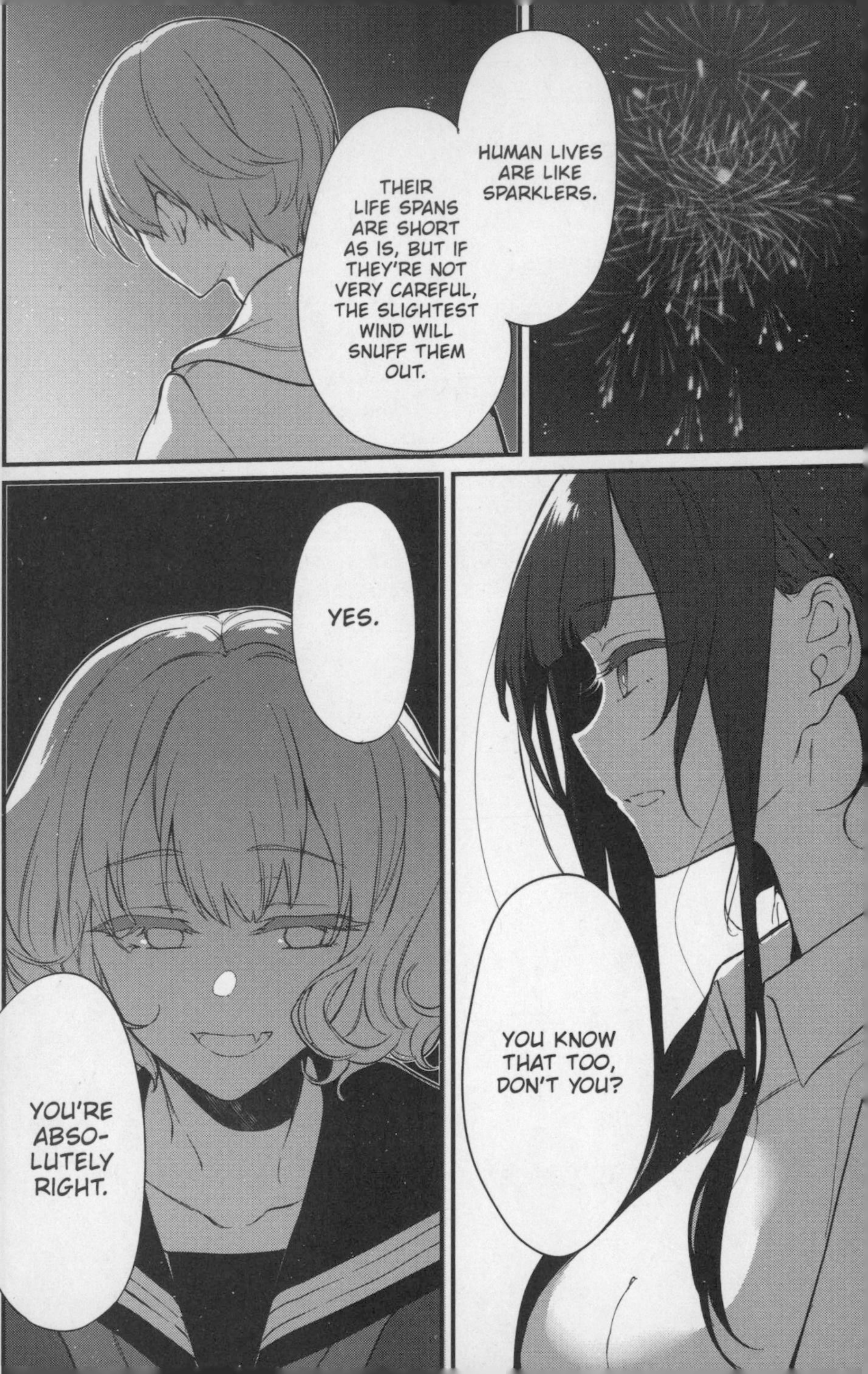
HUMAN LIVES ARE LIKE SPARKLERS.
THEIR LIFE SPANS ARE SHORT AS IS, BUT IF THEY'RE NOT VERY CAREFUL, THE SLIGHTEST WIND WILL SNUFF THEM OUT.
YOU KNOW THAT TOO, DON'T YOU?
YES.
YOU'RE ABSO-LUTELY RIGHT.

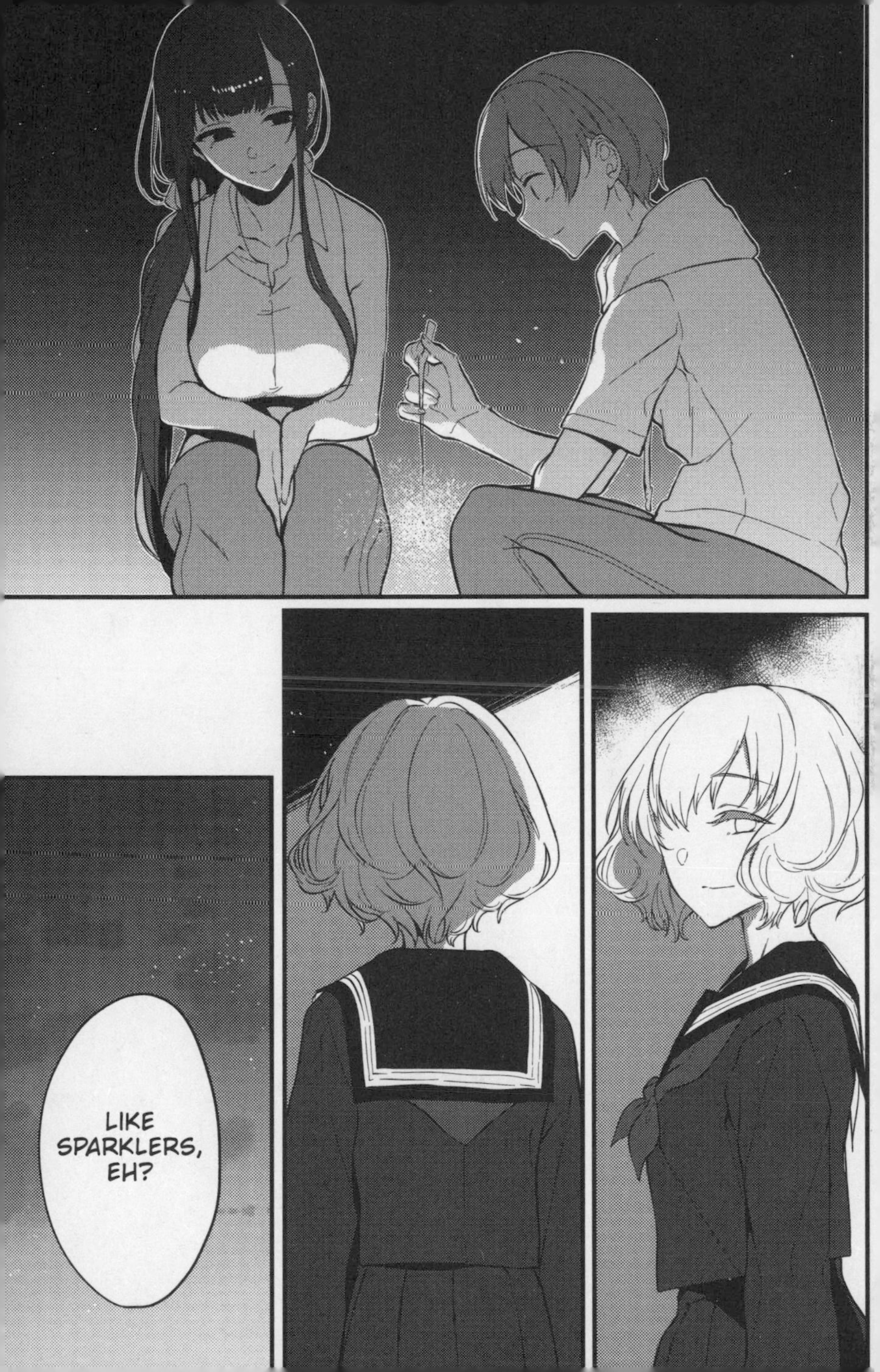
LIKE SPARKLERS, EH?

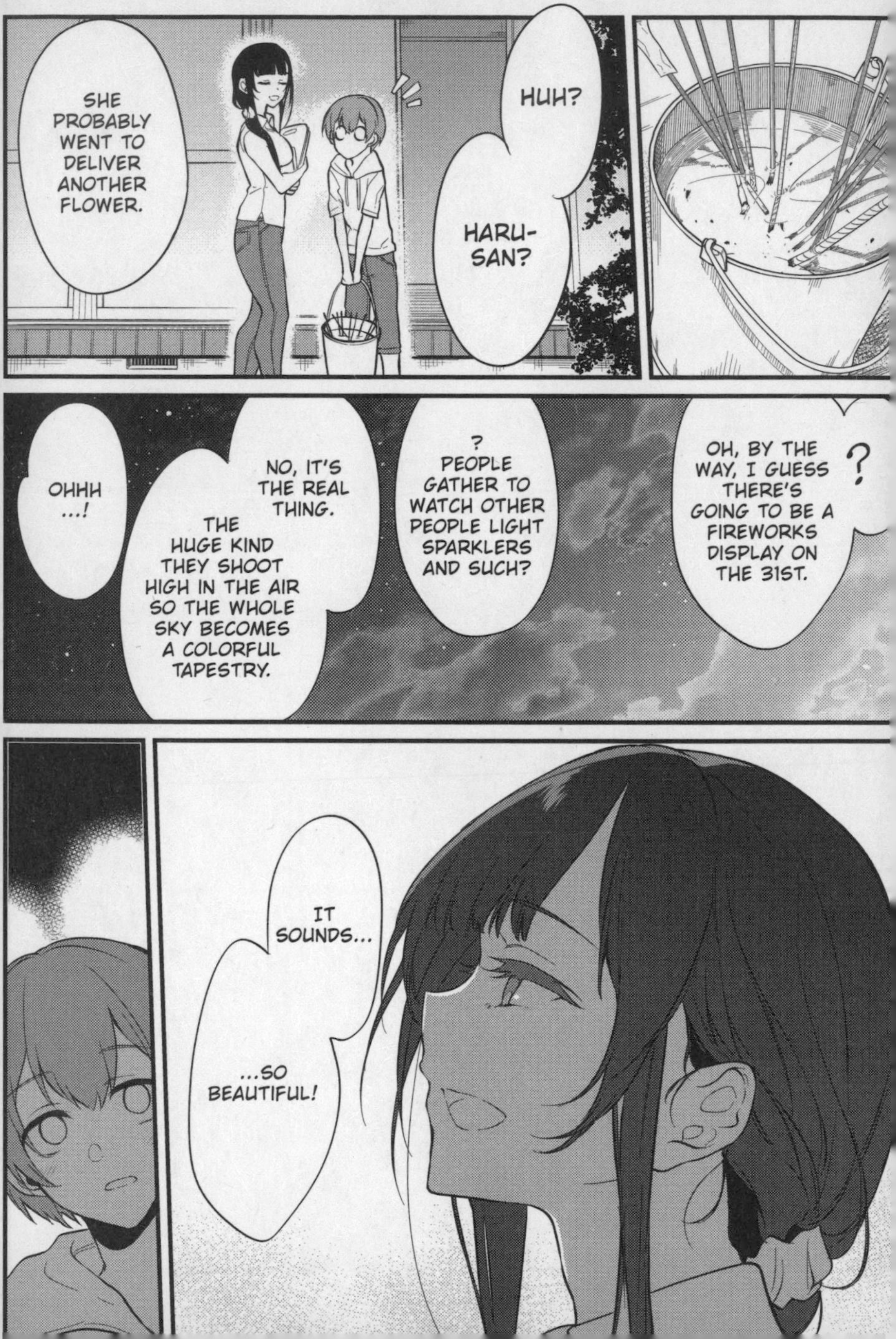
HUH?
HARU-SAN?
SHE PROBABLY WENT TO DELIVER ANOTHER FLOWER.
?
OH, BY THE WAY, I GUESS THERE'S GOING TO BE A FIREWORKS DISPLAY ON THE 31ST.
? PEOPLE GATHER TO WATCH OTHER PEOPLE LIGHT SPARKLERS AND SUCH?
NO, IT'S THE REAL THING.
THE HUGE KIND THEY SHOOT HIGH IN THE AIR SO THE WHOLE SKY BECOMES A COLORFUL TAPESTRY.
OHHH ...!
IT SOUNDS...
...SO BEAUTIFUL!

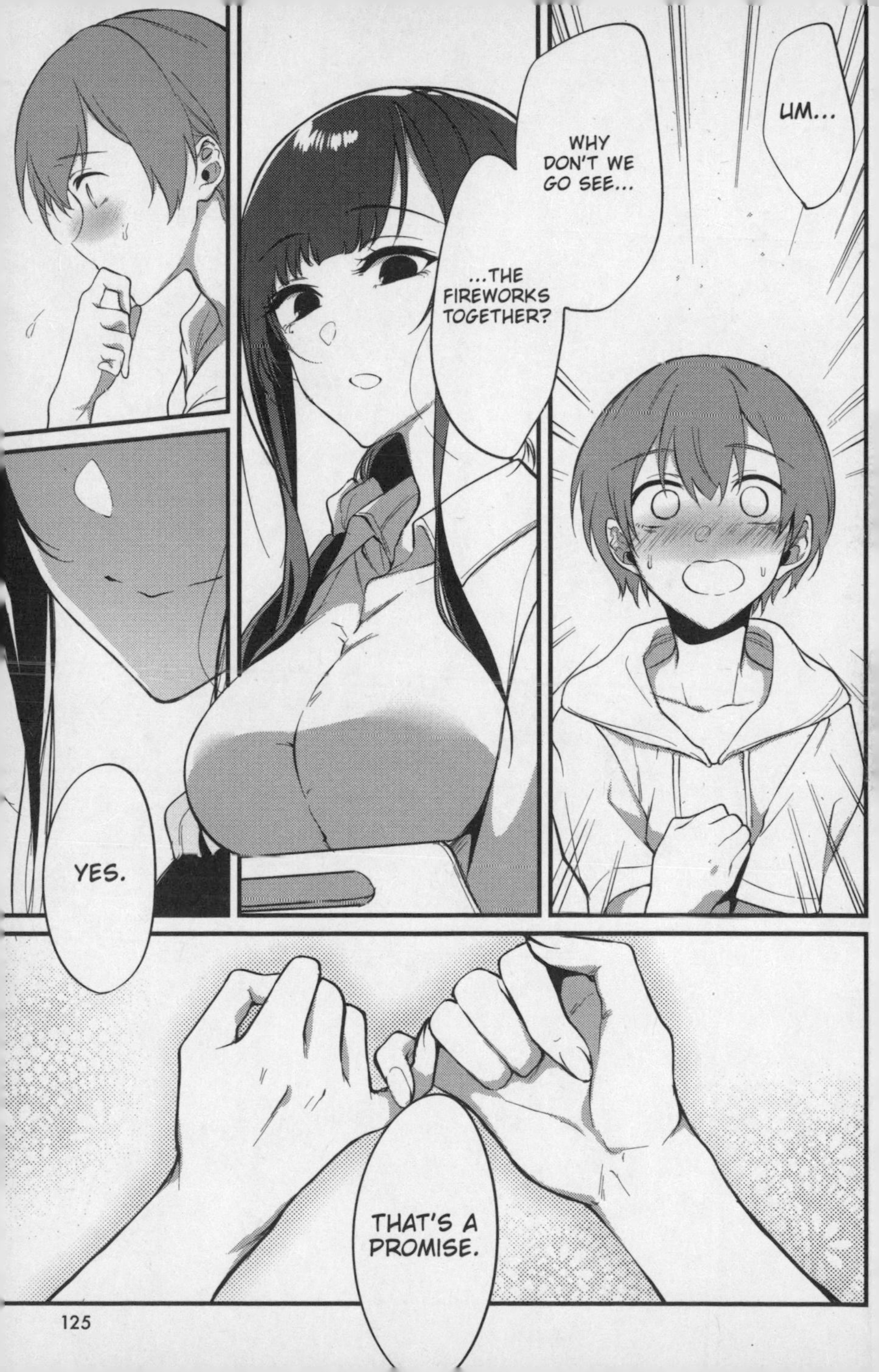
UM...
WHY DON'T WE GO SEE...
...THE FIREWORKS TOGETHER?
YES.
THAT'S A PROMISE.

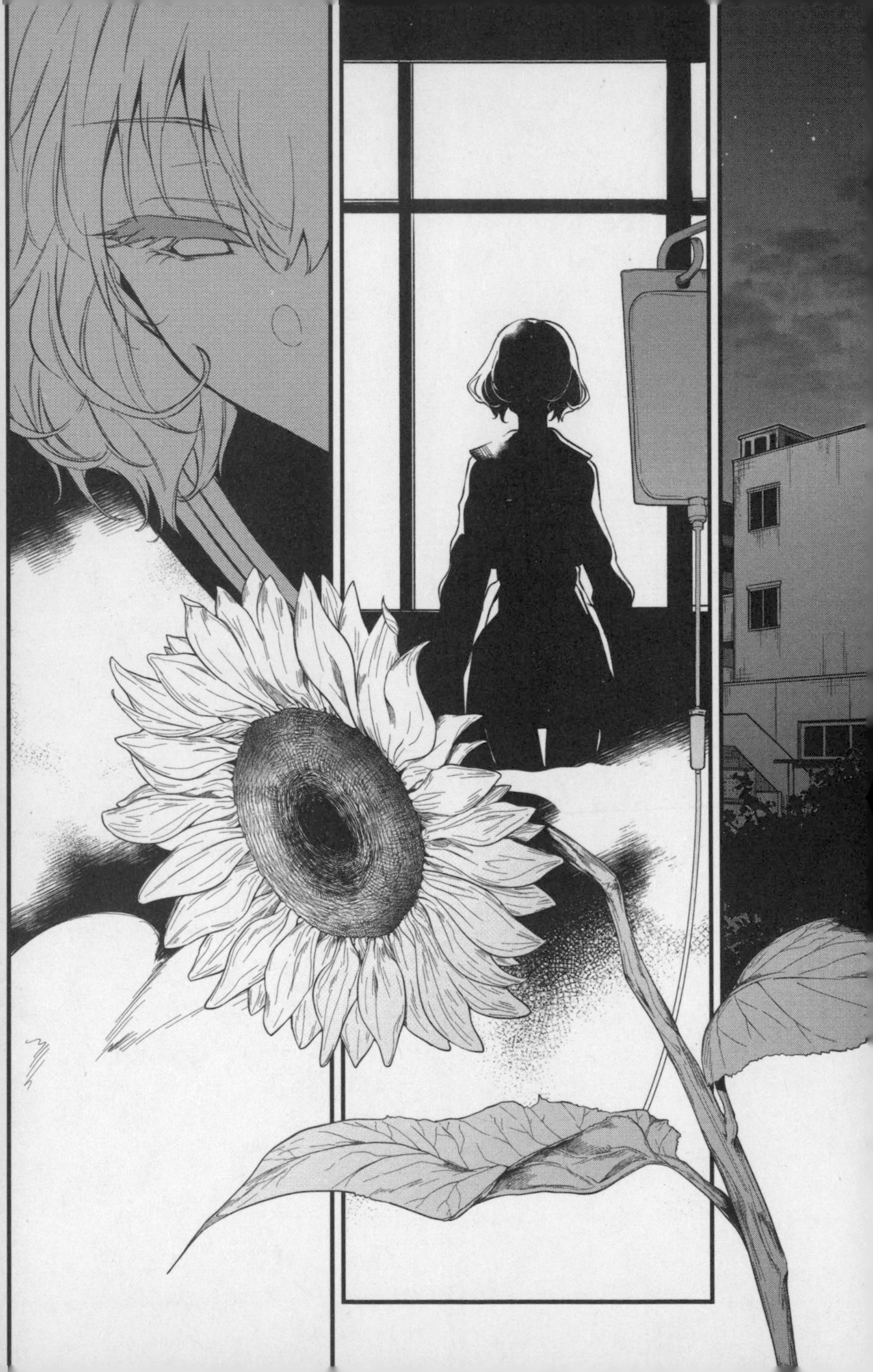

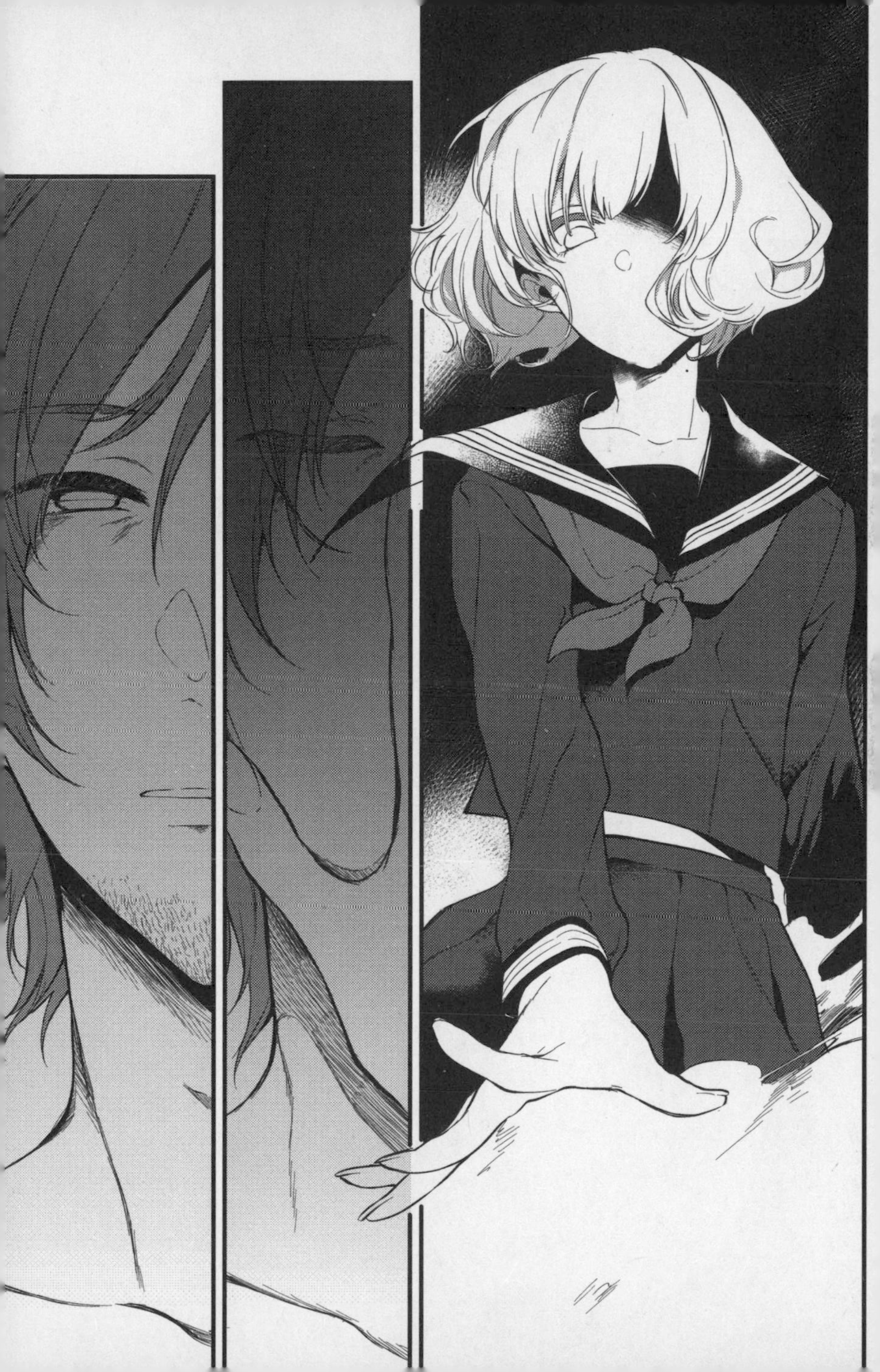

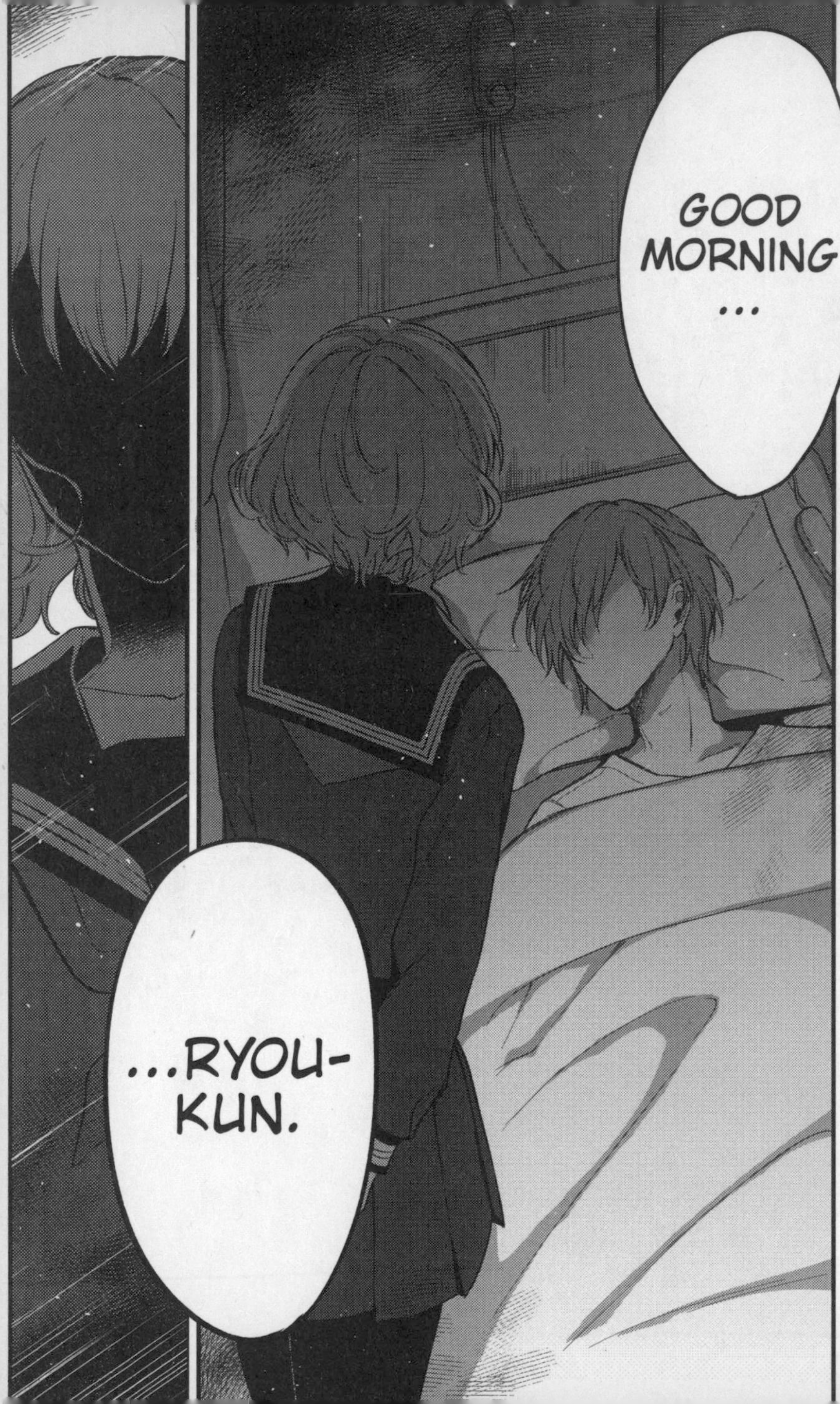
GOOD MORNING ...
...RYOU-KUN.

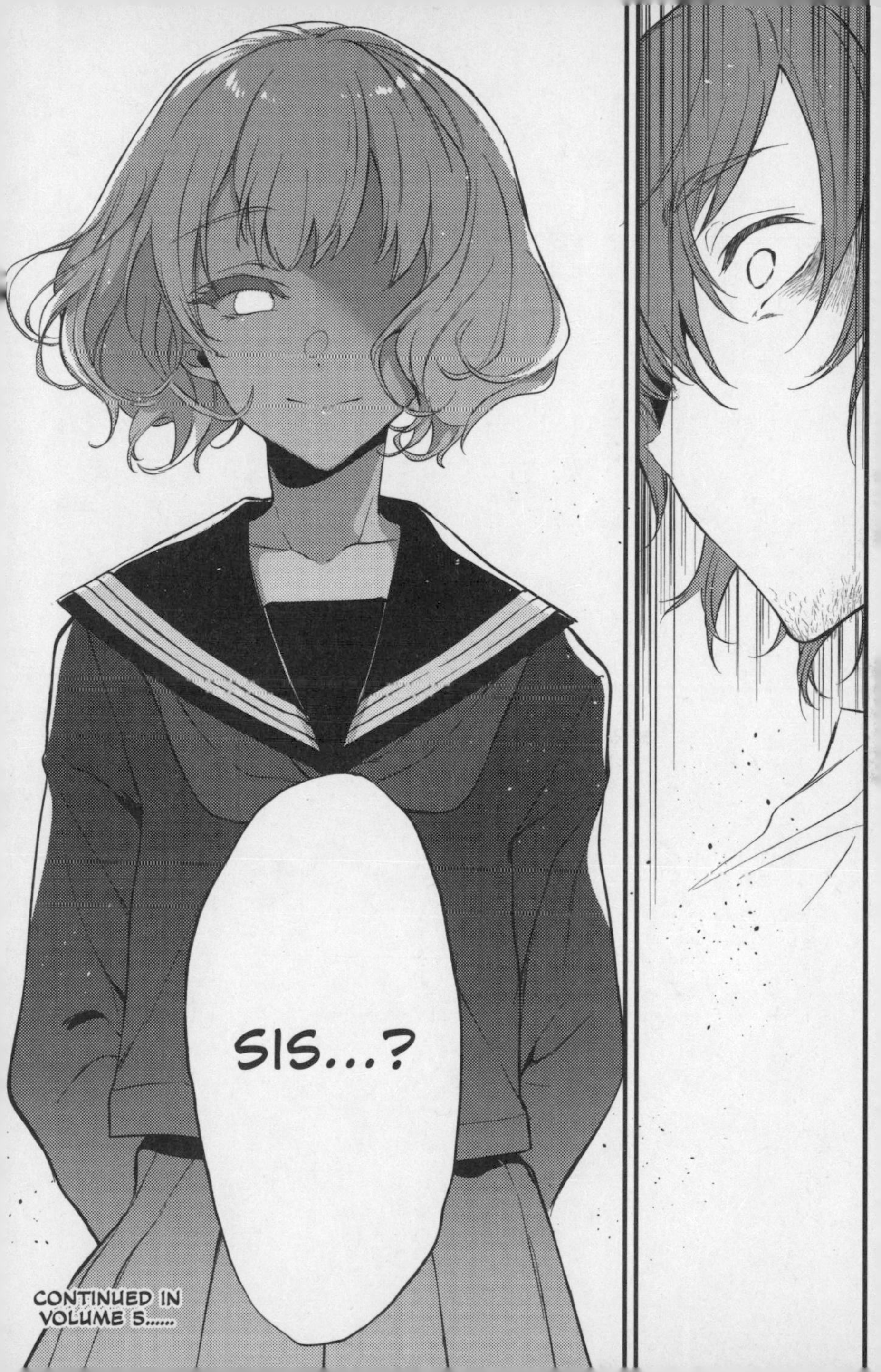
SIS...?
CONTINUED IN VOLUME 5......

The ELDER Sister-like ONE

4

IIDA POCHI.

Translation:
SHELDON DRZKA

Lettering:
PHIL CHRISTIE

ANENARUMONO Vol. 4
©IIDA POCHI./TEKERI STUDIO 2020
First published in Japan in 2020 by KADOKAWA CORPORATION, Tokyo.
English translation rights arranged with KADOKAWA CORPORATION, Tokyo
through TUTTLE-MORI AGENCY, INC., Tokyo.

English translation © 2020 by Yen Press, LLC

Yen Press
150 West 30th Street, 19th Floor
New York, NY 10001

Visit us at yenpress.com
facebook.com/yenpress
twitter.com/yenpress
yenpress.tumblr.com
instagram.com/yenpress

First Yen Press Edition: September 2020

Yen Press is an imprint of Yen Press, LLC.
The Yen Press name and logo are trademarks of Yen Press, LLC.

The publisher is not responsible for websites
(or their content) that are not owned by the publisher.

Library of Congress Control Number: 2017954162

ISBNs: 978-1-9753-1593-1 (paperback)
        978-1-9753-1592-4 (ebook)

10 9 8 7 6 5 4 3 2 1

WOR

Printed in the United States of America